PAUL SCHILDER
Mind Explorer

PAUL SCHILDER
Mind Explorer

Edited by

Donald A. Shaskan, M.D.
Department of Psychiatry
University of California
San Francisco

William L. Roller, M.A.
Mental Health Service
Group Health Cooperative of Puget Sound
Seattle, Washington

HUMAN SCIENCES PRESS, INC.
72 FIFTH AVENUE
NEW YORK, N.Y. 10011

Copyright © 1985 by Human Sciences Press, Inc.
72 Fifth Avenue, New York, New York 10011

Printed in the United States of America
123456789   987654321

Library of Congress Cataloging in Publication Data
Main entry under title:
Paul Schilder, mind explorer.
   Bibliography: p.
   Includes index.
   1. Schilder, Paul, 1886-1940. 2. Psychoanalysis.
3. Psychiatry. I. Shaskan, Donald A. II. Roller,
William L. [DNLM: 1. Body image. 2. Self concept.
BF 697 P324]
RC339.52.S35P38   1985   616.89'0092'4   83-22632
ISBN 0-89885-144-0

Dedicated to
Lauretta Bender, M.D.
and
William Thomas Snider, M.D. (1888-1965)
—A country doctor in Illinois

CONTENTS

CONTRIBUTORS

ALEXANDRA ADLER, M.D. Associate clinical professor of neurology, The New York University School of Medicine. Associate attending in neurology, Bellevue and University Hospitals, New York.

LAURETTA BENDER, M.D. Professor of Child Psychiatry, School of Medicine, University of Maryland.

WALTER BROMBERG, M.D. President Board of Directors, American Board Forensic Psychiatry.

S.H. FOULKES, M.D. Physician emeritus, The Maudsley Hospital and the Bethlehem Royal Hospital, London; Hon. President, Group Analytic Society (London); Editor, Group Analysis.

JOHN FROSCH, M.D. Professor of psychiatry, New York University College of Medicine. Director of Psychiatry Emeritus, Brookdale Hospital Medical Center, New York. Editor Emeritus, *Journal of The American Psychoananlytic Association.*

IAGO GALDSTON, M.D. Past President, The Schilder Society, New York.

DAVID G. HUBBARD, M.D. Director, Lauretta Bender and Paul Schilder Memorial Vestibular Projects.

JUDITH S. KESTENBERG, M.D. Director Child Development Research, Sands Point, New York.

NATHAN S. KLINE, M.D. Director, Rockland Research Institute.

SANDOR LORAND, M.D. Author, *The Technique of Psychoanalytic Therapy.*

SAM PARKER, M.D. Private Practice, Forensic Psychiatry.

WILLIAM L. ROLLER, M.A. Group Psychotherapy Coordinator, Mental Health Service, Group Health Cooperative of Puget Sound, Seattle.

MAX ROSENBAUM, Ph.D. Clinical Professor, Adelphi University.

PAUL SCHILDER, M.D., Ph.D. Clinical Director, Bellevue Hospital Psychiatric Division; Research Professor of Psychiatry, New York University Medical College.

DONALD A. SHASKAN, M.D. Department of Psychiatry, University of California at San Francisco.

ARCHIE A. SILVER, M.D. Professor of Psychiatry and Director, child and adolescent psychiatry, University of South Florida Medical School, Tampa, Florida.

CHARLES G. WRIGHT, Ph.D. Assistant Director, Lauretta Bender and Paul Schilder Memorial Vestibular Project.

ACKNOWLEDGMENTS

I wish gratefully to acknowledge Gentry Harris for his assistance with The Emotion of Motion; Max Rosenbaum for his interview of Sandor Lorand and his timely advice; Lauretta Bender for her encouragement and contributions; Frances Marsh Shaskan for her reviews; Sheila Young for her dedication; and Walter Bromberg for reminding me of his title (see reference 246).

Donald A. Shaskan
San Francisco, California

Special recognition is due those persons who helped in the conception and completion of this book. I want to acknowledge the work of David Rapaport, who laid much of the intellectual groundwork for scholarship on Paul Schilder; to thank John Adler of Berkeley, who first suggested to us the notion of a Frestshrift as a way to celebrate a man's life; our authors who tell Schilder's story and reflect his teachings in their own achievements; Robert Steele of Connecticut who read my notes on phenomenology; and thanks most of all to Vivian who was there from the very beginning.

William L. Roller
Berkeley, California

PREFACE

It seems particularly fitting at this time of continuing research into the conflictual areas of psychoanalytic and philosophical theory to review the extensive contributions made by the late Paul Schilder. For this purpose, we asked many of Dr. Schilder's former students or co-workers, as well as research workers in a field pioneered by Dr. Schilder, to give tangible expression to the influence of this teachings on their specific work.

The papers that follow give more than one could have hoped for in shedding light on the magnitude and originality of his thought and in penetrating the complexity of his ideas developed from acute clinical observations. What at the time may have appeared to be mainly speculation is now accepted as evidence of brain function or nervous system organization. Nonetheless, all who listened to Dr. Schilder during the years he was at Bellevue Hospital and New York University School of Medicine were deeply touched by his warmth and dedication to furthering their understanding of the connection and relationship between the reality of the world of forms and gravity and of the internal sphere of primitive origins.

We hope that in reading these impressions of Paul Schilder—in particular, his own unpublished work in the United States on Body Image contained in this volume—will provide a taste of the brilliance and richness of his thought.

Donald A. Shaskan

INTRODUCTION

There are indications of recurrent interest in the works of Paul Schilder published in Germany and in this country among student of psychoanalytic thought and laboratory research scientists in brain and sensory organs. The present volume is a compendium of responses to some of Schilder's earlier work in Vienna and his subsequent research in New York while he was associated with New York University School of Medicine and Bellevue Hospital.

In Vienna he had a close relationship with Sigmund Freud during the early years of the latter's formulations on personality structure. At that time he also worked with Wagner von Jauregg on a malarial treatment of general paresis.

It was then that he began his investigations into the recesses of the mind/brain organization and relationship and on the development of thought processes in the normal and schizophrenic personality.

From his early days and also in this country Schilder impressed his colleagues with his encyclopedic mind which ranged freely over the multidisciplines dedicated to the understanding of personality development, the physical and social adjustment of the individual, and the normal and pathological psychological states. He astounded his listeners wherever and whenever he lectured—particularly in university forums—with his skill in categorizing philosophical thought, descriptive psychological states, psychoanalytic theories of personality structure and function, and neuropathological formations in the brain and central nervous system. He would then extrapolate from each of these disciplines ideas that would serve as signposts in his unrelenting search to explain changes in brain morphology.

Through avenues of research into thought processes, he developed the symbol of the "sphere" and how it acts in response to stimuli generated both internally and externally by images which are often very faintly defined. He found this schema particularly useful in examining how the mind of the schizophrenic individual works, i.e., fails to accomplish its original intent to communicate desire.

Schilder has made major contributions to our understanding of the body image: its spatial attributes in reference to its own form and position and also to the body image of other individuals with which it comes in contact. These deductions on the importance and relevance of the body image to the healthy functioning of the personality or of the ''psyche'' gave rise to his interest in group formation and group activity at a time when treatment of an individual in the group situation was thought irrelevant, if not impossible.

Chapters in this volume reflect the impact of Schilder's inquiring mind, in his acclaimed function as a teacher, upon the subsequent work and research of the individual authors. They represent a variety of experience which has served as an extension of Schilder's substantive research into a field which is today exploding with new data on inner/outer experience and mind/brain interdependent functioning. The seminal thinking of Paul Schilder on whatever subject he touched in his search for understanding of essences of projection of the self into the outer world and of its return to its inner domain, lends authenticity to the writings and utterances of present-day investigators and, in so doing, illuminates their findings and conclusions.

This volume's contributors attest to the power and originality of Schilder's thought. Paul Schilder will in time be recognized for the magnitude of his productive mind and will take his place alongside the other eminently distinguished scholars in the field to which he dedicated his energies.

D.A.S.

PERSONAL NOTES
AND REMEMBRANCES

Chapter 1

REFLECTIONS ON PAUL SCHILDER[1]

Sam Parker, M.D.

When I first went to Vienna in 1924, I had already spent two years in various medical schools in Germany. My objective in going to Vienna was primarily to complete the clinical years of medical school and, at the same time, to enroll in the Freudian Psychoanalytic Institute. I achieved this objective, and at the same time ran into a number of intellectual giants and creative medical minds whose work attracted me almost as much as Freud's.

To be an academic in Vienna at that time and make any headway meant you had to make a lot of noise. By that I mean publish or spout new ideas. No matter what you were you always had to blow your own horn. You had to be highly individualistic, intellectually and socially aggressive, and as independent as possible.

Paul Schilder followed this trend with his own brand of eclecticism. He could not be tagged or categorized easily. Although he was definitely psychoanalytically oriented, he had never himself been analyzed. He did not belong to the Freudian Psychoanalytic Institute, and yet he was completely accepted by the Institute and the Freudians around town, with the exception of the older ones who felt he was a maverick.

At the same time, he was a professor at the University of Vienna, which was very unusual because Jews did not as a rule get on the teaching staff of the university. Schilder was there at the recommendation of Julius Wagner-Jauregg, who was head of the neuropsychiatric division at the University Hospital.

---

[1]Remarks by Sam Parker, February 17, 1980, Santa Monica, California (Taped interview.)

Wagner-Jauregg was himself a maverick. He was not a Viennese but a Tyrolean. The Viennese couldn't understand his German. He was not acceptable in Vienna because he was not one of them. He was a "hick." The fact that he was so outstanding annoyed them tremendously.

Wagner-Jauregg and Freud had been classmates. He wanted Freud to come into the university as a professor, but Freud would have none of it because he did not want to bother with the university politics. Freud was right—he didn't need the university: rather, the university needed him.

Wagner-Jauregg brought to the department of neuropsychiatry all kinds of people who were not establishment types. One of the people on his staff was Constantin Von Economo. He was the first to describe epidemic encephalitis just prior to the great pandemic of 1918 during World War I, and he gave it the name of sleeping sickness. Von Economo was a true renaissance man. He came from a very wealthy and titled family of several European bloodlines. But instead of being merely a socialite, Von Economo displayed many and varied talents. He was a flyer during World War I and became one of the first directors of Lufthansa. He helped to build the first airport in Vienna. He was also a champion bridge player, a musician, a breeder of fighting cocks and rare birds, and was the first scientist actually to count and functionally define the cells of the human cortex. He made the first complete cellular map of the human brain which serves not only as a basis for understanding the various motor and sensory controls of the brain, but also provides a norm against which any other brain damage or loss can be calibrated. I assisted him in this work in his laboratory and translated his original work on the subject from German into English for the Oxford University Press.

It must not be forgotten that Vienna in the 1920s was populated by a number of other historical luminaries in the psychological world beside Freud. One was Stekel, who had branched off from the original Freudian group and had become a world renowned sexologist. I became very friendly with Stekel at that time because I had been asked to translate some of his works for Boni and Liveright, the New York publishers. There was also Alfred Adler, an outstanding offshoot of the original Freudian circle who made history in his own right. His daughter Alexandra (whose contribution appears elsewhere in this volume) was a classmate of mine and we both became house doctors at the university neuropsychiatric division.

All of this activity was going on in Vienna at this one time. From a cultural point of view, it was a center without peer in the world. Professor Carl Schorske is absolutely correct when he describes post-Hapsburg Vienna as a "garden in transition to a wilderness." Vienna has always been a hotbed of anti-Semitism. All of that intellectual and cultural ferment that was taking place in the Art Deco period ultimately gave way to the disappearance of almost all of the Jews in Vienna. The place has now become a graveyard. The only achievements the people can point to are in the past. There are the beautiful buildings and collections from ancient times, but nothing is happening.

A great number of Viennese Jews in those days tried to overcome their handicaps by accepting proselytization. Many became Catholics in order to advance in their professions, since that was the predominant religion of Austria.

Schilder did not become a Catholic, but a Protestant—and that because of marriage. He did not marry until the middle of the First World War. As a medical officer in the Polish Army, he was slightly wounded and relegated to rest and recuperation somewhere in the Tyrol, or the lower mountain regions of Austria. In the pastoral village where he was billeted, he met a strikingly beautiful girl who was the daughter of an innkeeper. Her name was Mitzi and he fell in love with her. She was extremely immature and vulnerable.

They became intimate and wished to marry. But in Austria in those days you could not marry outside your own faith because the rules were quite rigid. The village happened to be Protestant, and so Schilder became a Protestant.

Despite being a Protestant Jew, Schilder made headway in Vienna because his thought was unique.

He joined the neuropsychiatric staff because Wagner-Jauregg was nothing if not open-minded. He even allowed me—a non-Viennese, non-Austrian—to become his assistant, mainly because I could understand his German. Since he became so famous, the world beat a path to his door and he needed someone to front for him.

This gives a picture of the cultural ambience in Vienna at the time.

I first met Schilder when I enrolled in one of his classes at the medical school in 1925. It was a shocking experience. His whole appearance, manner, and behavior were so offbeat that at first I was too preoccupied with him personally to pay much attention to what he was saying. Primarily this was because of his high-pitched, squeaky voice which was different from that of any other man I have ever encountered. Also, he had a strikingly unique personal appearance. He was only of average height, but he was quite slender, stoop-shouldered, swarthy, almost like a Yemenite, and had jet black hair and a jet black banker's mustache. He had a foppish tendency of dangling his wrists in a variety of gestures which, together with his voice, immediately gave the impression that he was quite effeminate. Nothing was further from the truth. Almost as if it were a defensive mechanism, Schilder completely ignored the effect he had on people around him or those who met him for the first time. He correctly estimated that the sweep of his thinking and the stimulus of his ideas would quickly transform people's initial reaction into affirmative identification.

Everybody else in Vienna, including Freud, Adler, and Stekel, established cults. Only Schilder did not. His restless mentality and universalist type of vision made such an objective impossible. Moreover, the people who were attracted to him were very individualistic as well.

Schilder never hestitated to appropriate the ideas of others, which he then would either expand with ideas of his own or would rework in a different direction, or would make into components of other theories of his own. It is for this reason that one finds Schilder experimenting with psychoanalysis, hypnosis, organic neurology, sexology, and much more. He was always in the forefront of current ideas. Making rounds with him was always a kaleidoscope of stimulating thoughts on various aspects of any case in point. Whenever any one of us came to him with a new observation, a special kind of case, or a project, Schilder always managed to support the objective but still have it worked up in such a way that it included his own ideas as well. Of course, that is always the prerogative of a clinical boss.

I began analysis with Schilder in 1926. The article I wrote in 1925 and published in 1926, *The Character of Modern Psychiatry* (excerpts of which appear in this volume), was my way of satisfying my new acquaintance with a famous man, Smith Ely Jeliffe, the New York neuropsychiatrist and editor of the *Journal of Nervous and Mental Disease*. He had come to Vienna to visit Wagner-Jauregg, who passed him on to me because he could not speak English. Jeliffe requested that I write the article on Schilder.

Heinz Hartmann, also a member of the Neuropsychiatric Institute in Vienna at the time, had already begun his work on ego psychology. Ego psychology was a development of phenomenology, and Hartmann was well read in philosophy and familiar with both Brentano and Husserl. Ego is a Latin word for "I" and without "I" there is no "you." In other words, a subjective consciousness presupposes the existence of others—and that is the philosophical foundation for a psychology of relationships and object relations. And that has been the creative and progressive contribution of phenomenology in the development of modern psychiatry.

Schilder's ultimate aim was a comprehensive textbook of psychiatry based on a wedding of phenomenology and psychoanalysis. He wanted to encompass the various lines of thought, including organic neurology. At that particular time and place, infusing a dynamic and psychological spirit into psychiatry was the unquestionable wave of the future. The special character of Viennese culture in the 1920s, which was equally reflected in its painting, music, and literature of the time, called for just this evolution from the purely nosological or purely organic background of previous psychiatric thought.

The development of psychiatry in the United States was something entirely different from what started in Vienna. Consequently the people in this country did not take kindly to Schilder. After he came to the U.S. and got an appointment at Bellevue Hospital, where I was once again his assistant, he joined the Psychoanalytic Society of New York. Later, the society dropped him as a member because they considered him a maverick and not a real psychoanalyst. He had been accepted by the analysts in Vienna but the analysts in New York were too cult-oriented to accept him. Many of his ideas quickly became institutionalized and thus neutralized.

Interestingly enough, the psychiatric community didn't want Schilder either, because the orientation of psychiatry in the United States has always been more biological. Adolph Meyer, a granddaddy of psychiatry in the U.S., always felt uncomfortable taking psychiatry anywhere that was too far from the organic. Meyer was always promoting the idea of mind and body as one. It was almost as if his guilt feelings were such that he constantly had to prove that psychiatry was pure and in no way denigrating the organic. He wanted so much for the organic and the psyche to be one. He made a ruling theme of this because he did not wish to offend the organic community.

Paul Schilder, however, wasn't bothered by that kind of guilt problem. Although he never expressed it in this way, I believe he was aware that in every language there is one word for logic and an entirely different word for the psychological. The world of the logical is an independent world; it exists apart from us—apart from me, apart from you. The world of the psychological does not. It exists only in you and me. This is a phenomenological approach. Psychology starts with *Ich und Du.* That is to say, it starts with a relationship. It is a dynamic, fluid, constant interreaction. However, because the possibility for a relationship is, so to speak, an effluent of the body or has its source in the body, it is in this sense only that psychology and the body are one.

Schilder did clinical studies to illustrate this idea. Once he asked me to pick out a half-dozen cases of syphilis of the brain. As assistant to Wagner-Jauregg, I was responsible for the work-up of new patients with syphilis of the brain. Before I would inject them with malaria, I would give them a physical and mental status examination. After injection, I would take care of them during the period of their fever reactions, and then kill the malaria.

Schilder wanted to examine several cases of organic brain deterioration before they received the malarial treatment. He tested their recall and memory. After they recovered and began to function more or less normally again, he would retest the same patients as to their recall and remote memory. He found that a great many of these so-called organic cases that had completely lost their recall and memory prior to treatment had regained memory after treatment. A strict organicist could not explain such a phenomenon because once the capacity was lost, a patient could not get it back, since the lesions could not be repaired. Schilder's theory maintained that memory was not simply organic but also psychological in nature. His conclusion supported the phenomenological approach.

Since Schilder's era, American psychiatry has given a completely different definition and direciton to the science of psychology. Instead of trying to simplify psychoanalysis and phenomenology, American psychiatry has developed mechanistic psychologies that depart from a psychology that is theoretically founded in human relationships. These are efforts to mechanize human behavior. The latest expressions are in biochemistry in which human feelings and behavior are reduced to the elucidation of chemicals.

Whereas the principles of physics and mathematics operate independent of human beings, psychology is a science distinctly related to human functioning. Science is a set of observations about which theories can be organized and rules formulated that are then tested and replicated by experiments. Both Bergson and Poincaré believed this was possible for psychology as well as any field of observation. Psychiatry and psychology may fruitfully employ scientific method, but the resulting theories do not have to be mechanistic. Paul Schilder succeeded in showing this. I believe the eclecticism in psychiatry today still tacitly represents the dynamic and analytical phenomenology that Schilder formulated.

Chapter 2

SANDOR LORAND, M.D.

Interviewed by Max Rosenbaum, Ph.D.

I met Paul Schilder for the first time in Poland during World War I. I am Hungarian and Schilder was Austrian, and we were both attached to the Health Corps of the Austrian-Hungarian Army. I got to know Schilder and liked him.

On my way to the U.S. in 1925, I went to Vienna to refresh my knowledge of gynecology at the (Algemeiner) Krankenhause, since I did not know what kind of employment I would find in New York and wanted a specialty to fall back on if necessary. As it was, I believe I became the first thoroughly trained psychoanalyst in the United States.

While in Vienna I renewed my friendship with Schilder, who was an associate professor at The University of Vienna under Wagner-Jauregg. At the time, Wagner-Jauregg was engaged in the malarial treatment of brain syphilis, for which he received the Nobel Prize. I believe Paul Schilder was instrumental in the implementation of that treatment.

When Schilder came to the United States, he renewed his contact with me in New York, and I helped him in various ways where I could. He was having a difficult time in his marriage. He wanted to divorce his Austrian wife, Mitzi, but feared Americans would react negatively if he did, and that it might affect him professionally. I urged him to live his life the way he wanted.

I suggested to A.A. Brill and Smith Ely Jeliffe the formation of the Paul Schilder Society to give stature to his achievements and ideas. I truly liked Paul, and we maintained a friendship through the years. He was a nice human being one could relate to. After the New York Psychoanalytic Society Education Committee deprived him of his status as a training analyst in the New York Society, we formed the Paul Schilder Society, which still functions today.

One example of Paul's objectivity and sensitivity comes to mind. He once referred a person to me saying, "He's a nice young man—but he wants to discover gunpowder." It was a play on a German expression meaning this man had to come to grips with the fact that he had positive qualities but limited capacities.

I believe there is no such thing as a passive analyst. Paul Schilder was a man both active and objective in treating his patients.

Chapter 3

REFLECTIONS ON PAUL SCHILDER[1]

Lauretta Bender, M.D.

I met Paul Schilder at Adolph Meyer's Phipps Clinic in Johns Hopkins Hospital, Baltimore, Maryland, on January 2, 1930, at 9:00 a.m. Adolph Meyer always had a morning session with staff, and on that day he introduced Paul Schilder, who had come as a visiting professor and would stay for three months. I immediately fell for him. During those three months we were associated quite closely. At the time I was doing follow-up studies on schizophrenic women who had been treated at Phipps Clinic and had been transferred to Springfield State Hospital outside of Baltimore. I was also just starting my work on what would later become the Bender-Gestalt Test. I first used it as a research tool for patients who were not communicative. Paul Schilder went with me to see those patients at Springfield State Hospital. We made several studies together there. One was on schizophrenics' reaction to pain, about which he wrote a paper.[11] He also showed me various motility tests and had me observe sensory phenomena in schizophrenic women. He became acquainted with my Gestalt test, which he liked very much and used, and he wrote a preface to the monograph when it was published in 1938.[15]

From the very beginning, I was attracted by his keen thinking, his imagination, his capacity to envisage so many things from his examination of patients, and his ready contact and affinity with patients, which enabled him to reach them and get them to talk to him and to demonstrate in each one the various motility and biological

[1] Taped interview 10/18/80 Severna Park, Maryland.

problems. Of course, this was consistent with Paul Schilder's belief that schizophrenia was a problem of the whole body, the body image, social life, psychological life, and biological life of the patient. I was impressed by the breadth of his mind and his ability and alertness in observing things about him that were significant to his whole philosophy of life.

Among his most outstanding contributions were his body-image concept, his grasp of the interrelationship between neurological functioning and perceptional and psychic functioning, and his capacity to correlate all these areas, as he did in *Medical Psychology*.[193] For instance, from the body-image concept came the realization that the drawing of the human figure by any individual was a self-portrait and a projection of the body image. We learned from that time on to use patients' drawings of human figures as their expression of the body image and problems connected with it. From this he went on to interpret modern art, classical art, and oriental art as expressive of human problems and of his total philosophy.[189, 190, 194, 195]

Although I believe Paul Schilder does have at least a floating and unorganized school, one of the reasons no formal school developed around him was that he simply didn't live long enough. After all, he was only fifty-four when he died. At the time, he was in the process of creating a global outline for psychiatry. He had several books in mind and expected to make a summary of his work. Although I have attempted to carry on as much of his project as I could by publishing his collected writings in English (five volumes) since his death, I obviously couldn't do it the way he intended. Only a small part of his extensive German writings have been translated into English.

If he were alive today, Paul Schilder would be tremendously interested in all the work that has come out of embryology, the new work that has come out of the perception of the two sides of the brain, and especially the new work on vestibular function, which Schilder really started. Another very important contribution was his ability to conceive and work out special research methods for delving into these different areas. He was not interested—and maybe the time hadn't yet arrived—in the present trend toward the statistical analysis and computerization of knowledge. He was more interested in individual patients, in what they could experience, and also in what he could learn from their experience. Paul Schilder was always a therapist. Every contact that he had with a patient was for the patient's good, even though the contact also gave Schilder new insights, information, and ideas for future thought. He contributed extensively to psychotherapy, psychoanalytic therapy, and group therapy, and used all forms of supportive techniques, such as art. He encouraged all of the therapeutic activities that my associates and I used with children.

Paul Schilder was both a humanist and a phenomenologist. This is demonstrated by the phenomenological paper he wrote on children's development of symbol formation and language.[211] He wrote extensively on the construction of thought processes, as has been noted by David Rapaport.[189] Paul considered himself a social psychologist as much as anything else.

But I have seen statements deriding his phenomenology as old-fashioned and, so to speak, not appropriate to the American scene. Such statements overlook not only Schilder's achievements but also those achievements and contributions of phenomenology to human understanding.

Schilder's legacy to psychiatry and the history of ideas will depend a great deal on what people do with his ideas—and how receptive they are to works like the present volume. I do see him quoted in the field of vestibular function.[204]

Schilder was definitely a help to me in my own professional career, very stimulating and responsive. He did everything he could to encourage me and pushed me in every way possible, almost beyond my strength at times, because during these years I had our three children. Many of the women who came from Vienna warned me about Paul. They said, "You won't get along with him because he puts women down." But it wasn't true at all; he did everything he could to promote my career.

We did quite an elaborate study on alcoholic encephalopathy[12] in which Paul did the clinical work and I did the neuropathology. In many of the papers we wrote together he would dictate the abstract part and I would contribute the clinical case histories. We always worked together whenever we travelled, which was frequently, and I always took a typewriter. When we went to Holland, they laughed at me because I took a typewriter and didn't take an umbrella. Often, he would dictate to me on our vacation.

He did more of the intense thinking and I did more of the concrete work.

As far as my own contributions are concerned, my own Gestalt test has been significant. The Bender-Gestalt Test demonstrates perceptual maturation. I think my concept of maturation and disorders of maturation, or maturational lag, is important. Also significant is my hypothesis that maturational lags exist in both schizophrenia and developmental language disorders. These matura-tional lags contribute to the degree of plasticity such patients exhibit in their functioning. This explains a great deal about their problems, but also explains the possibilities for growth and for correction of their problems, or even acceleration in some maturational functions.

Paul Schilder was a psychoanalyst; he considered himself one. I had trained through him and had been psychoanalyzed, but it was not one of my major fields. It was one of his major fields but, on the other hand, he was neurologically and neurobiologically trained, as I was. We did have that in common. He said that until he worked with me, he didn't know you could work with children. For that he gave me credit.

As a psychiatrist, a wife, and a mother, I was able to combine my career with my family life. I am surprised at the professional women of today because they are so self-conscious about it. I was never particularly conscious that there was any great problem con-nected with it. I just did what I wanted to do from one stage to the next. But different people may react differently. Though others may consider me as such, I do not consider myself as having been a pioneer in the area of women's liberation. I can understand how younger women might consider me as a model, but I was never very conscious that I did anything special as a woman. Fortunately, Paul Schilder had the idea that women should live out all their life possibilities and instincts. He was delighted when we had children. We were married only four years, but people coming from Vienna said those were the happiest years of Paul's life. His death was a terri-ble shock. It seemed so unnecessary to lose him at that age. But I had a job on my hands. I had three children, a full-time job at the Bellevue Hospital and New York University, and I also had much to do in keeping his work alive. But that became very rewarding—a labor of love.

Paul Schilder was a very warm individual, not only with me and our children, but of course with various people who knew him. He always had lots of friends around. He was the one that people coming from Vienna—like Judith Kestenberg, Josef Gerstmann, and others—would see immediately. As a matter of fact, after his death, many people would come to me saying they intended to come to Paul Schilder, but now came to me to help them get settled.

Paul always liked his students. He was very concerned that they be well taught and have really important learning experiences. Fur-thermore, he believed that these experiences should entail not only what he knew but also their relationship with patients from whom they might learn for themselves to better develop themselves.

Paul Schilder enjoyed giving credit to his students. Many of his papers are published with the other author's name first because his name comes late in the alphabet. I've had people say, "But, his name should have come first." It had been Paul who insisted that it should be in alaphabetical order.

For fun and recreation, Paul liked the art museums to the point of exhausting me. The Museum of Modern Art in New York was his particular favorite. Of course, he collected oriental art, and these works are all originals and very valuable. He had intended to gather an entire collection, and visualized a house on the East Side of New York in which he would display his collection. It was a goal he never realized. We had a fire in 1962 at the summer house in Long Beach, Long Island, in which some of the collection was destroyed.

He very much enjoyed children. He enjoyed having social affairs with his Viennese friends. He loved going to parties. However, he would often describe their parties this way: if the urging to eat was slight, the food was good; if the urging was strong, the food was sometimes poor. He enjoyed such affairs very much, but they could also be exhausting for me. He could talk Viennese and German until the wee hours, but I'd be falling asleep on a couch somewhere, either pregnant or nursing a baby.

With regard to the intellectual climate of Vienna, he talked about Wagner-Jauregg as the one who mostly supported him. He talked about Freud, and felt there were some differences between them. In the end he tried to reconcile some of them with Freud. Paul had me type a letter to him in English. Freud objected to this, maintaining that Schilder should have handwritten the message in German.

We used to go to Alfred Adler's meetings held regularly at his hotel quarters in New York. They were very pleasant evenings. Alexandra Adler and her brother were to join us later after they left Vienna.

And, of course, we had meetings at Bellevue Hospital, which Paul developed into the Society of Psychotherapy and Psychopathology—now the Schilder Society.

When Paul bought the summer home for me and the children at Long Beach on Long Island, he said he would never serve hard liqour there. If people visited, it would have to be for social reasons, for the beach, or for him. He was a very sociable person—quite open-minded and interested in people. That interest, of course, extended to his patients. He said, "Always believe everything a patient tells you." And many psychiatrists don't, you know.

Chapter 4

PAUL SCHILDER AND INTEGRATIVE PSYCHIATRY

Iago Galdston, M.D.[1]

Heinz Hartmann, who has made the most ambitious critical analysis to date of Schilder's psychiatric work, describes Schilder as "one of those men who would have achieved great things in every branch of science." Hartmann signalizes just those qualities of Schilder's personality and scholarship that endeared him to all who knew him and that gained him the esteem of the learned. He had an astounding memory. He was versatile; he possessed the faculties of imaginative and critical thinking. He exercised these competencies in both theoretical and clinical explorations. Schilder was able "to bridge the tension between contrasting worlds of thought, leaving relative independence to the subordinate viewpoints."[94] He "did not squeeze individual observations into the Procrustean bed of too limited theoretical formula, nor . . . on the other hand (did) the variety of the single phenomena get lost without being formed."[94]

In *In Memoriam,* Fritz Wittels wrote "It will be the task of the large community of his friends to collect and to organize his discoveries, observations, theories, and critical comments, in order to find the basic plan which exists in every life dedicated to scientific work."[248]

To seek the basic plan in Schilder's life is to engage on a most ambitious adventure. Fortunately Schilder himself, shortly before his death, published an *Apologia,*[216] which affords us a sketch of the basic plan of his inner life, that is, of his cultural and scientific life.

Paul Schilder was born of Jewish parents in the city of Vienna, Austria. His father, who died when Paul was but three or four years

[1]Past President, Schilder Society, N.Y.

of age, was of Northeast European origin. He was a soap merchant. Paul affirmed that he had little or no recollection of his father. His mother, on the other hand, had a profound influence upon him. She was a strong and intelligent woman who early recognized her son's extraordinary endowments, and encouraged him in their cultivation. Paul had one brother, with whom he appears to have had little in common.

The death of Paul's father, when Paul was so young, deprived him of normal economic and psychological support. It is likely that his early loss of the father and the urge to redeem the father image may have directed Paul's energies first into medicine, and then into psychiatry.

Schilder tells us that he became interested in philosophical problems at the age of thirteen. Given his superior mentality, it is reasonable to suspect that this precocious interest was in part the search for intellectual and emotional insight, and in part an effort to find security in a clear orientation toward "man and life." Buechner's *Kraft und Stoff* provided him with a materialist foundation. Schopenhauer, Nietzsche, and Kant, listed in this odd order, were his succeeding interests. Philology and philosophy tempted him further, but he chose medicine because, as he wrote, he "wanted to be in closer relation to human beings." Later he elected the specialty of psychiatry for similar reasons, because therein he saw an approach to "the fundamentals of human life."

In electing medicine Schilder did not turn his back on philosophy or philology. On the contrary, he remained a philosopher to the end. As his knowledge of the anatomy, physiology, and pathology of the nervous system increased, and as his experience with the mentally ill broadened, his awareness of the need for a philosophic matrix to bind together, to give pattern and meaning to the data of experience, increased accordingly. It is thus easy to understand why his work with Gabriel Anton at Halle an der Saale, and his absorption of the teachings of both Meynert and Wernicke nurtured his intellect but left him unsatisfied, and why he felt that the basic insights proffered by both these great neuropsychiatrists required deeper psychological study. Schilder made an heroic effort to dig deeper, to achieve the penetration he deemed essential. But in his first endeavor he fell short of his aim. Indeed he did not succeed until his knowledge and his thinking were transilluminated and redirected by Freud's teachings.

Schilder's first paper appeared in 1909. Between 1909 and 1914 he published a total of eighteen contributions. Only one among these dealt with a psychiatric subject in the strict sense of the term. All the others were neurological in content; and among them was a paper that fixed Schilder's name in the annals of neurological history: *Zur Frage der Enzephalitis periaxialis diffusa.*[184]

The single psychiatric paper *Ueber das Selbstbewusstsein und seine Storungen*[185] appeared in 1913. It was nine pages long and dealt with a theme to the elaboration of which Schilder devoted the major energies of his remaining years. In 1914 Schilder's first book appeared. It was 304 pages long and was titled *Selbstbewusstsein und Personlichkeitsbewusstsein.*[186] In the same year Schilder published what may be considered to have been his first psychoanalytically oriented paper. It was titled *Zur Kenntniss symbolahnlicher Bildungen im Rahmen der Schizophrenie.*[187] Schilder stated that by these studies he "was led to a closer approach to Freudian ideas." His "study on schizophrenia served to further increase his belief in the validity of Freudian symbolism."[215]

However, Schilder's volume *Selbstbewusstsein und Personlichkeitsbewusstsein*, published in 1915, reveals no analytical insight. It was evidently composed before he acquired an effective understanding of psychoanalysis. This volume is a most impressive witness of the impenetrable fog in which psychiatry was engulfed in the pre-Freudian days. Knowledge was vast, but understanding lacking. It was as in the days before the Rosetta Stone was brought to light, when all the accumulated hieroglyphics served only to deepen one's sense of frustration and impotence.

Selbstbewusstsein und Personlichkeitsbewusstsein is a substantial volume, wherein, besides reviewing what had been previously taught and written on the problem of depersonalization, Schilder presents numerous carefully and thoroughly detailed case histories. The pages literally cry out with a profusion of data which to the psychoanalytically attuned intelligence proffers etiology and dynamic causality, as well as clear insight into the patient's complaint and behavior. As one turns the pages of this meaty work, one expects to come upon that clinching section which shows that the author has grasped the meaning of the data he has so painstakingly, so fully and so competently gathered and recorded. These expectations, however, go unfulfilled. Only years later, after 1918, after the First World War, after he had come into personal contact with the Viennese Psychoanalytic Society, do we find in the works of Schilder that effulgent quality which makes it so outstanding in the literature of psychiatry.

At the outbreak of the First World War, Schilder volunteered for service in the Austrian Army, and for the duration of the war served first at the front, and then at base hospitals. It is noteworthy and so very characteristic of Schilder's demonic drive (demonic in the Socratic sense, i.e., to learn, to study, to experience) that during these war years and sometimes under heavy gunfire, he resumed and continued his intensive studies in philosophy and carried them through with such competence as to entitle him to a degree of the doctorate in philosophy. It was not, however, to wile the hours away, nor yet to cater to the ambitious demands of an "academic ego" that Schilder was moved to resume his philosophical studies. It was rather because he felt keenly the need for deeper insight into the data of psychologic and psychiatric experience, and because he was persuaded that such an insight could be gained only by reducing the data of experience to some encompassing generalizations. This to his own satisfaction he was able to accomplish. Two fundamental trends of thought were clarified for him during this period of intensive study: first, that the laws of the psyche and the laws of the organism are identical, i.e., that thought and imagination can be studied with methods similar to those used in the study of perception; second, that this biological process is a process of development which is clearly reflected in the development of each single thought, i.e., that thoughts develop from primitive stages through continuous contact with the motives of experience, passing from a protozoan-like stage to more and more complicated organic forms. In the process of this development the different parts of reality come into focus. Individuals strive towards the world, and through a constructive process arrive at configurations in perception and action. This leads not only to increased insight into the structure of the world, but also to a more satisfactory experience in the unified personality.[216]

This most compact summation of Schilder's psycho-philosophical convictions is not easy to comprehend. Yet it does afford us a key to Schilder's works, many of which on superficial inspection might otherwise appear like a motley mass of disjointed excursions.

In the above cited summation there are two departments of thought. Each stands compactly separate, yet both are organically united to yield a superior dynamic resultant.

Schilder first affirms that "the laws of the psyche and the laws of the organism are identical," and that both psyche and organism may be studied by similar if not identical methods. This affirmation, except that it excludes epiphenomenalism and the vitalistic separation of the psyche, is hardly a distinguished affirmation. Standing alone it would arouse suspicion that we have here the profession of an easy naturalism, one that seeks to reduce psychology to the elementary biology of nerve function. But it does *not* stand alone. It is linked to a second affirmation, namely, "that this biological process is a process of development." This too appears a relatively innocuous affirmation. However, on inspection we discern that the "dead weight" lies in the term "development." It is far too commonplace a term. *Emmergent evolvement* would have better served his intention.

The above quotation is taken from his *Vita* and Bibliography included in this volume. His words reflect convictions crystalized in his philosophical studies of some twenty years or more. In 1928 Schilder published a rather elaborate and remarkably comprehensive exposition of his philosophical convictions under the title *Gedanken zur Naturphilosophie*. A reading of these *Gedanken* affords one clear understanding of why Schilder was so receptive and responsive to Freud's teachings—and also why he took exception to a number of the psychoanalytic tenets. "No unbiased observer," wrote Schilder, "could afford to neglect the data which Freud had brought forward concerning human drives and the structure of the psychic apparatus." "The fundamentals of dream interpretation and of the libido theory seemed to be beyond doubt, and indeed have proved to be of lasting value for the understanding of the organism." However, Schidler critisized and rejected what he termed the "regressive character" of psychoanalysis, finding it senseless to believe that "life should intend merely to return to prior stages of satisfaction, and to rest," nor would he subscribe to Freud's ideas concerning the death instinct.

In 1919 Schilder became a member of the staff and faculty of the University Hospital of Vienna, and there he continued his services and studies until 1929, when he came to stay in the United States. These were fruitful and productive years. The Clinic of Wagner von Jauregg afforded Schilder a fortunate medium for the exercise of his skills and faculties. The Clinic was essentially neurologic and somatic in orientation, yet it tolerated psychoanalytic research and therapy. Poetzl, von Jauregg's assistant, tried to combine psychoanalysis and brain pathology; Schilder actually achieved it. How well he did this is reflected in his splendid monograph *Brain and Personality*.[201] This most pregnant, provocative, and stimulating work, representing the lectures delivered by Schilder at the Phipps Psychiatric Clinic of Johns Hopkins University from 1928 to 1930, still remains a shining example of what I would term Integrative Psychiatry. In this brilliant exposition of "brain and personality," free of all "parallelisms," and of the naive concepts common in the current psychosomatic doxy, we encounter a clear-eyed exposition of what we know and what we do not know, and numerous suggestions for further study and research.

The temptation to cite more passages from this luminous work, *Brain and Personality*, is hard to resist. Here Schilder appears to have been unfettered in inspiration and imagination. Little wonder that Adolph Meyer described Schilder "as a representative of European psychiatry combining the training in neurology and internal medicine and psychopathology generally and also psychoanalysis and keenness for the sciences and the philosophical and cultural background."

During the ten years of his stay at von Jauregg's Clinic, Schilder came into closer contact with Freud and with the Vienna Psychoanalytic Society. During this period he absorbed and incorporated into his own thinking much of psychoanalytic theory, but likewise there came to the fore those differences which led Schilder ultimately to separate himself from the so-called orthodox followers of Freud.

Wittels[248] reports the Freud once criticized Schilder for working in "too wide dimensions," instead of limiting himself to psycho-analytic microscopy. The criticism may or may not have been war-ranted, but it very aptly reflects the difference in their respective positions.

Schilder did not come to analysis, as did most of Freud's associates and pupils, a novitiate in psychiatry. On the contrary, Schilder brought with him a vast score of neurological, psychiatric, and clinical experience that validated analytical theory. But then—and here is where the fracture came—his experience, his knowledge, his understanding, in some directions outreached the compass of analytic theory, and there he could not but follow his own light. In this, one recognizes the kinship between Schilder and Ferenczi. Ferenczi, like Schilder, though not in the same measure, brought with him when he joined the analytic movement a sound training in neurology and in "classical" psychiatry. Ferenczi too was at odds with orthodox analytical theory and practice on the self-same scores that agitated Schilder.

Schilder never denounced nor renounced psychoanalysis. He merely disassociated himself from those who pretended to be the guardians of analytical orthodoxy, from the so-to-speak "Synod of Analysis."

Chapter 5

PAUL SCHILDER
Fragmentary Recollections

Nathan S. Kline, M.D.

There were many things that were disturbing when one first heard Paul Schilder—the Viennese accent, the high squeaky voice, the gesticulations. All of these initial distractions eventually led to vastly improved communication. Once a Schilderian presentation had begun, there was no possibility of confusing it with any other experience. All the unconscious associations, the "latent learning" and the *prima psychiatrica assaluta* performance created a special frame of mind conducive to profound comprehension.

By the end, of the second lecture that I heard Schilder give, I knew without question that I had found the therapist for the mildly agitated depression that I had been carefully nursing for many years. The analysis took a bit more than a year. By the end, the volume of material was substantial since it included not only Dr. Schilder's notes but also a detailed account of my dream-life during that period together with Schilder's exegesis. As a medical student I was allowed to register as a Bellevue outpatient and hence the record was retained in the Bellevue outpatient files. Schilder had already met with his tragic fatal accident at the time of my departure, and hence I took my case history along with me. I have guarded it carefully for forty years now. I feel that I am still a bit young to fully appreciate it but my sixty-fifth birthday is due shortly, at which time I will allow myself to review the material.

Treatment was obviously successful, since I can't remember a single thing about it. What I do remember is my third year when I spent three months as a psychiatric extern. Not only did Dr. Schilder approve of this, but assigned me to work as his amanuensis—an occupation which continued on a part-time basis for most of the next year as well. My function was to sit in an unobtrusive part of the room taking notes, which at the end of the session were turned over to Schilder. Unfortunately none of these contacts led to any other contacts with him. Although he was among the most kindly of men, he did not encourage familiarity; or perhaps it was my own diffidence.

My recollection is that all of his suits had vests and that he carried what appeared to be an inexpensive Ingersoll watch in the lower vest pocket on each side. Immediately before a session with the patients began, he would simultaneously remove the watches from the left and right side of his vest and place them on the table before him. I was never able to fathom the purpose nor did I have the courage to ask.

Schilder's wit was frequently based on observing what some saw and others did not. My own choice was the day he was berating an extravagant patient: "The trouble with you is not that you live above your income. Everyone should do that. But you live *too much* above it."

Chapter 6

GROUP PSYCHOTHERAPY AND GENIUS[1]
The World of Paul Schilder

Donald A. Shaskan, M.D.

The year 1965 marked the 25th anniversary of the death of Paul
Schilder, scholar, student, teacher, eminent researcher, precursor of
group psychotherapy. Let me recall a few incidents from my own en-
counters with him at Bellevue Hospital and again draw your attention to his position of prominence for the richness and depth of a
massive contribution to the field of psychotherapy.

His contribution, which it is hard to believe one man alone in a
comparatively brief lifetime could make, is not measurable in conventional terms. It has had an effect upon every serious student of
normal and abnormal psychology.

It was the product of an encyclopedic mind and an insatiable
curiosity about people. Whatever was provocative, whatever was being investigated relevant to his interest after he came to America in
the 1920s, was added to an already tremendous store of knowledge.

Bellevue Hospital provided him with the kind of case history
material which no other hospital in the United States could have offered. Its psychiatric service, housed in a large new building, provided treatment for every category of patient: children and adults alike;
alcoholics and prisoners—the social failures then as now; and two
wards of extremely disturbed patients. All the separate and individual disciplines were represented and all were of equal interest to
Schilder.

The term that fits him best is one used by the late David
Rapaport for describing his role among the top theoreticians and

[1] Reprinted from *Group Analysis* II,3, January 1970.

clinicians, namely "a minister without portfolio." By this is meant an observer who knows intimately the work and publications of leading exponents of all related fields. This role he could fill like no one else around him. He could report on the sequences of thought of each authority—where they agreed, where they differed, from what sources they had drawn their ideas. And what was the most remarkable feat of all, he could point out what they had failed to observe, without detracting from the significance and import of their contributions.

Into this phenomenal world which Schilder was always in the process of restructuring—so much so that he never repeated himself—he invited students and colleagues alike to enter and to feast upon its riches.

To make rounds with him on the psychiatric service was an experience of profound influence on students, colleagues, and patients. It was a scene of lively discussion and intense questioning of the patient by Schilder. (I need not remind you that these were the days before the drug therapies which have since made patients more amenable to treatment.) Schilder considered the doctor-patient relationship to be one of the highest order; he used it successfully to bring the patient into his world. In the same manner, he expressed a great respect for the integrity of students beginning their experience in psychotherapy. He encouraged them to give articulation to their opinions and observations on pathological processes. I recall with pleasure even now his words of commendation when, on neurological examination of a patient suffering from depression, I located a brain tumor.

Each new discovery would provide a new opportunity to draw from his wealth of knowledge of the nervous system. His background in clinical medicine, physiology, biology, and pathology was extraordinary. It served as a screen against which he projected his formulations on psychic functions and thought processes. It was easy for him to visualize things in a dynamic state—attributable, I believe, to his having perfected a mastery of relationships.

Any physical trauma of the body—no matter how slight—was reason for Schilder to inquire into how the patient responded psychologically to it. What effect had this on the body image, and what compensations did the patient make for it? I never saw him tire from the search for more precise information on how the patient measured the differing degrees on his or her feeling scale. Everything was comparative and the search went on continuously. Not only did he believe the psychotherapist should analyze expressed feelings, but that he or she should also be aware of the ideologies that the patient fosters, to the exclusion of leading a normally happy life. The therapist, too, should not overlook the nature of the ideologies which he or she defends as a "way of life." These, in Schilder's experience, can be serious deterrents to an individual's human growth. The experience of the group, however, he observed to be humanizing—what Slavson refers to as universalization.

Schilder's interest in the qualities enjoyed by individuals of genius led him to some formulations which provide the reader with new insights. What he had to say about creativity has been further amplified by Ernst Kris in his studies. Schilder observed in geniuses the existence of an uncommon ability, on the one hand, plus an abiding interest in the subject matter, on the other hand. The uncommon ability binds the interest. He used as one of his examples the scientist Gauss who had an uncommon ability in seeing relationships between numbers which escaped the notice of others. Using this ability early in life laid the foundation for an enormous interest in numbers. This same formula, it seems to me, can be applied to Schilder, whose powers of observation of human behavior led him to an ever-deepening interest in the human psyche.

David Rapaport, for whom Schilder offered such a rich challenge to his own search for psychological truths and who was during his lifetime one of Schilder's most devoted followers and disciples (although, as he says, he scarcely knew him personally), enriches one's appreciation of Schilder through his own selective commentary. He refers to Schilder as an "unsystematic genius" who sowed the seed without any thought of harvest which it has remained for others to reap.

Before passing on to what I think is significant to group psychotherapists, I would like to quote from a speech that Rapaport made before the Schilder Society in New York in the early 1950s. He refers to two points of departure for Schilder, which he describes as his articles of faith: (1) Human thinking is directed toward an existing world of objects, and without assuming the existence of such a world of objects, no theory of thinking can be built; (2)Socialization, just like reality-directedness, is not an acquisition of thinking or human psychological life, but a basic implication of it.

These he endeavoured to demonstrate through describing drive actions and expressive movements, showing that these forms of behavior, already directed to an audience, are communications. He linked language to expressive movements, tracing thus its fundamentally socialized character—socialization is not acquired but lies in the very nature of human psychic organization. Rapaport continues, "Here, again, Schilder did not break the continuity between drive and primary process on the one hand, and experience, learning, cultural influence, socialization, and secondary process on the other."

It seems that although the ego is strongly motivated to perform certain tasks, it adds to its functions that of adaptation to the object world which it has developed through the processes of socialization and acculturation. Schilder, though greatly impressed by the "environmentalists" like Fromm, Sullivan, and Horney, regretted their slighting of the concept of man's behavior as basically motivated from within.

Heinz Hartmann, in the development of his theory of ego psychology, pays tribute to Schilder's ideas on adaptation and automatization, which had not been fully developed by Schilder.[169]

What then prompted Schilder to form the first group of patients at Bellevue? In part, I believe, it was stimulated by his curiosity as to why people in New York were joining groups formed for the purpose of making public confessions of their shortcomings. This was the topic of the day in the early 1930s, as some of you may recall. The effect of the group on the individual challenged his interest. I even recall a demonstration of hypnosis before a group of students which he was leading, where the question of the effect of student reaction on the hypnotist and the subject stimulated his help in a questionnaire that I drew up and submitted to the students. The results indicated a correlation between the reaction of the students and the increased feelings of power of the hypnotist, plus increased feelings of submission of the subject, as compared to a simple hypnosis.

Some time later he invited me to sit in as an observer on this group which he was organizing. He selected four or five patients whom he was seeing in individual psychotherapy. He was rather cautious about this whole procedure. As I recall, we even met in some basement room, where he had his office. He had suggested to the patients that they write up a history of major events in their lives. He thought this might facilitate their participation in the group. The idea was that I should comment on the session, which also gave him a chance to interpret my relationship to him and to the group. He was most impressed with the way feelings of isolation were overcome in the group.

There was a lapse of several years before I resumed group therapy. By that time, Paul Schilder had died but, in retrospect, I have often thought of how I shared his "hunch" that we had started something that would prove valuable in the future treatment of patients. On the flyleaf of a book he published, *Psychotherapy*[213] inscribed most generously were his words: "To Donald Shaskan, in remembrance of common work together."

I hope this brief introduction into Schilder's world will give you some idea of its color, its complexity, its richness. For those of you who have never experienced it, may I suggest that you have no time to lose in beginning.

Chapter 7

COMMENTS ON PAUL SCHILDER[1]

S. H. Foulkes, M.D.

I am very pleased to add my own appreciation of Paul Schilder to that of Dr. Shaskan, the more so as my experience with Schilder is complementary to that of Shaskan's, insofar as it refers to the time when Schilder was still in Vienna where I met him fairly frequently, although I cannot say that I knew him very well as a person.

The first time I encountered Schilder was when he read a paper, on a psychoanalytic theme, to the Conference of Psychotherapists at Bad Nauheim in 1937. He made a strange impression with his birdlike face, and speaking as he sometimes did in a highpitched voice. However, I soon became submerged in what he said and his voice seemed to lower in tone, and when he finished I knew I had listened to one of the few exceptional people who had something original to say.

I remember very vividly when we celebrated (if that is the right word) his departure from Vienna in a kind of beer garden at a long table under beautiful old trees. Most of the staff of the Psychiatric University Clinic were present, including Potzl, Hoff, Hartmann, Herschmann, Stengel, and many others. When he left, Schilder shook hands with all of us. This was the last, alas, that I ever saw of him.

I knew Schilder principally in two different capacities: the one at the Clinic and the other at the Psycho-Analytic Institute. He was then still a member of the Psycho-Analytic Society in Vienna and taught there. At the Clinic I accompanied him often on visits which

[1]Reprinted from *Group Analysis* II,3, January 1970 (Comments following article by Donald A. Shaskan, M.D.)

invariably were also occasions for clinical and theoretical discussions. This was in 1931, in the interval between his first visit to the United States and his finally going to settle there.

There was another special occasion in which I took part regularly. This was his Clinical Lecture or Demonstration. He had an original way of demonstrating psychoanalytic mechanisms, such as repression, denial, symbolic expressions, displacement, and so forth, on what were clinically psychotic patients, especially schizophrenics, because they showed these features very much more clearly in brief demonstration than neurotics would have.

At the Psycho-Analytic Institute, I was one of five members—if I remember rightly—who took part in his course, and it was therefore quite an intimate affair. I remember that Isakower and Dr. Zingg were present, but cannot now recall the other two. I think the theme was psychoanalytic psychopathology in general way, but it may have had a more specific slant of which I cannot now be certain.

I have often mentioned Schilder in my writings, and those familiar with them will probably often see his influence. I counted him, after Freud and with Kurt Goldstein, as the most influential teacher I had in psychiatry or medical psychology· and psychopathology. Needlesss to say, Schilder's writings have a great deal to do with what I learned from him. I am particularly thinking of his book *The Body Image* and *The Blueprint of Psychiatry on Psychoanalytic Basis*—but also of quite a number of his other writings, such as *Brain and Personality* and *Psychoanalysis, Man and Society*.

After Schilder's departure for the United States I had only one more contact with him. I sent him a paper on Helen Keller thinking it might especially interest him. He wrote appreciatively about it and had it published in the *Psychoanalytic Review*. I still remember that he drew my attention in the same letter to his book *The Image and Appearance of the Human Body*, which was then about to appear.

Perhaps in this context a reference to Schilder as a precursor to group psychotherapy is not out of place. When I first started practicing in my own way as a psychoanalyst what I later called group analytic psychotherapy, I knew that Schilder had begun with similar experiments in the United States, but I had no details, as his book on psychotherapy was not on hand. I was so convinced that what he would be doing would be in line with what I was doing, that I boldly declared that I practiced group psychotherapy on the lines of Paul Schilder. Later, in view of his reports, I found that I had in fact gone much further in this than Schilder had ever done, although I was not at all disappointed to have been classified as his follower. He had in fact only gone a few steps towards a more full-fledged group analytic psychotherapy.

However, I have little doubt that had he lived, he would have developed this very much further, and I think in the same direction as I have done. His paper on the analysis of ideologies in groups is nevertheless one of the best contributions in this field.

Part II

PAST INVESTIGATIONS

Chapter 8

INTRODUCTORY NOTE ON PHENOMENOLOGICAL METHOD
The Intentionality of Consciousness

William Roller, M.A.

Many of Schilder's speculations and aphorisms make sense in the light of the phenomenology of Franz Brentano and Edmund Husserl.[1] Notes have been added to *The Body Image and Social Psychology* (included in this volume) to elucidate the many levels of significance of Schilder's thought. His remarks will open the reader's mind to perspectives seldom considered in the context of psychology and psychiatry. Phenomenology—in the broadest sense—attempts to understand the conditions for our knowledge of the world by paying attention to and describing our very experience of the world. Phenomenology is a detailed description of phenomena in which the point of view and assumptions of the investigator are carefully acknowledged and certain aspects or perspectives of the same phenomena are bracketed off or kept from view in order to obtain clarity for other aspects and perspectives.

An example is the synthetic psychiatry of Paul Schilder. One of Schilder's basic assumptions is the following: the intention of the human organism is to grasp and achieve reality in life's most obvious senses as well as its richest and deepest levels. Schilder describes this intentional process as a way of directing human attention:

> But what else is attention than being directed towards a situation by emotional needs? . . . Attention and action are not very different from each other. The individual is

[1] Brentano, Franz. *Psychologie vom empirischen Standpunkt.* (ed. by O. Krause) Leipzig, 1924. Book II, chapter 1, paragraph 5.

actively directed towards the acquisition of data concerning the world and his own body [208 p. 287] .

A parallel assumption is Schilder's belief that socialization and all adaptive social responses are understandable and comprehensible in light of fundamental human drives and instincts. What is bracketed off here in the phenomenological sense are other possible intentions of the human organism and other possible interpretations for the origin of socially adpative responses. The possible truth of other theories is not denied nor their relative value estimated. The empiricism of Locke, for example, is not denied but rather set aside in order to obtain a different perspective. As a matter of method, such considerations are concealed so that certain conclusions are revealed in bold relief.

What conclusions can be drawn by this method?

In Schilder's thought, we are no longer left upon the "reef of solipsism," as Sartre described the dilemma of modern thought. Schilder embraced the phenomenological idea of intentionally: human consciousness is intentionality directed and that implies the "intentional constitution" of others in the world. From Schilder's perspective, the question is no longer how it is possible for the human being to socialize with other persons, since socialization begins with the first strivings of the infant. This perspective is radical and sets him apart from other proponents of interpersonal psychology (Fromm, Sullivan)[2, 3] whose concept of social adaptation is a result of pragmatism and in no way attempts to rethink the very foundations of knowledge, perception, imagination, memory, and reflection.

Sam Parker's 1926 article (excerpts published in this volume) traces many of the phenomenological assumptions at work in the notions of intersubjectivity and consciousness that have come down to us intact in object relations theories, though seldom acknowledged.

Parker elucidated Schilder's phenomenology in the following way:

That which differentiates real thought from phantasy, successful conduct from dementia, is its emotionally essential capacity for comprehending reality and not distorting it.

---

[2] Fromm, Erich. *Beyond the Chains of Illusion.* Touchstone Book, Simon & Schuster, 1962.

[3] Sullivan, Harry Stack. *The Interpersonal Theory of Psychiatry.* W. W. Norton, 1953.

The phenomenological analysis is based upon the premise
that thinking, willing, and the like are directed toward this·
reality [162 p. 319] .

If we recall that the images preparatory to final thought or
concept are peculiarly susceptible to affective (wish)
transformation into symbol-like structures with the
spheres of other instincts, we will understand that
premature thought must be based upon a world produced
by phantasy. An action occurring upon this basis takes only an imaginary, unreal world into consideration [162 p. 325] .

Two assumptions stand out from Parker's analysis. First,
Schilder adopted the phenomenological precept of Husserl that all
consciousness, including all thought processes, are directed towards
objects in the world. This is called the notion of intentionality. Second, he believed that every thought of the human individual
undergoes stages of development from the least distinct and imageless to clearly imaged and verbalized meanings. This process may
be summarized as follows: an impulse which is delayed or conflicted
gives rise to a thought which is imageless, which in turn gives rise to
an image that is verbalized in a word which carries meaning that in-
tends or signifies an object or action in the world. The notion of intentionality is at work here also, since the intentional object of this
process is to grasp reality. A sense of reality is obtained by an individual's completion of these stages which comprise the origin of a
thought, although as Schilder points out, the picture of reality may
be only partial.

There is a world in which we live and which we perceive.
Although this knowledge and perception of the world is incomplete and although we see only phases of the reality,
there is no reason to believe that our approach to the world
is unreliable. . .In the process of experimentation, satisfactory patterns of perception (Gestalten) are reached. .
.During these constructive processes condensations, sym-
bolizations, transposition of parts take place; full contact
with the reality is not reached. The relation between sign
and referent exists but is not precise. [218 pp. 275, 277, 278]

The intentionality of consciousness is a powerful tool for investigating
the human body and its extraordinary capacity to perceive and act. (See
Walter Bromberg's article elsewhere in this volume.) Meaning in the

world implies consciousness and there is no meaning without the intention or the "intending towards" of consciousness.

Parker demonstrates how Schilder attempted to synthesize physiological psychology and intuitive psychology into a biological whole using the methods of phenomenology. He also points out how closely phenomenology can resemble philosophical speculation, and the need for analytic rigor in applying its tools.

Parker's manuscript can still be useful to the modern-day researcher who undertakes the task of categorical phenomenology that Ellenberger defines for the therapist as:

> attempts to reconstruct the inner world of his patients through an analysis of their manner of experiencing time, space, causality and materiality, and other 'categories' (in the philosophical sense of the word [53] p. 101.

The brilliant observations of Paul Schilder have opened our understanding of the categories of space and time to include the force of gravity and the human experience of weight and their impact on the development of the human psyche.

Chapter 9

THE CHARACTER OF MODERN PSYCHIATRY[1]

A Synthetic Presentation of the Work of Paul Schilder

Sam Parker, M.D.

The taxonomic work of Kraepelin, Bleuler, and their contemporaries united the effort to give the psychiatric clinic a plan by which the seemingly inconquerable variety of mental and nervous phenomena might be organized. The scientific formulations for this organization are to be found pre-eminently in the psychology of Wundt, and, more ultimately, in the materialism and the psychophysical parallelism of natural science. The forms of nervous disease were accepted as substantially the individual expressions of organs, hence the appreciation of them as defects per se, possessing few signs of any correlation with the organism. The principle of psychophysical parallelism was applied to the explanation of mental phenomena and rested on the presuppositions of materialism. Even the knowledge gained from the study of the glands of internal secretion, although it is a move in the direction of ''organismic'' biology, is adapted as such in strict accordance with the materialistic principles of direct cause. The scientific approach to the mind was physiological psychology: the full content of the most complex psychic structures as well as the process of perception were reducible to the same formula. Man's experience was built upon a base of perceptions and feelings, his individual reaction on an association of these beyond which the diverse forms of psychic expression were regulated by a quality of apperception. The mind and the soul of man were not only dependent

[1] Excerpts from the original article in *The Journal of Nervous and Mental Disease.* Vol. 63, No. 4, April 1926. New York.

upon nervous matter for their existence: the brain has been considered the substance of their manifestations. A reversal of the influence was inconceivable.

That there is another way to approach the human mind we know from the artists and the experience of our daily life. Indeed, our experience gives the method of intuition its validity. We understand human conduct quite apart from casual principles. The conscious dismissal of understanding from the psychiatric clinic and the analysis of the human mind according to the "disease," or, perhaps, the symptom has led to the confusion and misunderstanding voiced by clinicians in their controversies on the meaning of disease, symptoms, and symptom complex. The method of understanding mental conduct, however, is not only adapted to the needs of humans but, as will appear later, may be employed to meet the strictest demands of causal science. These possibilities for appreciating human psychology have been realized in more modern times and have been primarily fruitful in extending our knowledge of the springs of human conduct. Philosophically and logically the intuitive or nonscientific method was prepared by the work of Bergson and of Husserl, and clinically adapted in the methods of Jung, Adler, etc. The Freudian psychoanalysis is also a form of understanding the mind in practice, but it lays methodological claim to being causally scientific and has been extended to a principle of normal psychology.

The gap between the intuitive, the psychological method, on the one hand, and the scientific, or physical method on the other, is, however, one of principle: a difference which seems incapable of solution except in fusion to a higher unity. The attempt to bridge this gap has been going on in many branches of science and has resulted in the biological approach to natural phenomena. In psychiatry one of the most diligent exponents of the biological position has been Professor Schilder in Vienna, and we may follow the thread of modern method more concretely in some of the principles formulated and carried to their ultimate conclusions by him.

The stream of experience is not exhausted in an enumeration of the perceptions or sensations. It is, first of all, the experience of an ego, an individual. By the ego is meant the experiencing core of the individual, the individual quality; and psychology is the study of this ego in its various expressions in sensation, perception, thinking, etc. Conduct or experience are the result of a reaction of the ego to objects, whether they be of the external world or of the mind, and in each reaction the whole ego, the whole personality, is reflected.

The descriptive psychology or phenomenology developed by

Husserl and Scheler and transposed to psychopathology by Jaspers[108] has shown that the realms of sensation, thinking, etc. also possess a definite structure. It is to these structures as objects that the ego directs itself in the act. The act is simply the attention to an object, the experience. Quite apart from any sensation the act is the radiation from an ego to an object as such. Beyond the questions of epistemology as to the metaphysical reality of the object, it must be considered that the object appears first as such to the ego that perceives it, perhaps in one quality, perhaps in another, i.e., either desiring, acting, or imagining. The primary process of perception consists of three categories: (1)The ego which perceives and in so acting turns to the object that appears. (2)The contents of the act are the sensations that occur in the body. (3)The body thus stands as one sphere between the personality and the world of the object. It belongs, nevertheless, to the sphere of the ego although it may itself be the object of the ego. In the sensations it represents, so to speak, the personality and perceptions may be structurally differentiated into those further from the ego and closer to the external world, and those nearer the ego and further from the world. The act itself also possesses regular characteristics. It is of a different quality depending upon whether it is an act of willing, wishing, imagining, etc.

The ego is irreducibly a part of every act as the experiencing agent. But it can also know of its experience in an act. This does not mean that the subject becomes its own object but simply that the ego is then no longer in the act, let us say, of thinking, but in that of knowing. When, in an act of perception, the material of the act is changed, it is nevertheless always the same ego that perceives the object, follows it in all its manifestations. But there are cases in psychopathology in which the object world (our reality) remains unchanged, but the ego seems to have undergone transformation. It is in this field that the form and consciousness of its modifications may best be studied.

Schilder subjected the conditions of depersonalization, double consciousness, and similar forms of so-called split personality to a careful phenomenological analysis.[186]In the thesis that the ego is an irreducible psychic form of the the organism, the splitting of the personality can be nothing actually altering the psychic elements of this ego, nor such elements of the personality. The change is simply one of contradiction between the experience of the central ego and the experiencing individual. "The self appears soulless because it does not flow undivided from the ego. It is not enough that sensations, feelings, images, thoughts be imminent to the stream of consciousness, indeed it is not enough that these be grasped by the central ego. In the grasping of content all the actual tendencies of the ego must be uncontradictorily unified.'' [186, also 208, p. 139] The phenomenology of ego experience shows that in its adjustment to objects given, so to speak, in the immediate foreground of an act, the ego at the same time experiences tendencies toward the background of the experience or toward objects of a different sort. But the experience is never plural in nature. On the contrary, the ego tends to the unification of its acts and what we know as depersonalization is but the incompatible situation noted above: the ego cannot enter into the act of experiencing and the act of knowing of its experience at one and the same time. Neither is it divisible, for it is contained entirely in each act. The result is that the activity of the individual appears strange, external, and automatic to the ego, a condition not unknown to normal life.

Jasper's statement that the realm of perception is distinctly different from that of imagination was subjected by Schilder to the test of experiment.[188] The net result was that, in respect to the psychological content, the image may be objective to the ego in essentially the same sense as perceptions. Even distinct signs of the process of sensation were noted that possessed the usual relation to forms of perception, thus corroborating the notion of Lipps that the image has the tendency to become perception, a notion that is of philosophical importance. The phenomenological data, the morphology, of experience are thus of the same principle whether the ego turns to the external world or to the structures of the mind.

Following the work of Kraepelin and the development of Bleuler, psychiatrists have paid much attention to the problem of schizophrenia. Quite apart from its clinical aspect, the psychology of schizophrenia has been attempted, and these principles as well as the meaning of the biological point of view may be well traced in the studies Schilder has produced in this field. To begin with, the factor of irrationality cannot be primarily considered as a peculiarity of mental disease since such factors undoubtedly influence the highest forms of thought in a salutary way. That such highly valuable concepts may appear in apparently totally schizophrenic minds has been satisfactorily shown by history (Strindberg, Van Gogh). The difference between the products of the positively diseased and the healthy cannot, then, be a subjective one, since the most normal minds probably experience the same unification of the ego, the same sense of totality and completeness in a production as the mentally diseased. A descriptive analysis of a more typical and suitable case leads to the conclusion that the diseased mind shows itself in its failure to achieve reality. All the paraphernalia of the mind are put into operation, but instead of arriving at a point of action the process exhausts itself in a hallucination, symbols, dreams, etc. Schizophrenic reality is not the reality of the objective world, but a dream world, a scene in which the various objects are called up by the mind, formed at will, and experienced without the slightest activity.

Phenomenology gives us a description of psychic constellations at rest. It is a structurallly static analysis of a cross-section of the stream of experience. The analysis of even a static sagittal section of this flowing life has been with great difficulty. This is sufficiently illustrated by the fact that any variation of introspective psychology, in order to gain a view of the experience, must bring it to rest. The cardinal characteristic of living experience is, however, its existence in and appreciation of time, and any psychology approaching the nucleus of experience approaches a dynamic formulation. A phenomenology of experience can include the nature of the past, but this does not transform the method to a functional one.

In continuation of his contributions to the problem of the dementias, Schilder was fully conscious of this and stated the situation most competently in his introduction to *Seele und Leben* [p. 1]. "It is not enough only to observe the resting structures of the soul, to dissect and describe them, order and classify. It . . . is a necessary prerequisite but such work is incomplete and unsatisfactory. For it is of the essence of the psyche that it proceeds in time, that it has a past and strives into the future. Resting psychic life is but an abstraction and that which is at rest takes on meaning only in the stream of becoming. . . .Descriptive psychology must be completed by psychogenetic research. . . ."[192]

The experience of time is an irreducible psychic quantity, as for example, the direct experience of the relation between willing and acting. Here is not only the experience of purpose as between the mind and the object, but also the content of time as adhering only to that experience and not to objects that are, psychologically, timeless. This may also be recognized in its consequences in the primitive and diseased mind. The phenomenon as such, in its quality, is graspable in the phenomenological sense, and Jaspers and others have developed it on this plane to a dualistic platform of psychic understanding in which understandable relations (*verstandliche Zusammenh änge*) and causal relations are completely separated. This position precludes the possibility of its adaption to the forms of natural science, although, in a sense, the essence of its descriptive psychology remains biological. It does not, however, give complete satisfaction to the biological postulate, since in no way can one develop the very apparent relations between the body and the mind from the dualistic position. It becomes necessary to link the developments to the principles of natural science.

In the external world and in the world of nature, time is not experienced but postulated, and studied by means of the principle of causality in the object. As will be discussed more broadly later, the use of this principle in science or in the mind has nothing to do with the qualities of objects but simply with their consequence. In this sense the qualitative data produced by phenomenology are not in the least influenced by a causal analysis. The difference between causality in nature and causality in the mind, however, is that the latter is directly experienced. It is primary, so that it becomes easy to understand the adaptation of a scientific principle original in psychic life. A dynamic psychology, a method comprehending the element of time in experience, stands upon the principle of cause, and is, in essence, a scientific method. In this respect it is the invaluable service of Freudian psychoanalysis to have become a dynamic psychology that serves as a normative basis for the study of psychic processes, while at the same time comprehending the relations of the mind to biological changes. Essentially, psychoanalysis was a form of understanding psychology, but it has come also to lay claim to full recognition as a scientific method. The crux of natural science is, after all, a strict adherence to causality and, just as physical science approaches but a part of the world for the study of consequences, so also does psychoanalysis pass up the ultimate quality of mental structure for the study of effects and changes.

Normal thought develops, just as the image, from an unclear and general to a clear and sharply defined structure. This process is an associative one in which factually and affectively related images and notions are mixed. The more elementary and distant the images are, the more direct is their dependence upon the emotional influence, so that undeveloped images often possess a symbol-like appearance. A thought passes though the same type of development in which images and symbol-like structures play a great part.[189] A thought develops upon a basis of images, but the preceptual element becomes less important as the thought develops towards sharpness and meaning. An experience which is full of meaning is thus poor in perceptual quality and simple as, e.g., word images. The ultimate source of such a process is a single, unified act of will: in the language of phenomenology, a single intention directed toward an objective relationship. The origin of a thought process is in the instinctive tendencies of the organism; these are impulses which form and transform the pictures in the process of development and normally pass over them in their attention to the ultimate object. The final clarity of normal thought shines upon a dark background of mixed ideas, images, and tendencies, the matrix from which thought arises. For these formulations Schilder introduced the concept "sphere of consciousness" (*die Sphäre*) into psychopathology. The sphere, William James' fringe, is the base of experience of any kind; it is the foundation from which the most conscious as well as the shadier, more unclear, experiences spring.

Fully developed normal thought radiates from a sharply defined ego to an equally well-defined world of objects. Between these two categories is the body, definitely separated from both but situated nearer the ego. The body is at once the subject of the will and the point of contact with the world. This world is experienced not only in the act of the ego, but has its content in the sensations of the body. Although in normally regulated experience this differentiation is usually well guarded, there are many gradations of experience in which the disparity of the world and the body becomes less clear. In the tactile perception of an object, for example, the difference is still preserved, but it becomes immediately less clear when the tactile sensation becomes one of great pain. In such a case the object and the sensation (world and body) begin to run together in experience. This is precisely the process which appears in schizophrenia. All of sensation has a tendency to merge and thus to become less differentiated from the world.

The data of modern psychological and clinical research have shown the mind to be quite as much an instrument in the comprehension of the world as the organic structures. Indeed, the mind is also an organic structure not built up of others but meeting the needs of the organism with and by means of physical organs. Schilder stated his platform for modern psychiatry in *Medical Psychology* (published 1924):

> My attempt then is to unify in one framework, phenomenology, psychoanalysis, experimental psychology, and brain pathology. This may be called eclecticism. Yet each of these points of view and approaches has brought forth factual knowledge; and factual knowledge of different fields must, in its deepest fundamentals, hang together and somehow be amendable to unification.[193 p.19.]

Beyond analysis, it seeks the synthesis, for only so can science approach an insight into the essentially synthetic character of the individual.

As regards the methodology of modern psychiatry, the review of the questions dealt with in one of the chapters of *Medical Psychology* are relevant. We choose the chapter on action and speech. For considering the question of psychophysical relations, localization centers, and their prevailing appreciation, no chapter could be more apt. For how are the contents and purposes of psychic processes better represented than their motor consequences? This will, at the same time, lead us over into the philosophical preconceptions upon which these and similar methods are based.

An action is a biological process in which an individual directs his energies toward an object, thereby innervating diverse sets of motor organs. Speech may be viewed from the same angle, and apraxia and the asphasias in all their various forms are still actions and forms of speech albeit in incomplete form. Now, an action or movement requires for its execution, for its origin altogether, a plan of movement. Upon the basis of the work of Head, Liepmann, Pick, and Schilder, it is probable that these images are the parts of a normally well-defined schema. Originally considering the localization of tactile sensations, Head suggested that the individual possesses a sort of topographic arrangement of his body in the mind and that the localization of the sensations were effected by a relation of the sensation to such a scheme. In the work of Pick and of Schilder,[191] this idea has been developed by studies in the pathology of action (apraxia), and Schilder has postulated a body diagram (*Korperschema*) by means of which normal action or movement presupposes an intact consciousness of the elements of the body diagram. There is no more chaos in the appreciation of sensations than in any other form of psychic experience. As a matter of fact, the results of these studies lead to the legitimate assumption that just as thoughts and concepts stand in relation to the general sphere, so is there a matrix, a diagram into which sensations of the body are ordered and then relayed to their accurately corresponding motor expressions. It appears that the body diagram has optical, tactile, and kinesthetic qualities, all of which, as a union, go into the accurate localization of bodily sensation. The material and conclusions gathered by Schilder in *Das Korperschema* show that this scheme is also the prerequisite for the individual variations of movement and also for the appreciation, not only of bodily space, but external spatial relations. The presence and operation of such a mechanism may best be portrayed by the cases of amputation wherein the amputated limb is still felt and hallucinated in all its original qualities.

Schilder also concluded that the apparatus of the brain may be influenced in the same direction psychically and physically. Schilder speaks of the principle of double expression (*Prinzip des doppelten Weges*).[84] The symptoms of lesions in the subcortex as well as in the cortex, as exemplified in encephalitis and the aphasias, are susceptible to remarkable influence from the sphere of the psychic. Observations have been made on the emotional changes of such symptoms, and it is an old clinical fact that chorea is more acutely disclosed under the infuence of the emotions, attention, etc.

The manifestations of nervous symptoms and psychic disturbances become more and more clearly related. They are not isolated or sporadic dysfunctions speaking the language peculiar to an individual organ. They possess a common source in the whole personality of the individual and express, in manifold form only, the single biological meaning of the organism.

To some, it may appear as if many of these doctrines are not less than an adaptation of purely Freudian principles to the tenets of phenomenology and modern epistemology. At bottom, however, psychoanalysis, phenomenology, and biological science are no more at variance than psychic and physical phenomena, and may, like these, be legitimately associatied in a synthetic conception of the individuality. It was specifically explained above that a psychoanalytic consideration of psychic phenomena in no way disturbs or precludes a phenomenology of psychic structures, or vice versa. To a fruitful comprehension of the whole of mental problems they both lend a fundamental weight. The complaint of some psychoanalysts that other psychological approaches are characterized by an inevitable "degeneration" to philosophical niceties is not so acute when one remembers that all the prevailing psychiatric methods proceed from generally the same philosophical platform. The efforts of the phenomenologists, among them Schilder, to differentiate the subject of investigation accurately from philosophical preconceptions is at least more laudable than to promote such metaphysical postulates as manifest empirical evidence. In this sense the amalgamation of psychoanalysis with other principles to a synthetic science of the mind is legitimate, and in no way circumscribes the clinical or scientific procedure of the former.

Schilder's progress has been toward a synthetic appreciation of the form of experience as illustrated under pathological circumstances, and such is, in general, the character observed in the trend of modern psychiatry. To this end it has been necessary to do the following: to define clearly the philosophical ground upon which modern method stands—a primary spiritual monism; to analyze the mental structures formally (phenomenology) and functionally (psychoanalysis), a combination of intuitive and scientific methods; and to combine them under the principle of the biological unity of the individual.

Chapter 10

THE WORK OF PAUL SCHILDER[1]

Alexandra Adler, M.D.

It is with a great deal of humility that I approach the task of delivering the Memorial Address on the life and work of Paul Schilder. It is impossible to do justice to this outstanding man in one lecture; furthermore, one person alone would hardly be able to cover adequately the enormous volume of his work. There is scarcely any major field of neurology and psychiatry that Schilder did not investigate and enrich through one of his several hundred papers and also through his books. Consequently every worker in these fields will find something in Schilder closely related to his own special interest. Articles and books, each of them stressing a different angle, will continue to be written for an indefinite period about the life and work of Schilder. May I call attention to the hundreds of volumes written about personalities such as Goethe and others, each of them from a different perspective and doing justice only to a part of the subject's personality and work. An all-embracing study of any monumental figure just cannot be written by a single person since no one really knows another person completely. I shall be content here to point out some of the milestones in Schilder's many-sided life.

Paul Ferdinand Schilder was born in Vienna, Austria, on February 15, 1886. On December 8, 1940, at the age of fifty-four, he succumbed to injuries received when struck down by a passing car on a street in New York. He was then at the height of his career, and his per-

[1]Presented at the Schilder Memorial Meeting of the Schilder Society—The Society for Psychotherapy and Psychopathology—at The New York Academy of Medicine, January 28, 1965.

sonal life had been enriched by his marriage to Dr. Lauretta Bender and by their three small children.

Schilder was graduated from the University of Vienna Medical School in 1909. He was subsequently appointed assistant to Gabriel Anton in Halle an der Saale, Germany, and one year later, in 1912, became assistant to Paul E. Flechsig in Leipzig.

His scientific career started auspiciously: in the first 3 years after receiving his medical degree, Schilder published eight papers in the fields of neurology and pathology. His first paper, which appeared in 1908, when he was twenty-two years old, was on the malignant glioma of the sympathetic nervous system. Four years later, in 1912, he wrote his first paper on encephalitis periaxialis diffusa,[184] which subsequently made history and permanently associated his name with the disease he had described—Schilder's disease. In this paper, published when Schilder was only twenty-six years old, he gave clear evidence of his genius and immense working capacity.

The first of the two patients whom Schilder described in his now historic paper, a fourteen-year-old girl, came to his clinic on July 3, 1911, and died on September 17, 1911. Seven months later Schilder submitted his paper, 60 pages long, with five figures and six full-page colored illustrations, to the leading German periodical in his field, the *Zeitschrift fur die gesamte Neurologie und Psychiatrie*. In this short period the twenty-five-year-old assistant had thoroughly observed the patient, made a complete neuropathologic examination, using the latest histologic techniques, and reviewed all related cases previously published, 66 altogether. He then summarized his findings by pointing out the characteristics of his case, and differentiated them from those of similar cases in a way that has never since been surpassed.

Schilder started his paper in the succinct manner characteristic of his searching approach by stating what he was about to undertake. This is the first sentence of his paper in my English translation: ''The case that will be discussed in the following seems worthy of publication because of its peculiar, very characteristic histologic findings.'' The original German version reads: *''Der Fall, an den sich die folgenden Erörterungen anschliessen, erscheint mitteilenswert wegen des eigenartigen sehr wohl charakterisierten histologischen Befundes.''*

The fourteen-year-old patient had started to vomit 8 weeks before admission to the eye clinic. Her vision was impaired and she was found to have bilateral optic neuritis. After neurosurgical intervention, namely puncture of the corpus callosum, frequently done at the time, she developed, 2 weeks later, paralyses of her legs and, later, of her arms, gradually lapsed into a coma exhibiting rapidly spreading signs of bilateral neurologic disturbance, and succumbed finally to pneumonia with a fever of 105 degrees. Autopsy of the brain showed macroscopically the characteristic large masses of degeneration of both cerebral hemispheres. Schilder summarized the neuropathologic findings as massive, diffuse demyelination of the cerebral hemispheres that often stopped at the arcuate fibers and only rarely penetrated into the cortex. The axis cylinders were comparatively well preserved and sometimes surrounded by inflammatory cells. From this picture Schilder derived the name "encephalitis periaxialis diffusa."

The following year, 1913, he published the histologic findings of the second case he had observed; many more cases have since been described in the literature. In 1934, for example, 22 years after Schilder's original publication, L. Bouman tabulated 100 cases in his book, *Diffuse Sclerosis (Encephalitis periaxialis diffusa)*.[37]

I am myself in a position to demonstrate here a case of Schilder's disease, basing my observations on material of my own not yet published. The patient was a twenty-one-year-old girl who died after having been ill for about 2 months. As so often observed, her first symptom was impairment of vision, and optic neuritis was diagnosed. The nasal sinuses were opened, but the patient's condition deteriorated and, as is also typical of this syndrome, she became quite somnolent. One week after the sinus operation her left leg became paralyzed and she was admitted to the Neuro-Psychiatric University Hospital in Vienna, where I happened to be a resident at the time. There she showed bilateral signs of pyramidal tract disease, bulbar speech, and bilateral optic neuritis, also disturbance of sensation. Her neurologic symptoms progressed and she became increasingly somnolent, developed pneumonia with a terminal fever of 104 degrees, from which she died in May 1931. The autopsy revealed the large patches of softening on both sides of the brain characteristic of Schilder's disease.

Figure 1 shows a frontal section through the brain of the patient (Weigert stain). A large patch is visible on the left side of the brain, a smaller on the right. Characteristically, the demyelination stops at the arcuate fibers, and not all the myelin in the patch is destroyed, which gives the focus a diffuse appearance different from that of multiple sclerosis.

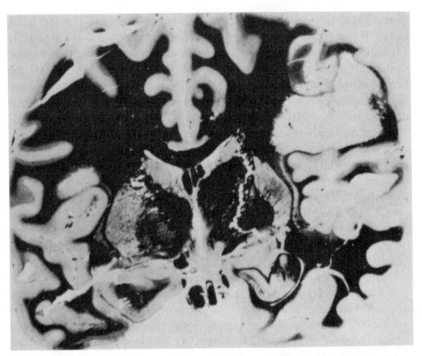

Fig. 1. Frontal section of the brain in a case of Schilder's disease. See text for discussion.

Figure 2 shows serial sections through the spinal cord of the same patient. Here one can observe what has also been described by others, namely that some patches in the spinal cord in cases of Schilder's encephalitis are identical with those of multiple sclerosis; that is, they are sharply delineated, as if punched out, with complete, not partial, disappearance of the myelin sheaths and complete destruction of axis cylinders.

For comparison, a frontal section of the brain in a case of multiple sclerosis appears in Figure 3. It shows much smaller foci of demyelination that go straight into the cortex, and the foci of myelin destruction are sharply outlined.

Figures 4 and 5 on pages 74 and 75 give microscopic pictures of areas of destruction in the case that I am reporting. In Figure 4 is shown a vessel from the spinal cord, surrounded by round cells, a condition that induced Schilder to group this disease tentatively among the inflammatory diseases, as expressed by the term "encephalitis."

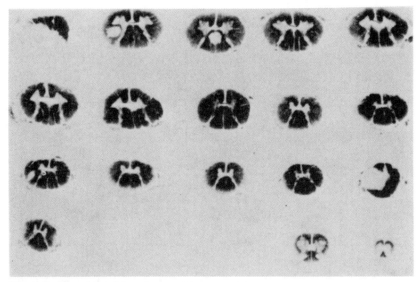

Fig. 2. Serial sections of the spinal cord in a case of Schilder's disease.
See text for discussion.

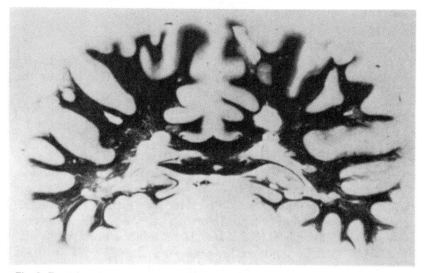

Fig. 3. Frontal section of the brain in a case of multiple sclerosis. See text for discussion.

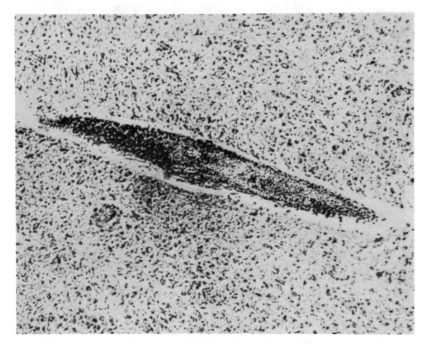

Fig. 4. Microscopic section in a case of Schilder's disease. See text for discussion.

Figure 5 is a high-power magnification of one of the foci of demyelination filled with scavenger cells: glia cells that pick up the debris and gradually change into granular cells.

Since Schilder's original paper, many investigations have been published that concern themselves with questions of whether those histologic conditions were inflammatory or degenerative in nature, which one of these conditions was primary, and whether the accumulation of round cells surrounding the vessels and axis cylinders conformed to the classic stipulations of inflammatory changes, or rather was an indication of reparative processes such as are habitually seen after destruction of central nervous substance. The most comprehensive discussions of this subject were published by Globus and Strauss[89] in 1928; by Bouman,[37] in the work already cited, in 1934; by Ferraro[65] in 1937; and, recently, by Adams and Richardson[1] in 1961. None of these authors in my opinion—as well as in their own opinions—has been able to advance any important facts beyond those published by Schilder himself in his comprehensive first com-

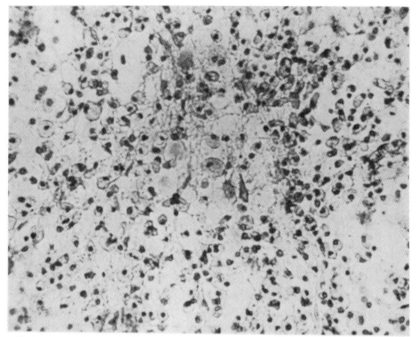

Fig. 5. High-power magnification of a section in a case of Schilder's disease.
See text for discussion.

munication of 1912. Many other names have been suggested for
Schilder's disease and for similar demyelinating diseases, such as
symmetrical cerebral central lobar sclerosis, progressive degenerative
subcortical encephalopathy, diffuse sclerosis, leukodystrophy, and
sclerotic inflammation. Some authors also have wondered whether
the name of Schilder should remain associated with this group of
cases showing, in Schilder's words, the "very characteristic
histologic findings." It should be noted, however, that neurologists
know well what type of syndrome to look for when a case is diagnosed
"Schilder's disease," whereas all the other names suggested denote
less specific clinical and pathologic pictures.

The disease has been found to occur more often in young people
than in older persons, but sporadic cases have appeared in patients
sixty years old and more. The illness may last from a few days to a
year and is nearly always fatal. In a very few cases, however, remis-
sions have been noted that have protracted the duration of the illness.

Instances of more than one case in the same family have been described, indicating the possibility of a heredofamilial basis for at least some of them.

In going over the case histories I was impressed by the frequency of major surgical treatment in the early stages of the illness, so often followed by a rapid progression of neurologic signs within a week or two.

The operative procedures consisted of rather extensive trepanations of nasal sinuses, performed in the hope of ameliorating the optic neuritis so often present in the early stage of the disease, or trepanation of the skull for ventriculography, puncture of the corpus callosum in the earlier years, and several other neurosurgical procedures when a brain tumor was suspected. In view of the admittedly close relation between Schilder's disease and multiple sclerosis, which was pointed out by Schilder himself in his first publication on this subject, could it be that at least some of the cases had started as multiple sclerosis and then changed into the malignant, rapidly progressive encephalits periaxialis diffusa? This possibility is given some support by the well-known observation that chronic cases of multiple sclerosis sometimes grow worse rapidly after surgery.

In 1913, one year after Schilder had published his basic work on the disease that carries his name, he wrote his first psychiatric paper, one on disturbances of self-consciousness— *Über das Selbstbewusstsein und seine Störungen*[185]—and, in 1914, when he was only twenty-eight years old, he published his first book, *Selbstbewusstsein und Persönlichkeitsbewusstein.*[185] From that time on, his investigations were divided equally between psychiatric and neurologic problems. In 1914, he also published a paper running to more than 40 pages on the meaning of symbols in schizophrenia[187]—a subject that continued to hold his interest—in which he makes extensive use and shows his thorough knowledge of the new trends in psychopathology, referring to the work of Sigmund Freud and Alfred Adler among others. This paper already gives clear evidence that Schilder's investigative spirit could not be forced into accepting the "all-or-nothing" attitude postulated by adherents of some schools. He writes that he does not agree with the uncritical extension of the concept of sexuality advocated by Freud and, particularly, by some of his pupils. Also, in the same paper as well as in subsequent publications, as in his book, *Gedanken zur Naturphilosophie*[195] written in 1928, he ponders the question of goal-directedness in human beings, especially in psychotics, and repeatedly comes back to the concept of teleology, which is the basic principle of Adler's school of thought and of other more recent philosophical systems.

The only period during which Schilder did not publish was the war years 1915, 1916, and 1917: except for this interval he published from 1 to 24 papers and books annually between 1909 and 1939. Psychiatric subjects predominate after 1934 and, during the last 2 years of his life, all his publications were in the field of psychiatry.

My own main reason for entering the Neuropsychiatric Hospital of the University of Vienna in 1926 was that, as a student, I had heard about the new and interesting interpretations that Schilder was introducing in his investigations of psychoses. My contact with him left many unforgettable memories; it stimulated constructive thinking and revealed to me his leadership as a teacher. Everyone who worked with him came under the influence of his personality, and many developed a deep abiding loyalty to him.

One of his outstanding qualities as a lecturer was his ability to induce even an apathetic audience into listening with the greatest interest. No one who was present will forget how, as the last speaker at one of the monthly meetings of the Vienna Society for Neurology and Psychiatry, he electrified a soporific audience by starting his communication in a loud voice with these animated words: "A man runs naked through the streets shouting 'the world has come to an end.' " After this, Schilder proceeded to elaborate on the symbolism in the delusions of the schizophrenic patient, the audience now in rapt attention.

Schilder accepted me on his staff very cordially, and, as I clearly remember, first asked me to examine a patient, one of the many he had seen that morning. This patient had made a suicidal attempt and Schilder felt puzzled about the motivation. I sat with the monosyllabic patient for more than 2 hours in an attempt to obtain statements from her. She then finally broke down and revealed the elaborate paranoid system that had driven her to attempt suicide. Accustomed to the authoritarian attitude of many European professors at that time, I was naturally somewhat apprehensive about how Schilder would accept all the new material that the patient had been hiding from him. I shall never forget the genuine pleasure and interest Schilder showed, to my relief, when I reported on this case. He replied that this clarified the whole situation and enabled us to handle the patient better.

Figure 6 is from a group photo taken in 1927. Julius Wagner von Jauregg, at that time head of the Vienna University Neuro-

Fig. 6. Julius Wagner-Jauregg's staff in 1927. Front row (*left to right*): Max Weissmann, Bernhard Dattner, Henrich Kogerer, Heinrich Hershmann, Julius Wagner-Jauregg, Joseph Gerstmann, Paul Schilder, Heinz Hartmann, Otto Kauders. Second row (*left to right*): Erwin Stengel, Edith Vincze, Lydia Sicher, Annie Reich, Ludwig Horn, Clara Strassky, Robert Stern, Fannie Halpern, Otto Isakower, Alexandra Adler, Hans Hoff, Edward Bibring. Back row (*left to right*): Gottfried Engerth, Friedrich Stumpfl, Stefan Betlheim, Ludwig Eidelberg, Edith Klemperer, Karl Hasse.

psychiatric Department and Hospital, sits surrounded by his staff. Around Schilder are grouped most of his collaborators, some of them probably familiar to most readers: for instance, Josef Gerstmann, with whom Schilder published papers on pseudosclerosis, disturbances of locomotion, micrographia, catalepsy, and tics; H. Herschmann, with whom he wrote, in 1919, on the dreams of the melancholic; Otto Isakower, co-author of a paper on apraxia and agnosia; Heinz Hartmann, co-author of two papers on dementia; Hans Hoff, later chairman of the department, with whom he wrote about 20 papers on the postural and righting reflexes; Otto Kauders, with whom he published a book on hypnosis; and Erwin Stengel, co-author of a paper on asymbolia of pain. I stand behind Schilder.

I missed the privilege of publishing a paper with Schilder for a very good reason. After a few exciting and greatly rewarding weeks of work under him, the chairman of the Neurology Department complained to Wagner von Jauregg that he had lost his whole medical staff to Schilder. There was actually about 20 on Schilder's staff in psychiatry, whereas Heinrich Kogerer, chairman of the Neurology Department, had been left with exactly one physician. When one morning, the whole staff met as usual in the conference room, Wagner von Jauregg asked for a list of those working for Schilder and, possibly because I was the last arrival, he ordered me to report for duty to the Neurology Department. When I started to explain that I was not interested in neurology, Wagner von Jauregg quickly turned around and stalked out of the room. While I stood there, dumbfounded, wondering whether I should resign from the staff of the hospital, Schilder came over to me and, after expressing his regret, assured me that this change would prove not to be so bad in the long run, that he also had stared working in neurology, and that I could return to him when my assignment in neurology was over. He was right in his first two statements, but wrong in the last assumption. When I was permitted to return to psychiatry after 2 years, Schilder had left the hospital to continue his work in the United States.

After his arrival in the United States, he continued to inspire others in their research through joint investigations. Particularly in his work with children he had the close cooperation of his wife, Lauretta Bender. Their first paper, on alcoholic encephalopathy, appeared in 1933. From 1936 on they published jointly papers on suicidal preoccupations on genetic psychology, and on principles of the play of children. During the 10 years Schilder spent at Bellevue Psychiatric Hospital in New York, he accomplished an enormous amount of research. In addition to his work with Lauretta Bender, important papers were published jointly with F.G. Curran, M. Hermann, D. Wechsler, W. Bromberg, L. Orenstein, S. Parker, H. Wortis, N. Roth, and others. Several of Schilder's books also appeared during this period. Some of these he wrote in English, such as *Psychotherapy*[213] and *Brain and Personality*;[201] others, such as the book that he considered his most important work, namely, *The Image and Appearance of the Human Body*,[208] were translated from the German. More and more his work showed his absorbing interest in consolidating his observations and integrating his profound knowledge of the functions of the mind and body. After Schilder's death in December 1940, several of his books then still unpublished, such as

Goals and Desires of Man[218] and *Medical Psychology*,[193] translated by the late David Rapaport, appeared.

Still, his untimely death left his work unfinished. Had he lived, Schilder undoubtedly would have proceeded to consolidate his work and to create from it a systemized body of knowledge—something that no one can do for him.

Schilder remained unanalyzed, in spite of his great appreciation of Freud's work which, he felt, no investigator of the mind could afford to neglect. In a revealing document, a four and one-half page autobiography written shortly before his death,[216] Schilder emphasized the lasting value of Freud's dream interpretation and libido theory, but he took exception to what he called the ''regressive character'' of psychoanalysis. It seemed to him ''senseless to believe that life should intend merely to return to prior stages of satisfaction and to rest.'' He also rejected Freud's ideas about the death instinct. He thus expressed an attitude very similar to one stated in his first psychiatric paper of 1912, only now more clearly. He felt ''convinced that life is not directed towards the past but rather towards the future; that psychological processes are directed towards the real world in a process of continuous trial and error.'' In this way, Schilder established important links to schools of thought that are based on a holistic approach, such as the Gestalt theory and the teleologic system of Adler's Individual Psychology, in which stress is laid upon the relation of the whole personality to its environment and upon action influenced by anticipatory thinking of the individual.

After Schilder's arrival in the United States, I saw him only on my occasional visits to New York, sometimes at Bellevue Psychiatric Hospital, where he invited me to his lectures and where I witnessed the same fascination with the subject discussed on the part of both the audience and the lecturer that I had observed in Vienna. I was also present at occasional meetings between him and Alfred Adler. Schilder published a note[213] about one of their conversations saying that he never quite agreed with Adler's statements but that he always found them intriguing and well worth consideration. This was exactly the reaction of Adler to Schilder, and their meetings were full of goodwill, humor, and inspiration.

The last time I saw Schilder was in 1939, at the New York Psychiatric Institute, where we both acted as examiners for the American Board of Psychiatry and Neurology. He suggested that we have lunch together. On this occasion he spoke with great animation about his various experiences in the United States, and also inquired about my work. I remember expressing some doubt about the advisability of continuing my academic career, since it had been geared to work in both neurology and psychiatry, as was customary in Vienna and in most other European medical centers, while in the United States a progressive separation between these two fields was taking place. To this Schilder's comment, which I recall almost verbatim was: "You know, America is so big and there are so many different opportunities here. If you fall down in one place, you get up in another—so different from the limited opportunities in Europe. There, once you are checkmated, you are through. Not so in America." These works have served me as a guideline ever since.

The lamps of learning have been made to burn brighter by Schilder, who left us all too soon. The influence of his personality and work will long be felt by those who were fortunate enough to be associated with him in his lifetime, by those who experience it through his books and papers, and by those who perpetuate it through the activities of the Schilder Society, of which he was the founder.

May we all help to keep burning the light that he kindled.

Chapter 11

THE SCHILDERIAN WORLD OF PHENOMENOLOGY AND PSYCHIATRY

Walter Bromberg, M.D.

THE PHILOSOPHIC BACKGROUND

The background from which Paul Ferdinand Schilder fashioned a psychological psychiatry was phenomenology. This philosophic development in the late nineteenth and early twentieth century in Germany represented a clash with prevailing idealistic metaphysics. It purported to analyze the "mind," consciousness, and other mental functions, through the immediacy of experiencing. The larger dimensions of Husserl's phenomenology are beyond this author's competence, but the general import of Husserl's thesis in the words of Fritz Kaufman, is that phenomenology "provided a methodical foundation . . . to all realms of being and experience, psychological as well as biological and physical."[113, p. 803]

In the philosophic world, Husserl's work made a tremendous impact. Its goal was to supplant previous philosophic thinking to form a "rigorous science of philosophy," as an "autonomous discipline which serves as a prelude to all other knowlege."[62, p. 19] Marvin Farber, a close student of Husserl's, states that phenomenology is prior to metaphysics as a description of being. In sum, phenomenology is a specific field of philosophic inquiry, whose basic premise is analysis of experience beyond the assumptions, deductions, presuppositions which a person ordinarily makes. Bringing these to light, that is, exposing the assumptions which appear obvious and otherwise would go unnoticed by the observer, allows him to experience his perceptions, and hence his subjectivity, directly. Among other technical areas of philosophy, phenomenology leads to a study of consciousness, cognition, knowledge, "through the subjective processes of experience and perception."[62, p. 561] It relates to "intuitively perceiving rather than explaining" and to a "reality as a correlate of real experience."[62, p. 529]

Psychology proper, and neuropsychiatry, where it deals with organic brain disease and consequent impaired perception and cognition, proved to be a fruitful field for the use of the phenomenological method. It was from this source that Schilder's work flowed, not only in uniting neurophysiologic psychology but in elucidating how the ego assimilates these elements and forms a social response and adjustment. The total Schilderian concept, or more accurately a bundle of concepts, appeared in *Medizinische Psychologie* in 1924, only reaching English readers in 1952 through David Rapaport's skillful translations.[193] Schilder himself regarded his *Medical Psychology* as a bird's-eye view of "one framework, phenomenology, psychoanalysis, experimental psychology, and brain pathology."[193, p. 19] Because of the wide horizon Schilder encompassed, Rapaport notes that it is not easy to follow Schilder as he branched off to psychology from phenomenology, nor that all of the ideas of the "rich, unsystematic genius" can be readily understood.[193,p.19] In any event, *Medical Psychology* adumbrated theoretically what he proved experimentally and clinically during the next 2 decades.

To state briefly the premises of Schilder's biologic-psychologic-social synthesis which grew into a constructive psychologic-psychiatry,[218] I shall rely on Rapaport's summary in his translation.[193] In essence, he states that the basic notion, originally of Brentano and Husserl, was that the human organism was driven (intended towards, the "intentionalism" of the phenomenologist), towards objects. These "drive intendings" arise from somatic sources (sense-data), becoming structuralized into the psychological apparatus. Both physiological changes, as in brain injuries, and psychological changes as in neuroses, can basically change behavior. Second, there is a *sphere*, an "unformed background of experience," which is similar to the unconscious, from which object-directed "intentions" arise to emerge as "reality-relevant" thought and actions. This concept represented the primary process of Freud in his "unconscious-conscious dichotomy."

Third, a related concept was that of the synthetic function of the psyche, similar to that imputed to the ego (the executive ego of psychoanalysis). Finally, the body-image concept, worked out in the agnosias and apraxias cases of brain injury and the perceptive changes in intoxication cases, was considered to be continuously built out of perceptive changes and integrated by the ego. These and other concepts were spelled out in Schilder's book in detail; some of them, as a theory of the "thinking process," represented an abstruse area of epistemology. As Rapaport puts it in his Appendix to *Medical Psychology*, "Schilder faced squarely . . . the question of what is . . . the relation between the primary and secondary process." [193, p. 342] In a word, what Schilder was concerned with was not so much the content of conscious and unconscious mentation, the sometimes exclusive concern of psychoanalysts, but the mechanism that underlies dreams, parapraxes, and drives that "translate themselves into behavior and symptoms."

The depth of Schilder's thinking as laid out in *Medical Psychology* is startling. But this early analysis of mind and behavior had its practical aspects which became evident in later work. Two main premises, as noted by Rapaport,[193, p. 352] have markedly influenced psychiatric theory and practice; "human thinking is directed toward an existing world of objects . . ." and "socialization is a fundamental form of human experience . . . the body image as well as the object (of perception), is built by continuous interchange with other human beings." All drives, motivations and object directedness "imply . . . the socialized character of man." This extension of phenomenology into psychiatry was profound, and, as Rapaport stated in 1951, the "full scope of his contribution has been hardly assessed."[193, p. 356]

Elaboration of the body-image development brought into view the characteristic of motility in relation to perception. "Perception of one' body image is followed by reaching out to other bodies, eventually building up a socialized picture of the outside world."[218] The "drive-intendings" toward objects, a phenomenological term, which involved motility tendencies, becomes in Schilder's thought a "construction of object." The child's mental growth becomes a constructive psychic process.[218, p. 57] Development of this concept led to a sociology where ideologies by which adults live—cultural traditions, attitudes toward life and death, social morality, aggression and passivity, the work ethic—all become extensions of the constructive process.

Schilder's wide-sweeping view of the human organism in the world, led to an understanding of such diverse symptoms of abnormal behavior as neuroses, hyperkinesis in children, and aggressive crimes such as murder and assault. The idea of motility in perception showed him that inner drives have a purpose; "desires and instincts cannot be understood as mechanical agents,"[218, 276] he wrote. This view of social behavior, difficult to trace in words, once it is grasped is sensible, verifiable clinically, and realistic. To trace the applications, one might say the investment of phenomenology in Schilder's later work is as impossible as it is to enclose his ideas in one paragraph or one book. Perhaps the following statement joins phenomenology with his medical psychology; "Phenomenology has shown clearly that human beings primarily do not strive for satisfaction but strive for the object which gives satisfaction."[218, p. 16]

THE MAN AND HIS TIMES

To understand the man and his times, we must be reminded that aside from psychoanalysis in its early phase, there was no unitary theory of how neurosis and psychosis developed psychologically. The diagnostic distinctions had been laid out following Kraepelin and Bleuler in the main. Neuropathology had a firm basis for interpreting neurologic illnesses; but the main thrust of psychotherapy was beginning to be in the direction of Freudianism, although the Meyerian tool of patience, kindness, and a longitudinal view of the patient's life story, were respected among non-analytic therapists. Generally speaking, the Great War (World War I) had forced a recognition that emotional and behavioral disturbances belonged to psychiatry, rather than to classifications of perversion and eccentricity. The Mental Hygiene movement, particularly in America, was making a beginning impact on medical and lay thinking in this direction.

Although the Age of Awareness had arrived, its comprehension by the patient-public was far from clear. Psychoanalysis was for the wealthy, not for the masses. The literate and intelligentsia were turning their attention inwards to analyze their existence and functions, but the middle class and lower socioeconomic groups had a minuscule interest in such sociopsychologic niceties. In those naive days, sex was a pleasure, not a preoccupation; aggression belonged to the criminal rather than the "normal" adolescent; psychiatry and medicine grew on observation and clinical acumen rather than on computer tabulations. Psychology for the literate layperson meant William James' introspectionism, his advice on how to strengthen habits and the will ("Make . . . your nervous system your ally . . . Keep the faculty alive in you by a little gratuitous exercise each day"),[107] and pragmatism. American academic psychologists were intent on intelligence tests (Terman's revision of the Binet-Simon test); on animal experiments with apes, (Robert M. Yerkes); on

Watson's Behaviorism; on Lashley of Harvard's ablation experiments in animals investigating cerebal lobe functions.[246] In Europe Gestalt psychology had replaced the laboratory analysis of mental states, based on Wundt's experimental sense studies. Pavlov demonstrated the "conditioned reflex"; Henry Head in Britain had described the concept of the "postural model of the body" or "body schemata" out of which the body-image notion grew; Goldestein, Pötzel, Weizsacker, and others in Germany and Austria were developing clinical sensory physiology.

It was in this climate that Paul Schilder meaningfully delineated a neuropsychiatry which illuminated human behavior and explained its malfunctioning. His dedication to clinical truths and his extraordinary perceptiveness flowed through empirical neurological and psychological observations to emerge as a total view of the functioning organism. *This amounted to no less than a clear picture of the perceptual organizational process; to the body-image concept in relation to the production of neurotic and psychotic symptoms;*[208] to a view of the maturation process in children (with Lauretta Bender); and to a philosophic basis for a social psychiatry.

To account for this broad base, this style of thinking, we can refer to Norwood Hanson's whimsical division of thinkers into two classes, the Lumpers and Splitters.[93] He characterized the former as those who:

> seek connections, analogies and symmetries between things apparently as different as cabbages and kings, while the splitters hunt out distinctions, differences and dissimilarities between things as apparently alike as peas in the pod.

Schilder, who was a Lumper, perceived connections and relationships as one constructs a graph from a few isolated points which later becomes filled in with detailed observations to form a completed curve. It was said that when he described the Schilder-Foix syndrome (encephalitis periaxialis diffusa), he did it from a single slide of the brain tissue from a single case and, some would add, from a single glance at that preparation. But Schilder was no armchair philosopher; he worked diligently with clinical material and with experimental observations. He had the charisma to stimulate younger associates to join in his studies who were not always aware of where they were heading.

When Schilder came to Phipps Institute at Johns Hopkins at

Adolf Meyer's invitation in 1930, he immediately plunged into implementation of the themes projected in *Medical Psychology,* starting with Leo Kanner in a study of optic images and optic imagination. When he arrived the same year at Bellevue Psychiatric Hospital as Clinical Director and Research Professor at New York University, the full flood of his energies became evident. With this development, initiated by Dr. Menas Gregory, Chief of the Bellevue Psychopathic Hospital from its inception as a Receiving Unit for the city's insane, 3 decades before the hospital sprang to life, the staff increased numerically and qualitatively. The diverse group of young psychiatrists soon became immersed in clinical research by contagion. David Wechsler developed his Intelligence Scale using workers in the W. P. A. (Works Progress Administration, Franklin Roosevelt's master-plan to stem the Great Depression); Lauretta Bender wrote on autistic children and evolved the Bender-Gestalt Test; Karen Machover worked out the Draw-a-Person Test; Frederic Wertham, an import from Johns Hopkins, announced his Catathymic Crisis theory of brutal murders in unstable criminals; Frank Curran worked with adolescents; Milton Abeles with amnesia; Sam Parker became involved in sense-physiology. I, myself, developed the psychiatry of marijuana and psychiatric criminology. In the years that followed, others on the staff contributed to dynamic psychiatry: David Impastato in electroshock therapy; Ralph Brancale in criminology; Irving Bieber as a distinguished investigator of homosexuality; John Frosch, the editor of the *Annual Psychoanalytic Yearbook*; Nathaniel Ross as supervising psychoanalyst.

Under the stimulus of Schilder, ward rounds attained the status of unversity conferences, research projects eventuated in important papers. For more than a decade, until Schilder's untimely death, the period was one of creativity. But our productions were small compared to Schilder's; his output was prodigious; lectures, books, papers, discussions at scientific meetings, research, streamed out uninterruptedly. As a man, he was impossible to dislike. A slightly built man, his coal-black eyes and hair and almost sepia-colored skin reminded one of a Turk rather than the Europeanized Viennese we had encountered among other expatriates. He exuded a true *gemütlichkeit* without stodginess, wit and urbanity without affectation, and a *joie de vivre* that covered intricate scientific, and mundane affairs alike. With patients he was friendly, yet incisive in his questioning. His neurological examinations were informal, almost haphazard, as if, in cutting short the details of a traditional neurological examination, he was automatically winnowing out the clinical chaff from kernals of significance. Although Schilder was intent on fashioning a system of psycho-physiology, a mental cosmology of the living individual, he did not extol his own accomplishments and rarely leveled criticism against others in the field. Some of the latter looked askance at his stream of writings. Once he intimated this to me and with a smile said, "If you don't write, you're autistic."

EXPERIMENTAL STUDIES

Before proceeding to discuss the phenomenological method and Schilder's use of it in psychiatry, some of his broader perceptions should be noted. In speaking of the unconscious and its relation to the mental life of humankind, Schilder enlarged the Freudian hypothesis. He placed the unconscious in the total stream of life and experience:

> The phenomenology of our experiences show that instincts and desires do not go into the past; they go into the future and they use the past only as a method to progress into the future. [220 p. 12]

In discussing the logic behind psychoanalysis, i.e., that causality underscores dynamic thinking in uniting unconscious drives to historical factors in a patient's life, he wrote:

> The essence of psychoanalysis is the causal chain from childhood to adult life, the inner connections to psychic life are causally related . . . but the meaning of the personality are beyond the causal chain."[220, p. 18]

Psychoanalysis, he noted, bases its attitude on an "absolute objective truth," (i.e., the facts of the patient's history of emotional trauma and conflicts), whereas the psychic life is "relativistic." Schilder's feeling for the psychological life of humankind went beyond the mechanics of psychic analysis, into its human meaning. He spoke in broader terms, as when he wrote:

> . . . every scientific attitude contains a code of action, i.e., besides causality there is a life to be lived, a moral and social life. [220, p. 10]

It has already been noted that phenomenology studies not only an object external to the self, but the "thinking subject" also, i.e., our subjective consciousness. This led Schilder to scrutinize the result when one experiences an object. What he assayed to do, when he came to America in 1930, was to examine the five senses, studying sense-data among normals and among brain-diseased, toxic, and psychotic cases. The first group of observations were made at the Phipps Institute with Leo Kanner on optic experiences. Here, optic aftereffects, representations, eidetic images, and autokinetic phenomena—the primitive optic experience when a point in darkness begins to move—were examined. When, for example, a subject was asked to image a line or geometric figure, or asked for afterimages from a picture shown him in the tachistoscope, the optic pictures showed characteristic multiplications of the image ". . .all inherent in the optic process itself and independent of the object viewed."[220, p. 16] Similar changes are noted in the illusions and hallucinations of cases of mescaline, marijuana, and alcoholic intoxication. It became clear that:

that which is peripheral in a normal person becomes the psychic foreground under pathological conditions . . . mescaline intoxication brings into the foregoing perceptual process (belonging) to the field of imagination.[220, p. 39]

These findings were considered a primary tendency of the optic perception itself brought into actualization by "movements of the object, movements of the eye or by toxic influences" in the body. Hence, Schilder felt:

There is no sensory experience which lacks spatial qualities. Every sense has its part in space perception . . . and furthermore spatial qualities . . . from the optic sphere have to be incorporated in the space continuum of the other senses.

From there he went on to investigate perception in hearing, smell, taste, and touch, noting the profound influence of the body tonus and the vestibular apparatus on visual and touch perception and ultimately on the postural model of the body. Influence on body movement, stimulated by the vestibular apparatus was perceived as being crucial in the *gestalten* which come to form our body image. Thus are developed specific attitudes towards our bodies which ultimately become reflected in neurotic and psychotic symptoms. These attitudes arising from spatial (postural) and motility perceptions are not in conscious awareness. They flood in from a subliminal level as seen with startling clarity in cases of alcoholic psychoses where the toxicity stimulates the emergence of anxiety accompanying illusions of decrease or increase in the size of limbs or head, hallucinations of moving small objects, castration and dismemberment delusions and so on.[39, p. 206]

Further, it was clear to Schilder that body attitudes, in mental health as well as in disease, become part of our social orientation. Beyond our conscious awareness, body-image perceptions are reflected in our social, sexual, and personal relations with others. As Schilder put it:

> The body image belongs to the community . . . . There is a continual interchange between our own body images and the body images of others . . . . We are never completely contented with our own body image . . . . We change it by dancing . . . . clothes change our body image . . . . We put on masks, we walk on stilts . . . and in carnival festivities we may grow immense noses and immense heads . . . .[220, p. 365]

To illustrate his manner of working, a few details of Schilder's and the author's research on Tactile Imagination and Tactile After-Effects will be cited.[38, p. 133]

In our experiments, normal subjects of varying ages, psychologic sophistication and personality types were used—with remarkably uniform results. We studied the aftereffects of touch effects when held for a prolonged time. The significance of this group of experiments was that ordinarily one does not pay attention to the disappearing phases of a sensation. One feels or does not feel, or one feels vividly or dimly. However, if after a light touch on the hand, attention is paid to what occurs *in* that sensory experience, it will be found that it undergoes spatial and temperature changes, variations in the wholeness of the perception, a tendency for the sensation to move away from the original spot of stimulation, all this being often accompanied by optic changes.

This is illustrated in Plate I, Figure 1 on page 92. Subject "L" is touched on the right hand with experimenter's finger at two spots and asked to report sensations:

I feel and see the spots. The feeling is one of warm tension. The second spot is darker and feels more intense, now the first one has disappeared. The remaining spot seems to be the apex of a triangle—it has a warmish sensation, and the triangle comes out clearly. The spot seems to move towards the finger and drifts back. Now it becomes an extended line; later a spot coming close to the knuckle of the third finger.

With another subject, "A," a triangle is traced on the left hand. (Plate I, Figure 2). Subject reports:

I feel light touch on my hand made by a finger. There are two lines apparently meeting like two sides of an angle. Now I feel a patch of tingling in the angle. The optic picture follows the tactile one. Now everything is gone but an indefinite tingling at the apex of the triangle.

Experiment repeated on right hand with same subject (Plate I, Figure 3), shows his visual and tactile perceptions:

I feel three light strokes forming two angles. I feel a small patch at the angle of two of the lines. The patch moves. All the lines are gone: I see them as straight black lines on a white background.

Then to test the influence of vestibular stimulation on aftereffects, we placed another subject, "S," in a Barany chair (a device for stimulating the semicircular canals controlling equilibrium), touched two spots on the right hand, turned him to the left three times (Plate I, Figure 6). Subject stated:

I feel both points. The second is stronger and larger. The second grows in size; the first disappears gradually. Now the spots move to the right. The tactile picture is sharper than the optic. After stopping (the Barany chair), the second spot moves in a circular way to the left. . . . At the same time there is a slow wandering of the spot to the right and upwards. As the spot disappears, the sensations seem to go deeper.

FIG. 1   **FIG. 2**   **FIG. 3**
SUBJECT "L"   SUBJECT "A"   SUBJECT "A"

CHANGES, MOVEMENT AND   MOVEMENT, SENSATION
FATE OF SENSATION   AND AFTER EFFECT

FIG. 4 SUBJECT "F"   **FIG. 5**

OPTIC AND TACTILE   CHANGES IN TACTILE
IMAGES   AND OPTIC SENSATIONS
                             AFTER STOPPING

FIG. 6 SUBJECT "S"

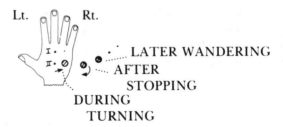

Lt.   Rt.

LATER WANDERING
AFTER
STOPPING
DURING
TURNING

EFFECT OF TURNING
IN BARANY CHAIR

PLATE I

To show how touch sensation, stimulated by visual images, develops into an ideational field, experiments with another subject, "F," (Plate I, Figure 4) are presented. A cross was drawn on his hand. Subject said:

> I feel and see the whole cross. It soon shrinks to a Greek cross. Now only a spot of vibrating feeling is left on the cross. It is penetrating into the hand. Now is superficial as if the skin were flattened. The superficial sensation has vibration in it. The optic picture of the cross follows the tactile sensation changes.

It will serve no purpose to present the minutiae of these and other sensory experiments. The main findings following a phenomenologic approach to the perception of sense data were (a) there are two groups of experiences, a sensation *of* the object and a sensation (or perception) *within* the subject; (b) an interrelatedness between tactile, optical, and vestibular perceptions. They also demonstrated movement tendencies inherent in perception itself. Further, they showed the fate of touch perception in terms of end-products, namely, irregular fading and fragmentation, terminating in disintegration and the close connection of movement tendencies to vestibular irritation. This study of the long-lasting aftereffects of perception sheds light on illusions and hallucinations of psychotics (the visual hallucination of delirium tremens), as well as dysesthesias in organic cases (neuritis, brain lesions, etc.), since disentegration products are directly represented in these phenomena. In other words, what is peripheral among normals becomes central in illness. Distortion in body image, the basis for many complaints among neurotic and psychotic patients, is often a matter of perceptual disintegration. Schilder discovered that subjective perception travels its own road, apart from the objective experience of sensation; usually the two types of perception merge together. Only in psychopathology or toxicity do we see the dichotomy.

As with symptoms, so with social reflections, we construct our worlds from subjective and objective experiences. "The relation between outer world, body and self, is a fundamental human relation," Schilder wrote.[219, p. 365] His total concept of the psychic organization of the human being rested on this insight.

Part III

CURRENT INVESTIGATIONS

Chapter 12

THE ROLE OF MOVEMENT PATTERNS IN DIAGNOSIS AND PREVENTION[1]

Judith S. Kestenberg, M.D.[2]

. . . rhythmic tendencies are in close relation to the system of emotions and the affective life. We may say that, ·in general, the primitive, the instinctive morality has very close relation to the medulla oblongata, brainstem, and the striopallidal system. Of course, we should not forget that there is no motility which is isolated, the tone is also under strong cortical influence . . . . We can say that all those motilities are closely connected with the instinctive life. They belong, psychoanalytically speaking, to the "id." Deliberate action, motility in which the pyramidal tracts play the leading part . . . has a much closer connection with the cortical region. Of course, it is not as if the cortex alone would then act . . . without the help of the subcortical structures no action is possible, but the cortex is the leader . . . This is the motility of the "Ego" in the psychoanalytic sense.[201, pp. 28, 29]

In my formative years as a budding neurologist, psychiatrist, and psychoanalyst, I had the privilege to work in Vienna where the enthusiasm of the teachers evoked in us a desire to fathom the connections between the brain and the psyche. By then, Freud himself had turned away from neurophysiology and devoted himself to

---

[1] Presented in a shorter version, with film illustration, at the Meetings of the American Psychoanalytic Association, Dec. 1971, and at the First International Symposium of Non-verbal Aspects and Techniques of Psychotherapy, Vancouver, Canada, July 1974.

[2] Child Development Research, Sands Point, New York

psychoanalysis which was to become a psychoanalytic psychology. In the Vienna *Neurologische und Psychiatrische Klinik*, the brain-injured provided an endless source for the understanding of mental functions. As aphasics recuperated, we not only saw the gradual return of speech, but we studied the ways and means by which thought processes were restored. Many of us became eager to see how sensation, perception, and motility developed in infants, but short of working in the department of psychology there was no way of studying infant development. At that time, Heinz Hartmann and Ernst Kris served as liaisons between psychology and psychoanalysis, but the pioneer who could combine the study of brain pathology and normal development of affect and thought was no longer in Vienna. Listening to Paul Schilder's students who had become my teachers, I hoped that some day I could profit from direct contact with him.

In my last year in Vienna I had worked on the development of eye movements, studying them in the awakening from insulin coma (1938), in a pontine lesion (1939) and in a frontal-parietal tumor (1941). Through the use of vestibular stimulation I could restore functioning in the child who could not move his eyes and in two women who lost their ability to orient themselves in the left hemisphere. What joy I felt to find Schilder's material about the influence of the vestibular apparatus on motility and psyche, neither of which could be separated from the other, and I looked forward to meeting him in New York.

I could not remain in Vienna and, fortunately, Paul Schilder helped me to get an internship in Bellevue Hospital in 1937. He wrote my friend and teacher, Hans Hoff, that he was going on his honeymoon with Lauretta Bender and would get me a position in Bellevue as soon as he got back. A few months later I met not only the most inspiring of teachers, but also a warm and unpretentious human being, forever helpful and encouraging his students to think, to study, to research, and to have the courage of their convictions instead of kowtowing to accepted and fashionable doctrines. I only hope that I have identified enough with Paul Schilder to convey his attitude to my students.

Working in Bellevue under the tutelage of Schilder, and then Bender, opened the world of childhood for me in a manner which prepared me for child analysis as a treatment method, without having to lose my neuro-developmental orientation. Twenty-seven years ago I began a study of movement which led me, with the help of the

Sands Point Movement Study Group[3] to construct a movement profile which could be correlated with Anna Freud's developmental assessment[70]. In writing for this *Festschrift*, I am grateful for the opportunity to communicate with Paul Schilder, posthumously, and let him "know" how his thoughts have influenced me to create a movement profile as a nonverbal tool for the assessment of development and for a base on which nonverbal preventive interventions can be designed.

In this paper I shall introduce, in a somewhat simplified form, the movement patterns on which the profile is based, and I shall use the movement profiles of a mother and her eight-month-old child[4] to illustrate the assessment of clashes and harmony between a parent and child, as well as the nonverbal methods used to prevent a pathological development in the child. I shall preface the main theme by a series of quotations, some from Freud, to whom Schilder adhered in many ways, some from Laban, a choreographer who introduced the effort-shape notation I used, but most will be from Schilder himself speaking. Moreover, each section of the paper will rely on selected quotations from Schilder's books to show the roots of my work in his.

FREUD, LABAN AND SCHILDER WRITING ABOUT MOVEMENT

Freud had in common with the neurologists of his era a keen sense of movement observation. In 1905, he coined the phrase "ideational mimetics" and explored the way we exercise the "art of remembering movement." He distinguished between small and

[3]Dr. Jay Berlow, Mrs. Arnhilt Buelte, Dr. Hershey Marcus, and Dr. Esther Robbins all belonged to this group. I am also grateful to Irma Bartenieff and Warren Lamb, who patiently taught me Laban's theory and their own. Appreciation is also due to Mark Sossin who helped me write the second volume of *Movement Patterns in Development* (1979) and to Susan Loman who, together with Sossin, teaches the course on movement notation.

[4]Johnny and his mother attended the Center for Parents and Children, sponsored by Child Development Research, an organization founded by the Movement Study Group of Sands Point, N.Y.

large movement which accompanies not only speech production but silent thinking as well. He spoke of the *"tension* by which a person indicates somatically the concentration of his attention and the level of abstraction at which his thinking is at the moment proceeding."[72, p. 193]

To Freud, movement was a model for thinking and thought, an " . . . experimental action, a motor palpating . . . "[75, p. 238]. To Schilder ". . . the sense datum does not exist without its motor response and the motor response is common to all senses"[219, p. 175]. Maintaining that the final unit of action is the object, Schilder went beyond his ideas of sensorimotor connections and showed us the basis of the development of symbols and representations. In a pioneering chapter on dancing, he made a statement which has become the theoretical base for movement and dance therapy.

> There is no question that the loosening of the body-image will bring with it a particular psychic attitude. Motion thus influences the body image and leads from a change in the body-image to a change in the psychic attitude.[208, p. 208]

Laban,[131, 132] a contemporary of Schilder, represented both Freud's and Schilder's points of view though he probably was not acquainted with either of them. He said:

> It is perhaps not too bold to introduce here the idea of thinking in terms of movement as contrasted to thinking in words.[132, p. 17]

Without knowing that he confirmed Schilder's concept of a stable and changing body image, he distinguished between body position and movement and marvelled how "an inner struggle can be transmitted to the spectator without perceptible movement and sound"[132, p. 115]. His fundamental effort analysis, which pertains to the ego-controlled movement, dealing with space, weight and time, could explain how we see " . . . in other people's movements what they feel and even how they think and we can sympathetically identify with them."[132, p. 115]

The art of observation through kinesthetic identification in which Freud and Schilder were so proficient, is almost extinct in psychiatrists now. They are too immersed in what people think and say. Laban was concerned with "how they think." Schilder went a step further and tried to uncover the road from form to content when he said:

> Where there is a specific motor sequence it changes the inner situation and attitudes and even provokes a fantasy situation which fits the muscular sequence[208, p. 208].

Freud (1905) gave us valuable hints as to how to observe and remember qualities of movement in adults and in children:

> I have acquired the idea of movement of a particular size by carrying the movement out myself or by imitating it and through this action I have learned the standard of this movement.[72, p. 191]

In observing children, Freud continued:

> You say to yourself: that is how he does it—I do it another way—he does it as I used to do as a child.[72, p. 197]

Schilder repeatedly stressed the developmental processes that lead from rhythmic to phasic motions. He was aware that " . . . there is a very complicated process in maturation from the primitive motility of the child into the graceful motility of the adult."[221, p. 191]

As observers of infants we need to have at our disposal a freedom of recalling our childhood which allows us to regress and accept the fact that we can still do things the way we did them in infancy. In our field of action and observation there is room for a continuous flow of motion and a rhythmic repetition that makes childrens' movement familiar to us. To understand the nonverbal behavior of children, observers must regress in a similar way as mothers do when they empathize with their babies.

A NONVERBAL METHOD OF APPRAISAL OF MOTHER AND CHILD AND THEIR MUTUAL INFLUENCE

In the recent massive literature on the interaction between mother and infant, it is hardly noted that Schilder, as neurologist and developmental psychiatrist, introduced the concept of helping the child develop optimally via a "motor education."[221] He said that a child " . . . should not be brought into a panic of equilibrium, or

more generally into a motor panic. . . . He should not have the feeling that motor restrictions are imposed upon him which are lasting.
. . . It seems to me that the motor education of a child is a preliminary step in all education and carries with it important emotional and libidinous implications. We may suspect that the mere knowledge on the part of the parents will not be sufficient to handle the problems of equilibrium in the child in a correct way. The parents will need, besides their motor equipment and their will, to help the child in his motor expression and security, an emotional inner balance."[221, p. 183]

As a young student of neurology and psychoanalysis in Vienna, I set for myself the task of understanding infants through the medium of movement. I was using Schilder's concepts to balance and supplement the verbal orientation of psychoanalysis. The welding of these two vectors led me eventually into the creation of a movement profile designed to assess infants' and parents' emotional development and also the creation of preventive measure that would counteract infantile traumatization via nonverbal methods of treatment. At first I designed a movement notation which contained the germ of what was to become tension- and shape-flow notation respectively.[116, 118, 123] By notating tension changes in human movement, I could classify temperamental and affective differences which are expressed in high-strung and abrupt or in low-key and gradual motions. By notating changes in the shape of the body, I could classify patterns of expressivity which are seen in frowning, strutting, or cowering. After some research, it became apparent that ordinary need-satisfactions, such as sucking, defecating, or urinating could be achieved only if appropriate rhythms of tension-flow were used in corresponding body zones. Moreover, rhythmic changes in shape-flow were also required to maintain a balance between intake and output. For instance, when breathing in air, the body expands (grows) and in exhaling, it shrinks a bit.

Tension and shape changes are related to one another, creating a basis for the intertwining of affect and expression, of need and object, within the recipient of the expressive communication. From the moment life starts, elastic tension-changes and plastic-shape changes can be recognized as the intrinsic elements of all movement. A preference for certain qualities of tension- and shape-flow could be detected early and a comparison could be made between the preferences exhibited by the caretaker and the infant. To aid optimal development, an attempt could be made to reconcile the differences between mother and baby which lead to clashes. These insights evolved in a longitudinal study of three infants which was begun in 1953. When the infants in this study grew older, more advanced movement patterns could be noted. The infants began to move in a reality-oriented fashion which presaged their growing into in-dividuals like their parents. Motions, which according to Schilder,[201] could be classified as serving the aims of the id became subordinated to those which were controlled by ego.[5] I learned to classify them in intensive studies of Laban's[132] effort-shape notation system under the guidance of Irma Bartenieff[6, 9] and Warren Lamb[134, 136]. Joined by the members of the Movement Study Group, I came to recognize that Laban's *effort*, used in dealing with space, weight, and time, as a motion-factor largely responsible for the expression of our attitude towards reality, and Lamb's *shaping patterns*, which carry our move-ment into multidimensional space, were the principal mediators bet-ween ourselves and others. The study of these patterns opened up the world of comparison between the mother's and the child's ego func-tions, as seen through the medium of movement rather than language.

In ontogeny, there is progression from the exclusive use of tension- and shape-flow in rhythmic and phasic movement sequences to precursors of effort and effort proper and to shaping the space around us in directions and in planes. From early preferences for cer-tain tension or shape changes there evolve corresponding preferences for the ego-controlled effort and shaping patterns. We can predict the potential for certain ego-controlled movement and compare this potential with what is already developed in the mother. As ego-controlled motility develops, the interplay between maternal and in-fantile adjustment to reality and to people comes into focus. It can be appraised and if necessary redirected towards a better functioning of mother and child. The emphasis from the start was on working with

[5]A basic assumption of Judith Kestenberg's theory is that inborn reflexes are the core of later reality-oriented mechanism, including the notion of self- and object-representations. By primary kinesthetic identification with Mother, a child transforms primitive reflexes into ego-controlled modes of coping with the external environment. And yet, as she remarks elsewhere, "the early reflexes do not altogether disappear."

Another basic assumption of Kestenberg's theory is the notion of kinesthetic memory. Without such a mechanism, the human being would be incapable of kinesthetic identification and therefore unable to pass along to offspring the coping behavior so necessary for survival in the adult world.(See Frosch on identification.)

both and helping them use their motor equipment for mututal ad-
vantage and to achieve a balance between body needs, requirements
of reality and mutual interests in a self-object continuum.

Out of the study of the isolated patterns and their intertwining
in one individual as well as their impact upon others, the Sands Point
Movement Study Group created a Movement Profile from which a
psychological assessment can be made, a comparison between
Mother and Child can be drawn, and a program of retraining can be
suggested that suits the best interest of the new family. (Anna
Freud),[70]

In the following sections I shall discuss in a simple form the in-
gredients of the Movement Profile. I shall do this by discussing each
of the patterns which is represented in the profile diagrams (profiles 1
and 2) and by using as examples actual profiles of a mother and her
eight-month-old child, Johnny. The notation and scoring can only be
presented here in a rudimentary fashion; the reader is referred to a
detailed explanation of the method in the second volume of *The Role
of Movement Patterns in Development.*[123]

WHAT IS A MOVEMENT PROFILE?

The notation of movement patterns, represented in the profile,
can be taught to all those who are interested in the subject and are
capable of kinesthetic identification with the mover, adult or child.
The interpretation of the profile depends on the orientation of the interpreter. Data from the profile can be correlated with a Rorschach
and with various clinical assessments of child or adult. To interpret
the profile so it can compare to Anna Freud's developmental assessment,[70] the interpreter must be familiar with the latter.

Retraining methods, based on the findings from the profile,
should be developed in collaboration between psychiatrists or
psychologists and movement specialists.[234] The following movement
profiles are based on a detailed notation and classification of movement patterns in a mother and a child. The upper portion of the
movement profile (see diagrams 1, 2, 5 and 6, profiles 1 and 2) help
us see how mother and child contribute to the creation of a holding
environment in which empathy and trust is generated through
mutuality in tension-flow and shape-flow patterns.[120] Where maternal and infantile pattern distribution differs considerably, we can
detect the existence of clashes between mother and child which
disturb the holding environment.

PROFILE 1–JOHNNY'S MOTHER

Solid lines–Pure rhythms. Broken lines–Mixed rhythms. All subsequent broken lines (2–9) –Patterns observed in gestures, dotted lines = patterns observed in postures. Load Factors–LF indicate how many qualities are used all at once in a single action (33% is lowest and 100% the highest LF). Horizontal lines on diagrams 2–9 indicate frequencies of variations. Horizontal lines on diagram 1 indicate frequencies of repetitions.

Body Attitude not included

1. RHYTHMS OF TENSION-FLOW

Oral sucking	Oral biting
Anal twisting	Anal straining
Urethral "walk-run"	Urethral "run-stop-go"
Inner-gen. undulating	Inner-genital swaying
Phallic jumping	Phallic leaping

2. TENSION-FLOW ATTRIBUTES

LF 44%

Flow adjustment	Even flow
Low intensity	High intensity
Gradual change	Abrupt change

Free: bound flow 1 + :1

3. PRECURSORS (PR.) OF EFFORT

LF 37%

Flexible (Pr. of indirect)	Channeling (Pr. of direct)
Gentle (Pr. of light)	Vehement or straining (Pr. of strong)
Hesitating (Pr. of deceleration)	Sudden (Pr. Accelerating)

4. EFFORT

Gesture LF 52% ----
Posture LF 50% ••••

Indirect	Direct
Light	Strong
Decelerating	Accelerating

5. BIPOLAR (symmetrical) SHAPE-FLOW

LF 33%

Widen	Narrow
Lengthen	Shorten
Bulge	Hollow

6. UNIPOLAR (asymmetrical) SHAPE-FLOW

Lateral widen	Medial narrow
Cephalad lengthen or shorten	Caudad shorten or lengthen
Frontal bulge or hollow	Dorsal hollow or bulge

7. SHAPE-FLOW DESIGN

Not reproduced

8. SHAPING IN DIRECTIONS

LF 33%

Sideways	Across
	Downward
Upward	
Forward	Backward

9. SHAPING IN PLANES

Gesture LF 41% ---
Posture LF 33% ••••

Spread	Enclose
Ascend	Descend
Advance	Retreat

PROFILE 2-JOHNNY, 8 MONTHS OLD

Solid lines = Pure rhythms. Broken lines = Mixed rhythms. All subsequent broken lines (2–9) = Patterns observed in gestures, dotted lines = patterns observed in postures. These do not occur in infants (see diagrams 4 and 9 in profile 1). Load Factors = LF indicate how many qualities are used all at once in a single action (33% is lowest and 100% the highest LF). Horizontal lines on diagrams 2–9 indicate frequencies of variations. Horizontal lines on diagram 1 indicate frequencies of repetitions.

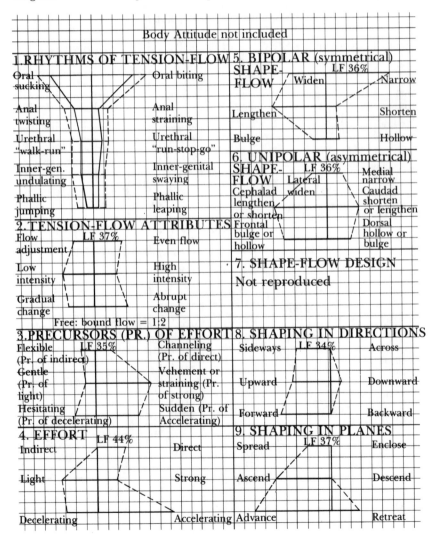

The mobile patterns which characterize early human life—tension-flow and shape-flow rhythms—require a stable framework which protects the child against loss of contact and falling. The caretaker uses ego-controlled coping patterns called efforts and shaping (see diagrams 3, 4, 8, and 9, profiles 1 and 2) to create such a framework.

DATA COLLECTION AND SCORING

The data for diagram 1 and 2 are obtained from the notation of tension changes. (See Illustration 1.) The notator looks at the mover and traces the changes in his tension on paper. He can do so as regards a limb, the torso, or the head, or he can observe and notate how changes of tension travel through the body from one part to another. A horizontal line is used as a time abscissa. Above the line one notates all changes of free, inhibited flow of tension, and all changes of bound, uninhibited flow are notated below the line. The vertical abscissa relates to the intensity of tension (bound flow) below the line and of intensity of release of tension (free flow) above the line. Not only must the notator synchronize his writings with the tension changes of the mover, he must also observe whether the same tension level is held for a time or readjusted, whether intensity rises or falls and whether the rise or fall are achieved abruptly or gradually. The resulting curve, as seen in illustration 1 is scored in two ways.

We count the repetition of rhythmic units which are used not only during need satisfaction (Illustration 1a), but also in many other activities. The rhythmic units are designated by letters (*Os, o, as, a us, u, fs, f, ps, and p*). Their meaning is explained in the section on pure rhythms (Figs. 1, 2 and 3, 4, 5). In addition to pure rhythmic units, there are mixed rhythms like *fps*, for instance. The distribution of both types of rhythmic units is computed in simple percentages and both are reproduced in Diagram 1 in the profile, (See Illustration 1a). The solid line in diagram 1 indicates the distribution of pure rhythms and the interrupted line of mixed rhythms.

The same curve is scored in accordance with the frequency with which attributes of tension and releases vary. For instance, graduality in illustration 1*b* is scored only twice and flow adjustment only once. The immediate repetition of these attributes is not taken into account. In one action we can note one or two or three changes. On illustration 1*b* we note an even level of tension in low intensity (*el*)

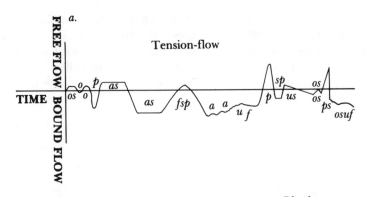

Computation		Rhythm
Pure Rhythms ——— Mixed Rhythms ---		Diagram 1

Pure Rhythms		Mixed Rhythms
os	3	2
o	2	1
as	2	–
a	2	–
us	1	–
u	1	1
fs	–	1
f	1	1
ps	1	–
p	1	3
	14	9

Total 23

Transferred in percentages on diagram

Definitions for Pure Rhythms Symbols

os	oral sadistic	f	feminine
o	oral	ps	phallic sadistic
as	anal sadistic	p	phallic
a	anal	osuf	oral sadistic urethral feminine
us	urethral sadistic	fsp	feminine sadistic phallic
u	urethral	usp	urethral sadistic phallic
fs	feminine sadistic		

Illustration 1a

We arrive at this factor by multiplying the number of attributes by 100 and dividing it by the number of actions, multiplied by 3. Instead of having a simple percentage, we have a percentage which takes into account that three attributes can be combined in one action. In this example, there were 22 attributes and 15 actions.

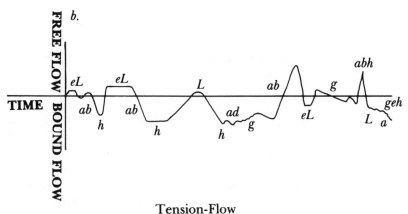

Tension-Flow
Attributes

Diagram 2

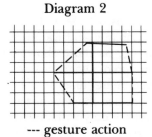

--- gesture action

Definitions for Attributes of Tensions and Release Symbols

eL	even level
ab	abrupt
ad	adjustment of tension level
h	high intensity
L	low intensity of tension
abh	abrupt high intensity
geh	gradual even level high intensity
g	gradual ascent or fall of tension
abh	abrupt high intensity

Illustration 1b

and, later, a gradual rise to high intensity which remains on an even level (*geh*). Since only variations and not repetitions are scored and there can be several changes in one action, we compute the load factor, that is the degree to which tension changes are loaded with 1 to 3 new attributes, and we represent the distribution of patterns on horizontal lines of Diagram 2. These then represent ratios of tension flow attributes in a given sample of observation (Diagram 2 in the profile). In a 20-unit scale, that is, 20 squares on the graph, a 100 percent load factor would use up the entire space available to form the diagram. With lesser load factors, less of the 20 units allotted to a diagram are used. The completed diagram shows a frequency distribution of elements in a mathematical ratio, each line of a diagram on the right and the left representing the relative frequency with which a given pattern was used during the observation on Profiles 1 and 2.

The notation of patterns represented in Diagrams 3 to 9 is done in symbols, devised by Laban[132] and Lamb.[134] All symbols are computed in the same manner as those shown on illustration 1*b*. All diagrams, with the exception of Diagram 1 are, therefore, numerically comparable. Because these diagrams show the frequency of distribution of certain specified movement patterns, we can compare the ratio in each diagram not only with one another but also with the diagrams of another person. In progressive development, the comparison of present and past diagrams yields data regarding development or improvement.

The distances between the three horizontal lines on the diagrams are 3 squares of graph paper. The choice of this distance is arbitrary. The outer lines which connect the horizontal lines are broken to indicate that only changes in gestures were noted. The dotted line in Diagrams 4 and 9 of Profile 1 indicate that only postural changes have been counted. This allows a comparison between the distribution of patterns in gestures and in changes of posture.

It takes time and practice to learn notation. The method of scoring has been adapted from Lamb[134] and is subject to changes if we can find a simpler procedure. Because so many of our profiles are available in this form we hesitate to institute changes which will make it harder to compare past and present results.

How is a notation sample obtained? Tension-flow curves and symbols of other patterns are written, making sure that all body parts are taken into consideration and equal time is alloted to each pattern. The average time of notating an adult's movement patterns is an hour, during which the observed is engaged in a normal conversation. An adult's gesticulation during a conversation is a sufficient source for tracing typical tension-flow changes, while in children one needs to notate tension changes during a variety of acitivities and in various states. Experience shows that adults display their usual repertoire of tension changes during average daily activities. As is well known, childrens' feelings and moods vary considerably so that notating only during one type of activity or during a special affective state (anxiety, exuberance, quiescence) would give a misleading impression about the child's drives and affective range. To obtain a representative sample in children, the infant must be seen in all states and the older child in all activities, as during eating, sleeping, playing, locomoting, and vocalizing or speaking. A 10-minute sample of each such activity is usually sufficient, but has to be longer if certain patterns cannot be observed at all during that time. The samples are also judged within the context of interobserver reliability. While there is a discrepancy between observers, the notation has to be repeated. Notating from films supplements live observation.

The profile is arranged in such a way that a description of the body attitude (not included here[118]) precedes it. It is then divided in two by a vertical line. On the left are listed diagrams representing the distribution of:

1. Tension-flow rhythms which convey to us the state of the mover's needs and drives;

2. Tension-flow attributes which convey to us dynamics of affective changes, especially those related to anxiety and freedom from anxiety;

3. Precursors of effort, which are the motor components of defenses and certain modes of learning;

4. Efforts which are the motor expressions of adaptation to the forces of nature.

On the right are listed diagrams representing the distribution of:

5. Bipolar shape-flow changes which convey to us the relative states of comfort and discomfort and the expressive range of the individual;

6. Unipolar shape-flow changes which convey to us the

realtive distributions of patterns of response to stimuli of a descrete nature;

7. Shape-flow design (not covered here) which deals with styles of moving;

8. Discretional shaping of space which conveys to us how a person tends to localize objects in space;

9. Shaping in planes which conveys to us how the individual uses the three-dimensional space around him or her to convey relationships to others whom he or she invites to ineract (See Tables 1, 2 and 3).

Table 1

Tension-Flow reflects needs, drives and affects		*Shape-Flow* expresses self-feelings, such as comfort-discomfort or attraction-repulsion to stimuli
Tension Qualities- *Intensity Factors*	*Affine Sets* *of Patterns*	*Shape Qualities* *Dimensional Factors*
1) *Bound Flow* (Inhibition, caution)		1.1) *Shrinking* (Discomfort, withdrawal)
2) *Free Flow* (Lack of restraint, feeling safe)		2.2) *Growing* (Comfort, approach)
3) *Even Level of Tension* (Indifference, sameness, poise, a.o.)		3.3) *Narrowing* (Constriction, shying away)
4) *Adjustment of Tension Level* (Affect modulation)		4.4) *Widening* (Expansion, seeking)
5) *High Intensity of Tension* (Intensity of feeling, as high strung, upset, a.o.)		5.5) *Shortening* (Becoming smaller, downcast, crying)
6) *Low Intensity of Tension* (Low intensity of feeling, as low keyed, delicate, a.o.)		6.6) *Lengthening* (Becoming bigger, elated, looking up)
7) *Abrupt Change of Tension* (Impulsivity, quickness of responses, a.o.)		7.7) *Hollowing* (Emptying, feeling rejected, yielding)
8) *Gradual Change of Tension* (Patience, deliberateness, savoring, a.o.)		8.8) *Bulging* (Feeling full, satiated, gratified, taking in)
9) *Neutral Flow of Tension* (Loss of elasticity, deanimation, loss of distinctness of feeling, a.o.)		9.9) *Neutral Shape* (Loss of plasticity, feeling and looking shapeless, losing structure)

Table 1. Tension and Affine Shape Qualities combine to give content and structure to *affects*. Lack of affinity between them connotes an intrasystemic conflict between feeling safe or afraid and feeling at ease or feeling malaise.

Table 2

Precursors of Effort Reflecting defenses against rives and learning modes	Affine Sets of *Learning Patterns*	*Directions in Space* Expressive of defenses against objects and of object-related learning
1) *Channeling* = Keeping tension levels even to follow precise pathways in space Precursor of directness, used in isolating, disconnecting and learning to define	Learning to define issues and preventing distractions	1.1) *Moving Across the Body* in one direction of the *Horizontal Plane*
2) *Flexible* = Changing tension levels to move around in space Precursor of indirectness, used in twisting, avoiding, and in learning by random association.	Learning by association and by generalization Learning to attack problems through explanations	Barring access to the body, preventing distractions 2.2) *Moving Sideways* in one direction of the *Horizontal Plane*
3) *Vehement* = Increasing tension to overcome difficulties in dealing with weight Precursor of strength, used in defensive attacks and in learning to conquer problems	Learning to seek explanations Learning by illumination, derived from past events	Displacing, eluding, generalizing 3.3) *Moving Downward* in one direction of the *Vertical Plane*
4) *Gentle or Delicate* = Decreasing tension, to feel confident in dealing with weight Precursor of lightness, used in reaction formation, appeasement, and in learning without resistance	Learning to make step by step deductions with proper sequencing and by anticipating consequences	Provoking, putting down, learning to explain *Moving Upward* in one direction of the *Vertical Plane* Looking up, trying to please, seeking guidance
5) *Sudden* = Increasing or decreasing tension abruptly to beat time Precursor of acceleration, used for defensive rushing, for counterphobic defenses, and in learning by sudden insight		5.5) *Moving Backward* in one direction of the *Sagittal Plane* Preparing to protect oneself, backtracking, and remembering
6) *Hesitating* = Increasing or decreasing tension gradually to prolong time Precursor of deceleration, used for defensive postponing dawdling, and in learning in a deliberate manner		*Moving Forward* in one direction of the *Sagittal Plane* Testing, initiating, anticipating the teacher, preceeding sequentially

Table 2. *Precursors of Effort and Shaping of Space in Directions* combine to give structure to *defenses and learning-modes* with special references to establishing maintaining motor *contact with people and objects.* Lack of affinity between the patterns connotes intrasystemic conflicts between certain defenses, associated with learning and modes of attaining or relinquishing contact.

Table 3

Precursors of Effort Reflects coping with the forces of external reality: space, weight and time	Affine Sets of *Patterns*	*Shaping Space in Planes* Expressive of multi-faceted relationships to objects, which structure adaptation to reality
1.) *Space Effort:*	Used in *communication and investigation*	*Shaping in the Horizontal Plane* (Aid to balance)
2.) *Directedness* (focused attention; to the point; discrimination; visual fixation)	Used in *in presentation, understanding and explanation*	1.1) *Enclosing* (exploration of small areas of space, especially in dyadic relationships and with stationary objects)
3) *Weight Effort*	Used in *operations and procedures*	
4) *Strength* (intentionality; determination)		2.2) *Spreading* (exploration of large areas of space, especially in multiple relationships and with moving objects)
5) *Lightness* (intentionality; light touch; tact)		
6) *Time Effort*		*Shaping in the Vertical Plane* (Aid to stability)
7) *Acceleration* (decision, inambiguous, without alternative)		3.3) Descending *(confronting people; demanding cooperation)*
Deceleration (decision with deliberation)		*4.4) Ascending* (confronting them with one's aspiration and looking up to theirs)
		Shaping in the Sagittal Plane (Aid to mobility)
		5.5) *Retreating* (anticipating consequences on the basis of past experiences, also terminating)
		6.6) *Advancing* (anticipating consequences of actions, initiating)

Table 3. *Effort and Shaping Space in Planes* combine to give the motor basis for *communication, presentation, and operation* (Ramsden, 1973). They mature at the same time as the cogitive structure which support secondary process thinking, symbolization, and deductive reasoning. Observers of young children often infer the existence of such precepts from motor behavior, conveyed through efforts and shaping. Lack of affinity between effort and shape connotes an intrasystemic conflict between coping with internal and external reality and relations to self and object. There is an *epigenetic* sequence in the maturation of:
Tension-Flow Control (Table 1)   and   1.1) Shape-Flow Regulation (Table 1)
Precursors of Effort (Table 2)   and   2.2) Directions in Space (Table 2)
Effort (this table)   3.3)Shaping in Planes (this table)
Clashes between 1, 2 and 3 reflect intersystemic conflicts between drives, defense and reality testing.
    Clashes between 1.1, 2.2 and 3.3 reflect intersystemic conflicts between self-feelings, object-directedness, and multifaceted relationships.

It should be noted that the left side of the profile represents motions related to the state of needs and to responses to inner and outer pressures while the right side represents reaction to stimuli and to objects. There is an intrinsic relationship between all patterns which can be studied by comparing diagrams. The vertical progression conveys to us a hierarchiacal line of development, with upper diagrams representing what is available at birth (Tension flow 1-2 and Shape flow 5-6) and the lower lines representing more advanced patterns which evolve from the former (Precursor of Effort 3 and Effort 4, Shaping in directions 8 and Shaping in planes 9). A heirarchiacal sequence is also seen in each diagram. The top horizontal line pertains to patterns which mature earliest, most of them in the first year of life, the second to those which become more apparent in the second, and third line to those which mature in the third year of life. For instance, on Diagram 4, the top line pertains to our orientation in space which develops earlier than our control of weight and time, quantified on the second and third line, respectively. Of course, these patterns continue to mature and differentiate and can become more advanced even in adulthood. Postural movements, in which a pattern is supported by an integrated participation of the whole body, mature in latency, but do not become highly differentiated until adolescence and adulthood. As will be seen later, these postural efforts and shaping patterns (Diagrams 4 and 9, dotted lines) express the functioning of the superego via movement.

By comparing pattern distributions in the left upper and lower diagrams, we gain insight into the relation between drives (Diagram 1), affects (Diagram 2), defenses (Diagram 3) and coping reactions (Diagram 4). By comparing pattern distributions in the right upper and lower diagrams we gain insight into the relation between moods and states (Diagram 5), reactions to stimuli (Diagram 6), simple (Diagram 8) and complex relationships to objects (Diagram 9).

By comparing the diagrams on the right with those on the left side of the profile, we develop an overview of the manner in which drives and ego-tendencies are interconnected with reactions to stimuli and objects. Schilder's view that all functions converge to create an object can be confirmed. However, by looking at the profile, we can say that all object-centered motion-factors structure our attitude towards our needs and towards our outer reality. They provide a form through which we begin to understand what is inside and what is outside of us.

In this paper, my attention is centered not so much on the individual profiles, but on a comparison of profiles of a mother and a child and on the retraining program that can be instituted once we can appraise how mother and child influence one another.

The Developmental Sequence on Which the Profile Is Based

My views on development are based on psychoanalytic theory, but they have been greatly influenced by observations of movement in various developmental phases. As a result, the developmental sequence which I find most useful in assessing development differs from the accepted chronology of psychoanalytic phases.[117, 118, 124]

Each phase is characterized by a confluence of drives and ego attitudes, related to external reality and to objects.[124] This becomes the basis for a predominant organization of the psyche. Movements, serving needs, and drive-discharge are classified as libidinal or sadistic with the understanding that these terms signify the nature of the aims pursued through movement. Other patterns serving affective, defensive, and coping actions are divided into indulging and aggressive.[132, 122] In phases in which sadistic wishes and corresponding movement patterns predominate, as for instance in oral-sadistic and anal-sadistic phases, aggressive ego-controlled motion factors predominate as well. A baby who likes to bite, also tends to isolate as a defense and will hit out, pull hair, and pinch. A baby in whom oral-libidinal wishes and corresponding movement patterns predominate, may turn away from unpleasantness and gingerly pat objects and people. We refer to these motion factors as indulging. On the basis of data from movement profiles, we have divided phases into libidinal-indulging and sadistic-aggressive, and we think that pregenital phases can be classified as:

1a. Oral b. Oral-Sadistic
2a. Anal b. Anal-Sadistic
3a. Urethral
3b. Urethral-Sadistic[6]

---

[6] Psychoanalytic authors assign urethrality interchangeably to the anal and phallic phases.

In each of these phases, we encounter all drive discharge patterns available to the human species, but some are predominant over others.

Psychoanalytic phase-hierarchy conspicuously omits a feminine phase while asserting that both sexes pass through the phallic phase in which the penis or the clitoris are the primary erotogenic zones. Femininity is supposed to develop in the positive oedipal period. This implies that a girl has to pass through a masculine phase before she can become feminine. In my view the pregenital phases are followed by a feminine, inner-genital phase in which feminine type rhythms predominate in girls and in boys.[118, 125] Through the integrative effect of feminine trends in drives and in corresponding ego attitudes and through the influence of the pre-oedipal mother, both sexes in this phase become maternal and creative. The indulging gentleness and patience of the maternal child is succeeded by an aggressive, expulsive quality which in adulthood will become the substrate of maternal discipline and maternal severing of close bonds to the child.

The phallic phase follows, at first with an influx of libidinal narcissistic tendencies and later with an increase of sadism and aggression in all aspects of behavior. This phase is followed by latency and then adolescence. While the inner-genital feminine-maternal phase is the cradle of parental love and concern, all subsequent and all prior phases contribute their share towards the development of parenthood.

One of our most fruitful discoveries concerns the fact that we can notate movement patterns which are aggressive or indulging in separation from those motion factors which are primarily directed towards oneself and objects. Attitudes towards objects, we discovered, are neither aggressive nor indulging, but they give form to these tendencies. To support aggression, the mover refrains from exposing too much of his body and he makes closed-shaped configurations in space; in contrast, indulging motions are coordinated with movements in which the mover exposes his body to objects and makes open-shaped configurations in space. When these two systems of aggression versus indulgence (left side of profile) and taking cover versus exposure (right side of profile) are not in harmony, we encounter conflicts, as for instance when an aggressive individual tends to use open-shaped motions which expose him to others.

In each phase of parenthood, parents, especially mothers, regress with their children. This give them a second chance to reorganize their psyche. In the process of reorganization, parental clashes with babies, toddlers, and older children can be ameliorated.

The clashes may be based on inner conflicts, as when a parent is indulging but distant; or they may be based on external conflicts, as when a mother counters a child's loving approach by not allowing him access to her body.

Because parents regress in the service of parenting, they are open to changes. That is the reason that we can successfully institute retraining procedures at this time but cannot always do so before parenthood has been attained.

DEFINITIONS AND DISCUSSION OF PATTERNS REPRESENTED IN THE MOVEMENT PROFILE IN DIAGRAMS 1 TO 6 AND 8 TO 9

In the following quotation from Schilder's early paper (1928) published in 1964 in English,[221] we find an overview of the development of movement patterns from the rhythmic, symmetrical to the phasic and asymetrical.

> The child's motility has the function of maintaining the posture (his position)[7] as the basis for subsequent action. The mouth, an organ with a fixed posture (position) in the face, has specific functions. However, there is, at least at an earlier stage of development, reaching of the mouth for objects and rhythmical sequences of mouth movements. The child needs security in posture (maintaining his position and shape) and freedom of action which brings him in relation to objects, and to the world . . . . He guards himself, with resistence, against postures (shapes) imposed upon him. . . . Grasping, at first a function in the service of the maintenance of (position) posture, later on serves in relating to objects. Pointing is derived from grasping. There is a muscular tension as an expression of the resistance against imposed postures (positions) . . . . At first symmetrical movements and primitive rhythmical movements . . . prevail. Unilaterality and arhythmicity follow. The further development of motility is guided by contact with the world (see diagrams 3 to 4, 8 to 9). However, the basic problems of equilibrium, posture (shape), grasp, freedom of movement, and efficiency of

[7]All words in parentheses within this extract are introduced by the author to help the reader translate Schilder's terms into ours.

movement remain. . . . No child is satisfied merely with
security (with being held). There is, continually, the urge
to experiment (continuous freedom of movement). The
motility is dependent on impulses and the energy of impulses.[221, p. 181]

The love of the mother (father) does not merely consist of
stroking the child, but also in protecting the equilibrium
and posture (shape and position) of the child, without im-
pairing his freedom of motor expression, and without imposing postures (positions) on the child which he does not
want. The emotional problems connected with motility
blend with the intrafamilial emotional problems. The help
the child needs is also motor help.[221, p. 181]

It should be noted that Schilder uses the word "posture" to
denote what in German has been called *Haltung*. The latter pertains
to "positions held" by the individual. For instance when he speaks of
the fixed posture of the mouth, he seems to be referring to its position
in the face. When he speaks of "postures imposed upon children,"
he seems to be referring to the way parents hold children, not allowing the child's body to assume an attitude and a positon of limbs to
each other which is natural to him at a given stage.[8]

Not only does Schilder outline the development of motility, not
only does he advocate that parents respect the child's positions,
shapes and motility-modes, but he suggests that the child needs
"motor help." Our retraining procedures are developed to prevent
the development of emotional disorders resulting from inhibitions
and distortions of movement.

In the following sections the reader will recognize for himself
how Schilder's visionary ideas have been carried out in practical
terms in the developmental assessment of children and adults,

[8]In our terminology (see page 121) we would speak of the child assuming
shapes which he or she can hold as for instance flexing one side and stretching the other in response to head turning (tonic reflex). Righting reflexes
(to which Schilder refers as postural reflexes) guarantee that the child will
assume a body shape in response to changes in position of a body part that
will be suitable for resisting of gravity. As will be seen later we reserve the
term "posture" for postural patterns in which the whole body serves the
same goal. These lead to changes in posture in the adolescent and adult.

through the use of movement notation and in the retraining procedures which are based on this assessment.

TENSION-FLOW RHYTHMS AND ATTRIBUTES (DIAGRAMS 1 AND 2)

Every movement flows. When flow ceases, movement ceases. In our view the flow of movement in living tissue is maintained or interrupted by changes in muscle tension. We concur with Schilder who formulated in a general way that:

> . . . Actions of the voluntary muscles are always connected with reactions in the vegetation and sexual systems which concern themselves with the protrusions and openings of the body. Since we deal with general attitudes, it is unnecessary to ask whether the motility of the voluntary muscles or the involuntary muscles of the gut are the origin of the impulses. It has already been shown that this is an artificial separation.[218, p. 28]

Tension, be it in the visceral or skeletal muscles, is mediated by the gamma system, the reticular formation and hypothalamic centers which also serve the neurophysiological regulations of needs and affects. There are many more apparatuses of tension control. One of the most important structures in this respect is the vestibular apparatus which, according to Schilder, assumes

> . . . a special position as uniting factor among the senses and as a general organ of tone and motility . . . . [219, p. 83] When there is a special pull in a special direction due to tonus, the amount of this pull is added or subtracted from the gravity of the body.[219, p. 101]

Before a child can deal with gravity in an adaptive way by combatting it with strength and indulging in it with lightness (see pp. 137-140), he or she uses tension changes to deal with his or her own weight. Tone is the tension of the muscles at rest. Schilder distinguishes between tonic and clonic movement as is customary in neurology. This must refer to tension changes during movement. Laban[131, 132] distinguishes between bound and free flow of movement, the former resulting from simultaneous contractions of the antagonists and the latter from lack of opposition in the antagonists. Bound and free flow, in our view, refer to the flux of tension-changes, with the former acting as inhibitor of impulses and the latter as releaser. Bound flow promotes discontinuity and cessation of movement and is experienced as caution. Free flow promotes continuity and it initiates movement, being experienced as freedom of action. When Schilder stressed the need to allow the child a freedom of movement to safeguard his independence, he referred to what we call free flow of tension.

Bound flow is seen in the tightness of the young infant's fist, especially when succeeding in holding it near the mouth. The grasp reflex is performed with bound flow and the head is held erect in bound flow. A tight fist and a tight neck can be observed when a four-year-old holds a pencil in order not to lose aim and stiffens the head in order not to derail his or her motions. A mother may hold her infant in bound flow in order to prevent his or her falling out of her arms.[9]

Free flow is seen in young infants' flinging their arms or kicking their legs; in the ten-months-old infants' banging their high-chair; in a mother's nodding to the baby and friends waving to each other. Rocking a child in predominantly free flow promotes kinesthetic sensation in him or her that underlies feelings of freedom and safety. Rocking in predominantly bound flow promotes sensations underlying anxiousness. Free flow frequently initiates movement and bound flow ends it.

The word "tension" has been used by Freud to connote drive pressure, but he did seem to model his theories of tension and energy flowing freely or becoming bound on actual observations of movement.[124] In one of the very rare instances when Schilder spoke about "tension" rather than tonus, he used this phenomenologically rather than metaphorically:

> In some way every movement is based upon the structures which extend between the beginning and the end of a movement. . . . The movement as such continually provokes new sensations of the kinesthetic and tactile type, which go into the field of tension and changes of tension.[208, p. 57]

---

[9]Films of these and other examples used in this paper are obtainable from Child Development Research, Sands Point, N.Y., or the author.

Patterns of perception and motility can be rhythmic or phasic. Underneath all motor rhythms there is the rhythm of tension-flow, expressive of needs and drives which call for bodily and psychic satisfaction. The repetition of rhythmic units must be distinguished from a repetition of qualities or attributes of tension. For instance, the sucking action is a rhythmic unit, repeated until satisfaction is achieved. Similarly, straining to defacate is a unit which repeats itself until defacation is completed. These rhythmic units are composed of tension changes in specific sequences. For instance, sucking consists of a simple alternation between free flow (used for pumping) and bound flow which helps the child to hold the nipple while he swallows. (See figure 1a p. 126). A straining rhythm begins in different ways, gradually or abruptly, but always leads to a holding of tension on an even level for some time before there is a release.

In looking at the notation of tension-flow changes, we recognize special shapes which certain rhythmic units assume, as the sinus curve of the sucking rhythm. We must note that although repetitive changes in bound and free flow occur continuously in every motion, not all motions follow a sucking rhythm. Similarly, repetitions of "holding the tension level" on an even keel are frequent, but they do not necessarily produce straining rhythms. We distinguish therefore between rhythms of tension-flow and attributes of tension-flow.

RHYTHMS OF TENSION-FLOW

Schilder recognized the all-encompassing quality of rhythm, but he was also familiar with the flow of rhythm and saw clearly that in the organism rhythmic discharge forms are evoked in the service of satisfaction. He said:

> In the so-called normal development, there is continual, almost rhythmic, flow between activity and passivity, aggression and submission.[218, p. 49].
> All senses function in a rhythmical way. . . . The vegetative organs function rhythmically; so does the bowel movement. The electric phenomena connected with the activities of the nerves and the central nervous system are rhythmical. . . Rhythm signifies continuous dissatisfaction.[219, p. 378]

When we speak of rhythm we must specify what is repeated in

regular or irregular intervals. Our own study is concerned with repetitions of rhythmic units in which muscle-tension changes in typical sequences. It is our impression that underneath all motor rhythm there is a rhythm of tension-flow which expresses needs and drives, calling for satisfaction. Some of the rhythms of tension-flow are put in the service of predominantly erotic (libidinal) drives, others serve sadomasochistic drives. All rhythmic discharge forms serve both aggressive and erotic aims, but one can distinguish those in which libidinal aims predominate from others in which there is considerable admixture of aggressive aims.

Schilder spoke of "an inner tension of an organ" and pictured energy lines connecting erogenic zones.

> Individuals in whom a partial desire is increased will feel the particular point of the body, the particular erogenic zone belonging to the desire, in the centre of his body-image. It is as if energy were amassed on these particular points. There will be lines of energy connecting the different erotogenic points and we shall have a variation in the structure of the body-image according to the psychosexual tendencies of the individual.[208, pp. 124-125]

Diagram 1 of the Movement Profile is based on these observations by Schilder.

We have classified tension-flow rhythms in accordance to their suitability for functioning in specific erotogenic zones (oral sucking and biting, anal twisting and straining, urethral walk-run and run-stop-go, inner-genital undulating and swaying, phallic jumping and leaping rhythms) as seen on Diagram 1 or the Profile. Our observations and notations revealed that all these rhythms occur in various parts of the body, not necessarily always in the erotogenic zone which evokes them. When Schilder speaks of "energy lines" (a hypothetical force) I think he refers to intensities of tension that wander throughout the body and concentrate on certain lines, perhaps the Chinese meridians which connect various zones of the body. Schilder empahsizes that grasping and sucking have a special relationship. We observe this in a wider sphere when we see that oral rhythms are more likely to be used by the upper part of the body than the lower. Conversely, anal rhythms are more often seen in the lower part of the body.

The tension-flow apparatus has as its base the elasticity of tissue. Its rhythmicity is based on the continuous changes of elasticity which will be discussed in the section on attributes of tension-flow. The well-differentiated "pure" rhythmic units of tension-flow rhythms are adapted to the zones to which they are best suited. (See Profiles, Diagram 1, lines bordered by solid lines). Rhythms become more differentiated in phases in which they are dominant. For instance, sucking rhythms are more pronounced in the oral and straining rhythms in the anal-sadistic phase, but they can be noted in the newborn's movement. Mixed rhythms consist of combinations of several rhythms which add to or modify one another (see Profiles, Diagram 1, lines bordered by broken lines). As a rule, the newborn moves with more mixed than pure rhythms, but that is not always the case. Mixed rhythms reflect individual endowment. When certain components in mixed rhythms are more frequent than others, it indicates that there has been a tendency to use them more than others since birth. For instance, if someone has had a congential proclivity for oral-sadistic type of rhythms, he or she will mix them with other rhythmic units more frequently than someone who favors phallic rhythms since birth. The congenitally preferred rhythms become even more prominent when they differentiate into pure rhythms in developmental phases in which they normally increase. This may lead to fixation in a phase and to a tendency to regress to it later in life.

Diagram 1 in both profiles represents the relative distribution of rhythms of tension-flow detected in the flow notation of Johnny and his mother, respectively. Figures 1 through 5 explain how the various rhythmic units are classified. (See Illustration 1.) However, only pure rhythms are explained here. Mixed rhythms (denoted in Diagram 1 by broken lines) are the result of confluences between two or more pure rhythms. For instance, an oral rhythmic unit can be mixed with a feminine or phallic rhythm. These are scored separately and shown on the periphery of the pure rhythm diagram.

The basic elements of tension-flow are free and bound flow. A simple biphasic movement, such as turning to a stimulus and away from it, is performed with free flow initiating the motion, bound flow preventing it from overshooting its goal, a renewal of free flow which brings the arm back to its original position, and a bound flow which stops the movement. Many authors, including Schilder, use the term "tension" interchangeably with "energy":

> Psychologically, the tensions and energies at the beginning of a movement are of course completely different from those at any other point in the course of the

movement. The fall of energy has a complicated structure and every specific movement has its specific melody.[205, p. 57]

When we speak of the rise and fall of tension, we refer to the differences in tension (not energy) which are more complex than mere alternations of free and bound flow. We call them *Intensity Factors* and score them according to the manner tension-intensity increases and decreases. The graduation of intensity in tension provides the melody of movement of which Schilder speaks. Intensity factors are composed of six attributes of tension-flow through which we express our feelings and attune to the feelings of others. In ordinary life we are not conscious of the changes in our tension and we often think that we know only intuitively how another person feels from minute to minute. Yet even a superficial scrutiny of tension attributes, classified as aggressive, reveals that keeping an even flow of tension is often a preparation for a surprise attack, that high intensity of tension is an ingredient of anger, and an abrupt rise of tension makes the onlooker fearful in face of the mover's impatience.(right side of Diagram 2) Conversely, tension-flow attributes, classified as indulgent (left side of Diagram 2) are used in actions in which adjustment of tension levels is used for fine nuances of feelings, low intensity of tension for pleasantness and gradual changes in tension for the expression of patience. The combination of free and bound flow with one, two, or three attributes of tension-flow makes possible a myriad of combinations which may be used to express feelings for which language does not provide words.

The reader is reminded that Diagram 2 as all others represented in Profiles 1 and 2, with the exception of Diagram 1, are obtained from the computation of a load factor, in such a way that the more space a diagram occupies, the higher its load factor. In terms of tension-flow attributes, high load factor indicates a greater complexity of feelings.

On the left side of Diagrams 2, 3, and 4 we score the relative distribution of indulging, passive motion factors, and on the right side, the aggressive and active elements.

Thus, on the left side of diagram 2 we see the *indulging tension-flow* attributes:

Adjustment of tension levels (first line)
Low intensity of tension (second line)
Gradual ascent or descent of tension (third line)
(go to page 131 for continuation of discussion)

FIGURE 1

PURE RHYTHMS

a) Oral Sucking   b) Oral snapping and
                        biting rhythms

Figure 1. *Oral sucking* rhythms can be best observed during suckling, not only in ther perioral region, but in the baby's fingers and toes as well. His mother's rocking harmonizes with this rhythm. Oral-sadistic rhythms can be subdivided into snapping and biting. Oral sucking has smooth and oral snapping and biting has sharp transitions from free to bound flow and vice versa. Biting is held for a short time in the same intensity of tension. Both rhythms are characterized by changes from free to bound flow. During the oral-sadistic subphase, the infant snaps, jerks and 'bites' with all parts of his body. The older child uses biting rhythms more selectively.

In Johnny's rhythms we note a definite preponderance of oral and oral-sadistic in both pure and mixed rhythms (first line on diagram 1 on profile 2). This was in keeping with his developmental phase. It is interesting to see that Johnny's mother matched his preference for oral rhythms (diagram 1 on profile 1). The degree of her orality in pure and mixed rhythms suggests that there was an oral fixation which enhanced her regression at this time. We must also keep in mind that she may have regressed to attune to her child in the service of her maternal ego.

FIGURE 2

PURE RHYTHMS

a) Anal twisting   b) Anal straining
                        rhythms

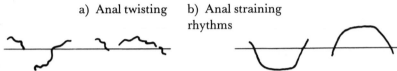

Figure 2. *Anal twisting* is characterized by subtle adjustments of tension levels, either in low intensity of tension or in small changes in high intensity. They often appear in spiral motions which emanate from the anal sphincter and spread over the rear of toddlers who wiggle as they creep. Facial mimicry, based on anal type rhythms, is common at the end of the first year and in the second year of life. Twisting rhythms give way to *anal-sadistic straining* rhythms, which are characterized by evenly held intensity of relatively long duration. Most of the time they reach high intensity, but not always. Toddlers pull themselves up, climb and let themselves down in rhythms like these. At the same time they may strain more when they defecate.

At eight months, Johnny had quite a few anal twisting rhythms and very few anal-sadistic straining rhythms (second line of diagram 1 on profile 2). His mother was in tune with the former, but did not, through her own rhythms, encourage the latter (second line of diagram 1 on profile 1). Had she not been able to increase the frequency of straining rhythms in the following year, she would have found it difficult to train Johnny.

FIGURE 3

PURE RHYTHMS

a) Urethral "Walk-run"   b) Urethral "run-stop-go rhythms"

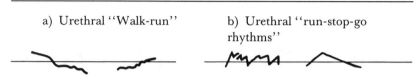

Figure 3. In transition from the anal to the urethral phase, boys begin to hold their penis and girls put their finger on the urethral or orifice. Both become interested in the flow of urine. *Urethral* type *"walk-run"* rhythms which are on the increase at this time, are characterized by smooth transitions and small gradual changes in tension increase and decrease. Urinating passively and "walk-running" may merge. Accidents of urine flowing and falling because of lack of control may be frequent. A young toddler may begin a running rhythm by touching the front of the body and end it by touching an object that bars further progression. During the *urethral-sadistic* subphase, *run-stop-go"* rhythms are used to initiate and stop urinating as well as running. At that time, toddlers tend to rush away abruptly, often to get to the bathroom on time. The acquisition of control over urination converges with the achievement of control over urethral rhythms, used in running, walking and stopping. (Kestenberg, 1975).

Johnny's mother used a great many urethral rhythms of the "run-stop-go" variety. (diagram 1, line 3, profile 1). These reflected her impatience with Johnny, but also came her change in good stead when she was learning to increase here abruptness to cope with Johnny. At eight months, Johnny tended to yield passively to urethral impulses and judging by his tendency to combine urethral "walk-run" rhythms with others, one could predict that his urethral-passive needs will increase further in the beginning of his urethral phase, when ordinarily urethral, passive-libidinal impulses predominate (diagram 1, line 3, profile 2). This may bring him in conflict with his mother who evidenced a propensity for active urethral-sadistic rhythms.

FIGURE 4

PURE RHYTHMS

a) Inner-genital undulating   b) Inner-genital swaying
                                     rhythms

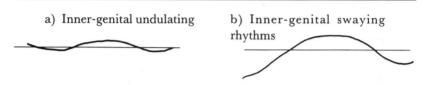

Figure 4. The *inner-genital (feminine) undulating* rhythm rises gradually, but remains in low intensity of tension. Sometimes, one can see how a languid feminine rhythm, emerging in the pelvic region, spreads upward and becomes a mixed feminine-oral rhythm, eventually approximating an oral rhythm in the upper part of the body. This is especially noticeable when a nursing mother rocks her baby. The practiced eye can detect the frequent use of undulating rhythms in groups of three-four year old children who are in the midst of their inner-genital phase (Kestenberg, 1975). *Inner-genital (feminine) swaying* rhythms are characterized by a gradual rise to high intensity of tension which reverses from free to bound flow and vice versa. They are infrequent in children and most pronounced during labor and delivery. It is likely that the low intensity-undulating rhythms (figure 4a) are based on those occurring in the inner portion of the vagina. That type of rhythm in the male can be observed in the contractions of the tunica Dartos of the scrotum. The more intense, surging and swaying inner-genital rhythm resembles uterine explulsive movements. To be consistent we refer to it as an inner-genital sadistic rhythm.

FIGURE 5

PURE RHYTHMS

a) Outer genital (phallic) jumping

b) Outer-genital (phallic) leaping rhythms

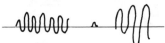   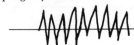

Figure 5. *Outer-genital (phallic)* rhythms are characterized by an abrupt rise and fall of tension. They have a smooth transition from free to bound flow and vice versa and they frequently reach high intensity of tension. Phallic rhythms can be noted in masturbatory activities and in those concerned with intrusion into space (Erikson, 1950). *Phallic-sadistic leaping* rhythms are characterized by sharp transitions from free to bound flow and vice versa. They are used in aggressive butting, pushing, punching and are most clearly seen in broad jumps and leaping.

Neither Johnny nor his mother used many phallic rhythms (line 5 of diagram 1 in profiles 1 and 2). In this, as in many other ways, they were functioning in attunement with one another.

On the right side of Diagram 2, we see the *aggressive tension-flow* attributes:

Even level of tension, as in holding (first line)
High intensity of tension, as in excitement (second line)
Abrupt ascent and descent of tension, as in jerking (third line)

A predilection for *adjusting tension-levels* can be seen in a variety of twisting movements in working with uneven surfaces or when a change of position is desirable. A three-year-old kneading clay will successfully change levels of tension as he or she creates new shapes. The child may use the same tenion-flow adjustment to modulate his or her smile. A mover who keeps *tension* on an *even level* gives the impression of being unconerned, uninvolved, poised, or serious. This attribute is required for easy resting and for preventing derailment, that is, being distracted from a steady course of movement by an interruption of some sort. Readjustment of tension-flow can be seen in carefree smiling and stretching. Combined with bound flow, adjustment of tension-levels may lead to a grin or to rigidity. Free, even flow of tension in meeting a stranger may indicate a steady and safe watching. Even bound flow indicates cautious steadiness.

Control over flow adjustment in free and bound flow is acquired in the first year of life. When mother and infant attune in these attributes, they develop empathy for change and sameness in each other.

Low intensity of tension is seen in all actions performed with delicacy and in low states of excitement. Picking up little specks of dust often has the same low intensity as a friendly little smile. A slap on the head, performed with low tension, is a love-pat, expressing friendliness and indulgence rather than aggressiveness. Low intensity in bound flow is used for precision work, in free flow for whimsical actions (middle left line of Diagram 2.)

High intensity of tension occurs in states of excitement. High intensity in bound flow can be seen in the way a newborn stretches the legs stiffly. Straining for defecation is a typical example of high intensity in bound even flow (holding). High intensity of tension in free flow is seen in the baby's flinging the arms, hitting out, or derailing. Clutching a railing without letting go may have the same high intensity of tension as the expression of anger in a face. In rage as in exuberance we see a high intensity of tension. In the former there is a preponderance of bound flow and in the latter of free flow.

The regulation of ranges of high and low intensities of tension is the achievement of the second year. When mother and child attune in these attributes, they develop empathy in excitement and in calmness.

Gradual changes in tension are the expression of leisure, patience or delayed reaction time and similar qualities. *Abrupt changes in tension* are the expression of alertness, impatience or impulsivity. Much depends whether graduality and abruptness combine with bound or free flow or with low or high intensity. Graduality in free flow is seen in the newborn's athetoid finger movements. A gradual increase of vitality is seen in the recovery from illness or depression. Abruptness allows for an immediate response to internal or external stimuli while graduality is used in calming down of excitement which is impossible to switch off on command. Abruptness is a feature of laughter and of spasmodic crying. It is clearly seen in the newborn's startles. The regulation of ranges of graduality and abruptness of tension increases and decreases is the achievement of the third year of life. When mother and child attune in these attributes, they develop empathy in leisure and alertness. Patterns over which control is being acquired are practiced more than others. Developmental preferences combine with congenital preferences for the selection of patterns of tension. Regulation of levels of intensity is begun in the oral phase; the regulation of heights of intensity starts in the anal phase; regulation of rates of tension changes begins during the urethral phase that follows. Tension variations are the basis for affect changes and they underlie differences in temperament, which are described by the following terms: uninhibited or tense, adjusting to novelty or even-tempered, low key or intense, and deliberate or impulsive.

Attunement in tension-flow is the empathic core of communication, mutual understanding, and acting in consonance.

In comparing the diagrams of Johnny and his mother which represent variations in tension-flow attributes (Diagram 2), one notes the greater degree of affective combinations in the mother. This is expressed in the difference in loading (37 percent in the child and 44 percent in the mother). The mother can use several qualities of tension all at once while the child more frequently resorts to only one and sometimes two. At a given time, Johnny's mother would adjust her tension-level gradually and decrease her intensity. Johnny was more likely to add abruptness or flow adjustment to whatever his tension-flow was at the moment. Mother's affects were more complex than Johnny's, not only because of the differences in maturity, but also because Johnny's restlessness and motor push did not give him enough time to develop deep feelings.

When Johnny came to the center at the age of four months, his excessive abruptness and high intensity jarred with his mother's gradually developing low tension. Attending courses for Movement in Child Care and in individual sessions, Johnny's mother learned to attune to her baby and to teach him how to attune to her. At first, when Johnny abruptly flung himself in his crib and cried, mother always picked him up and carried him. When he abruptly flung himself backwards in her arms, she would become anxious and tighten her grip on him. Our first step was to show her how she could help him calm down by presenting him with visual and acoustic stimuli which enhanced the use of even flow and flow-adjustment. As a next step, mother learned to use abruptness to synchronize with that pattern in Johnny. This enabled her to break his fall when he threatened to fall or would derail himself. Johnny became less intense and attuned to his mother's graduality and low tension (Profile 2, Diagram 2, third line on the left and second line on the left).

In addition, maturational advance fostered attunement between mother and child. Johnny was coming closer to the anal phase which enhanced both flow adjustment and the use of low intensity (Profile 2, Diagram 2, left upper and middle line). (See also figure 2 in "Pure Rhythms".) Through attunement, mother met Johnny's need to be abrupt and Johnny met her need to be gradual (Profiles 1 and 2, Diagram 2, bottom line). A decisive difference between mother and child could be seen in their respective distribution of free and bound flow. Mother alternated between free and bound flow in a ratio of 1:1, while Johnny at eight months used bound flow twice as often as free in a ratio of 1:2. His primary control consisted of excessive inhibition of impulses.

Three sources of this pronounced characteristic suggest themselves. Johnny was born a "tonic" (tense) child, that is, in our terminology he was more bound than free from the beginning. His mother's early difficulty in controlling and soothing him when he used high intensity of free flow prompted her to respond with bound flow, because she became very anxious. Johnny learned from her to respond to his dangerous impulses (climbing on high tables or ramming into things) with inhibition. In addition, when he practiced attuning with his mother's low and gradually developing tension, he would do this only when he inhibited his natural impulses. Much later, when Johnny reached the phallic phase, free flow threatened to overwhelm him and a clash between inhibition and release of impulses resulted in a head tic. At this point, the clash between Johnny and his parents re-emerged in full force. At this time, it was the father who tended to use bound even flow, and became a model for Johnny. When he entered latency, Johnny began to use many more ego-controls which allowed him to relinquish some of his newly developed bound flow.

Returning to Johnny's behavior at the age of eight months, we note that his attunement with his mother was quite good. Correspondingly, theirs was an affectionate, congenital relationship which was disturbed primarily by a clash in their respective defensive behavior.

EFFORTS AND THEIR PRECURSORS (DIAGRAMS 3 AND 4)

Efforts[6, 131, 132, 116, 118, 124, 123] are ego controlled patterns for adaptation to space, gravity, and time. When they mature, the child begins to adapt to space by paying *attention directly or indirectly*, to *gravity* by expressing *intent* with *strength* or *lightness* and by making *decisions* through acceleration and deceleration (Diagram 4).

Precursors of effort develop before effort. They evolve from related tension-flow attributes and they merge and transform into related effort elements. Aggressive and indulgent tension-flow attributes are affine or closely related to aggressive and indulgent precursors of effort and effort-elements, respectively.

	Tension-Flow	*Precursors of effort*	*Effort*
Aggressive	Even flow	Channeling	Direct
	High intensity	Vehement or straining	Strong
	Abrupt	Sudden	Accelerating
Induling	Flow adjustment	Flexible	Indirect
	Low intensity	Gentle	Light
	Gradual	Hesitating	Decelerating

When discussing space, Schilder usually referred to shapes and objects in space, but he did on occasion address himself to the objective qualities of space through which we move as contrasted to movement concerned with the body. He noted that:

> . . . the primitive outside world has more motion, more rhythm, more color and less sharply distinguished spatial relations than has the perceptual world.[221 p. 10]

and

> . . . The term perception or impression means that
> something is going in space. There is no sensory ex-
> perience which lacks spatial qualities. Every sense has its
> part in space perception. Effort and experimentation lead
> to a more unified space experience. Behind the variety of
> different spaces of the various senses the unified space of
> all senses is a given experience. The experiences of all
> senses lead to actions by the same motor system.[219]

The prerequisite for perceiving objects in space is an attitude
towards space. For stable optic images a directed attention is
necessary. There must be a tonic (at tension) response with the
stabilizing evenness of tension which leads into channeling our movement. For moving optic images and for sound which " . . . has in-
herently the quality of wandering in space,"[219, p. 76] an indirect attention is necessary. There has to be, at least, a flow-adjustment in tension which leads to flexibility that prepares the perceiver to attend
whatever moves in space.

Among neuropsychiatric and psychoanalytic researchers
Schilder was the only one who was concerned with our attitude
toward *gravity* rather than just toward space and time. He made the
pioneering discovery that sucking and grasping are not primarily
related to contact with objects, but are apparatus of support:

> . . . grasping does not (primarily) serve to incorporate an
> object into the mouth; rather it serves as a help in the fight
> against gravitation.[221, p. 41]

By giving support, the caretaker (mother or father) offers herself
or himself as an object which satisfies the basic needs of the organism.

> The grasp reflex is only one line of defense in main-
> taining one's position against gravity; the other one is an
> attempt to get support by clinging. The mother is not only
> protection in general and an agency for food for the child,
> but she protects the child against the everpresent enemy:
> gravitation. Dependence also means the wish to have help
> in standing upright.[219, p. 216]

However, gravitation not only evokes defenses, it also promotes adaptive active-aggression responses. In speaking of the play of children who experimented with gravity by pushing down objects and allowing them to fall, Schilder observes that:

> . . . . their delight in power and aggressiveness was obvious. The formal elements are, of course, not isolated parts in psychic life, but are a part of the biological orientation of children. Knocking toys down satisfies the aggressive impulses of the children, but it also helps them to acquire a better working concept of the problems of physics connected with gravitation. To be upright or to lie down is partially a moral problem (aggression and submission), but is is also a problem of the orientation of the organism to gravity and the physical world. Orientation means, for us, not only perception and knowledge, but also the motor side of the adaptation of the individual.[221, pp. 30-31]

The labyrinth which regulates our tension during rest and movement is ". . . another organ which helps us perceive gravity . . . skin and muscle sensitivity also play a part in the perception of gravity."[219, p. 83, 10] It is the labyrinth and its cortical representations which mediates in the transformation of tension-flow attributes into space tensions, weight pulls and time considerations.

A condition for perceiving one's own weight and secondarily the weight and mass of objects is an attitude towards gravity. for moving heavy objects there has to be a preparedness to overcome obstacles, an intent to develop an aggressive stance through strength. There must be a heightened intenstiy of tension which leads to vehemence or straining. For moving light objects an attitude of lightness is necessary. A person must be able to reduce tension to a low level before developing gentleness, a precursor of lightness.

When we investigate time experiences we must distinguish between such time factors as duration and intervals which operate in rhythms, between feelings of time passage we derive from kinesthetic sensations, and between the defensive and adaptive uses of time. Schilder wrote that

> . . . . we experience time as an expression of our strivings and that every change in the libidinal situation changes the time experience.[221, p. 22]

[10]See citation 204. Quotes correctly express Schilder's thesis.

On the other hand, he said:

Time experiences are always connected with experiences in the outer world. Time experienced cannot be isolated from our aim in life nor from our relations to the future.[219, p. 219]

A necessary condition for perceiving motion in time, our own and that of other objects, is our attitude towards time. To achieve control over motion and time, and thus become decisive, we must be prepared to react aggressively with acceleration. There must be some ability to react by abruptly changing our tension, which leads to suddenness of action. To indulge in the feeling of having time so that action can be delayed, we need to assume an attitude of deceleration. There has to be some control over evoking gradual increases in tension which lead into hesitation, a precursor of deceleration.

When the infant and child learn new skills and/or defend themselves against dangers they employ *precursors of effort* rather than effort proper (Diagram 3 and 4). Only when specific skills become automatized and the child can maneuver well in the environment does he or she employ effort elements to adapt to the forces of nature which are either opposed or accepted. However, precursors of effort never disappear; they are employed in learning new things and in defensive actions throughout life.[116, 118]

Precursors of effort are dependent on tension changes and guided by them while effort proper controls tension changes and makes them subservient to its goals. Efforts are oriented toward reality. Precursors of effort draw upon form feelings in the body to achieve external changes.

As earlier indicated, Johnny used to be a very intense (Diagram 2, Profile 2) and abrupt baby. This tendency has diminished greatly. However, it influenced the choice of his favored precursors of effort so that at eight months Johnny was vehement (Diagram 3, right middle line) and sudden (Diagram 3, right bottom line), using aggression and counterphobic rushing into danger as defenses. When Johnny needed to overcome obstacles before the appropriate skills had been automatized, he became frustrated and succumbed to temper tantrums in which vehemence and suddenness predominated. His mother became frightened by his defensive temper and responded by channeling her attention and by straining (Diagram 3, Profile 1, right upper and middle line). The former underlay her attempts to isolate affect from thought and action, and the latter served her identification with her aggressor child. The high-intensity even bound flow she used at such times was an expression of her anger and her contained anxiety. The result was that mother and child became locked in aggression and counteraggression. Neither used enough reaction formations to transform their defenses into gentleness, a precursor of lightness (Diagram 3, left middle lines in Profile 1 and 2).

The staff of the center took great care in teaching Johnny's mother to match Johnny's vehemence and suddenness, but they also showed her how from this initial stance she could calm both herself and the baby by transforming vehemence into gentleness, and suddenness into hesitation or deceleration. As a result, mother has become gentle at times, and with lessening of her anxiety, she would use lightness and deceleration as well as directed attention to guide Johnny towards a more adaptive behavior (Diagram 4, Profile 1, left middle and bottom lines and right upper line).

When acting in an adaptive rather than a defensive manner, Johnny's mother succeeded in teaching Johnny the art of indulging in weight and time by lightness and deceleration. However, she did not have enough indirect efforts at her disposal to use diplomacy in approaching the child. The staff was vigilant in helping her develop indirectness and increase her repertoire of strengths so that she could combine an indulging approach with an authoritative manner (Diagram 4, left upper and right middle lines, Profile 1).

Johnny not only transformed his excessive abruptness (Diagram 2, right lower line) into suddenness (Diagram 3, right lower line), but his attitude to time was also influenced by his congenital preference so that he used acceleration (Diagram 4, right lower line) much more often than other elements. His dynamic potential was great as he achieved a load factor of 44 percent in effort. However, in almost all of his combinations he accelerated. In contrast, mother's direct approach predominated over others and was used in many effort combinations.

Having examined the motor expressions of affects, defenses, and ego-attitudes of Johnny's mother, it is worthwhile to turn our attention to the influence of the superego on her actions towards the child.

GESTURES AND POSTURES REFLECTING THE FUNCTIONING OF THE EGO AND THE SUPEREGO

Motion elements can be divided into those used in *postures* and in *gestures.* [136, 170, 118, 123] I have noted earlier that babies do not assume postures and that it is more correct to speak of the shapes they form. Not before the ages of five and six do children develop postural efforts and not before adolescence do they integrate gestures and postures into phrases. Mature postural motion elements are a feature of the adult movement repertoire. Comparison of profiles with clinical assessments suggested that all three psychic structures (id, ego, and superego) are involved in postural movements (see dotted lines in Diagram 4, Profile 1). Thus we can judge from the distribution on postural patterns, as compared with those performed in gestures, how the superego functions.

A gesture-effort can be noted when one or more of the effort elements is used in a part of the body such as the arm, leg, torso, or neck. A posture-effort can be noted when one or more effort elements are used by the whole body. This presupposes total involvement in the action. The first postural efforts are global; that is, all parts of the body simultaneously display an effort such as strength or acceleration. More mature postural efforts are integrated; that is, all body parts act together but differentially to involve the mover in an effort action. Schilder was aware of this difference when he observed:

> . . . . we gain the impression that, from the point of view of sensory-motor development, the child brings more or less isolated and unrelated experience into a complete form by continual effort. Even then the parts are not in such a close relation to the whole as they are for the adult. [221, p. 54]

Postural efforts (see dotted lines in Diagram 4, Profile 1) reflect the superego's attitude towards space, weight, and time. Since spatial efforts are used in attention, weight efforts in the expression of intentionality and time efforts in decision-making processes, postural efforts reflect the superego's influence on these three functions. Under the pressure of the superego we encounter a restriction or an increase of certain efforts.

In the case of Johnny's mother, fear of penalties, imposed by her superego, reduced the aggressive components of directness and acceleration and increased all indulging efforts in her effort repertoire. (Compare dotted lines with broken lines in Diagram 4, Profile 1.) It is interesting to note that her postural strength increased over and above the frequency with which she used strength in gestures. We knew that she was angry at herself for not being strict enough with Johnny and this was reflected in her gesture-posture-ratio in strength. Her conscience was on the side of becoming more indulgent and less aggressive, as far as attention and timing was concerned, but she became more aggressive in expressing her intentions to Johnny. Her conscience supported the staff's retraining procedures. It accounted for what in therapy is called the "therapeutic alliance." Johnny's mother was allied with the staff in their joint efforts to help her become a more loving and yet stricter mother to Johnny who needed both indulgence or laissez-fair and a determined setting of limits to safeguard his integrity.

In this section I could discuss only the influence of the punitive and indulging aspects of the superego on the effort profile of an adult. The ego-ideal which becomes incorporated in the superego in latency pertains to an individual's aspirations which shall be discussed under the heading *Shaping in Planes*.

SHAPE-FLOW AND SHAPING

Tension-flow attributes, precursors of effort and effort proper, are dynamic patterns which reflect the changing forces within the individual as regards internal and external reality. In contrast, shape-flow and shaping in directions and planes are formal patterns reflecting the relation of the individual to environmental objects, to stimuli, and to objects in the surrounding space.

Schilder believed that the primary aim of motion is to seek support. This is complemented by his insight that, as the child seeks support, he or she attaches himself or herself to an object. In this connection, he repeatedly stressed ". . . the universal importance of the perception of motion in relation to the perception of form."[218, p. 36]

The shape of the body changes continually during breathing, and in turning to and from stimuli. Through kinesthetic memory of this rhythmic repetition, the infant develops an image of his or her own body which, to the baby is also an object. Schilder discovered that:

In the sensory field, in the development from primitive perception to organized perception, it seems that rhythm becomes subordinated to the impression of the stabilized object. . . . We always speak of unchanging objects. However, objects are continually changing—and still remain the same objects (Boring, 1933). Not only do objects change, but there is a continuous change in the sensory impulse which is the basis for the perceptual object. The static object is a product of late development. The primitive object is in motion internally and externally.[218, pp. 9-10]

The rhythm of the repetition of tension changes is associated with a rhythmic repetition of changes in the shape of the body. Attributes of tension-flow are coordinated with the attriburtes of shape-flow which give them a structure. At first the maternal body and the infant's body merge, especially if there is attunement and adjustment between them. Through distance from the mother, the child learns to differentiate between their bodies. To reach her, the child traverses space and learns about directions. In order to give structure to adaptive movements and efforts, the child shapes his or her body in multidimensional configurations, which are reproductions of the object in relation to the child's self.

Changes in shape are symmetric or bipolar (Diagram 5), as in breathing; they are asymmetric or unipolar (Diagram 6), as in turning to stimuli and away from them.

> We may draw the conclusion that a differentiation of action into a left and right action is not a complete one, and we see indeed, that in primitive forms of activity, symmetrical bilateral action is common. In the child, in the first few months of his life, the asymmetrical mechanisms of gait and creeping vie with symmetrical flexions and extensions (Schilder).[221, p. 163]

> The whole path from visual perception, or hearing, or smelling an object, through tonic or phasic action to final solutions is, from the beginning, connected with the reactions of secretions, the smooth muscles of the intestinal tract, and the whole vasovegetative system. The entire system gets its final shape by the continuous interaction between the tendencies toward and away from objects. . . . The construction of an object is essential in itself, and not merely because the object might sooner or later be of immediate use.[218, p. 41]

Symmetry refers to the two sides of the body. Bipolar shape-flow extends from the middle of the body to both sides, to the upper and lower ends of the body, as well as to the front and the back. It contracts from the sides to the middle of the body, from the head and the feet towards the middle and from the front to the back towards the middle. Unipolar shape-flow extends and contracts in one direction of the body axes. In Laban's (1960) terminology we speak of growing and shrinking of body shape. Schilder refers to the same phenomenon when he expounds on the psychological meaning of shape-flow and static shape:

> . . . Every expressive attitude is connected with characteristic changes in the postural model of the body. . . .

(Note here that postural model refers to the shape of the body.)

> Thus the postural model of the body is changing continually, and goes back to the typical primary images of the body which are dissolved and crystalized again. The image of the body thus shows characteristic features of our whole life. There is a continual change from crystallized rather closed entities to states of dissolution and to a stream of less stabilized experiences, and from there a return to a better form and changed entity. It is therefore the continuous building up of shape which is immediately dissolved and built up again . . . . every emotion is either connected with expressive movements or at least with impulses towards them. Every emotion therefore changes the body image. The body contracts (shrinks) when we hate, it becomes firmer, and its outlines towards the world are more strongly marked . . . We expand (grow) the body when we feel friendly and loving. We open our arms, we would like to enclose humanity in them. (See section on shaping below.) We expand (grow), and the borderlines of the body-image lose their distinct character.[208, pp. 209-210] [11]

Variations in body shape are used to express our affective relationship to environmental objects and discrete stimuli. Through symmetrical, bipolar shape-flow, the organism responds to the environmental changes of air-composition, temperature, light, and air-pressure (Diagram 5). The organism responds with unipolar shape-flow to inner stimuli projected on the outside and to outer stimuli, by growing towards beneficial and shrinking away from noxious

[11]Terms in parentheses are mine.

substances which are felt in certain parts of the body (Diagram 6). Changes in body shape are based on the organism's plasticity. Referred to as "dimensional factors," they occur in one, two, or three dimensions of the body.

DIMENSIONAL FACTORS

Open shapes: widening in width, lengthening in length and bulging in depth.

Closed shapes: narrowing in width, shortening in length and hollowing in depth

Growing and shrinking of the body shape are practiced by the infant not only in breathing, but in continuous rhythmic alternation between shrinking back into the intrauterine flexed positon and growing into the newly provided extrauterine space. An example of a similar pattern in older age groups is the coiling up of a swimmer before he stretches out to spring into the water.

The apparatus of bipolar and unipolar shape-flow provides structure for tension-flow. Free flow is congenial with growing shapes and bound flow with shrinking. These three apparatuses are at the core of body-image formation. Harmony between them has an integrative effect on the development of self and objects. Conversely, dysharmony or mismatching has a temporary or permanent disorganizing effect. Clashes between tension-flow and shape-flow distort the image of one's body and the image of objects which, when motion continues, can be rebuilt in a subsequent phrase in which harmony prevails.

The apparatus of *bipolar shape-flow* (Diagram 5, Movement Profiles) is used to express comfort and discomfort through growing and shrinking in the three dimensions of the body. Rhythmic changes between comfort and discomfort are at the core of the changeable, mobile body image, while states of comfort and discomfort underlie the stable body image. In comfort we feel big, in discomfort we feel small. The newborn infant uses bipolar shape-flow profusely. As the infant matures,he or she uses it more differentially for the expression of emotions. Frowning is done in bipolar *narrowing*, smiling is bipolar *widening* (first line of Diagram 5). Nursing in the mother's arms, the infant breathes in coordination with the sucking, narrowing as he or she exhales, and widening as he or she inhales. Widening is the

motor base of feeling omnipotent, and narrowing deflates omnipotence. When there is a balance between widening and narrowing, a feeling of *trust* is generated.

There is an affinity between narrowing and an even flow of tension and between widening and flow adjustment (Table 1) as can be
seen in frowning and in modulated smiling, respectively. When the
affinity between these patterns of tension- and shape-flow is preserved,
the infant preserves the trust in his mother when she remains the
same or changes a bit. This ability to trust develops by the end of the
first year.

Bipolar *shortening* is seen in coiling up and *lengthening* in stretching out (2nd line of Diagram 5). Diaphragmatic breathing involves
both these tendencies. After raising him or herself to standing, the infant maintains this postural shape by bringing pelvis and thighs
closer together through shortening and stretching out, upward, and
downward away from the pelvis which is the base of support.
Lengthening is the base of feeling grandiose (''so big'') and shortening (without lengthening) is at the root of inferiority feelings. When
there is a balance between those two tendencies, as seen in secure
standing, there is a feeling of *stability*.

There is an affinity between shortening and high intensity, and
between lengthening and low intensity of tension (Table 1), as can be
seen in clenching the teeth and in the opening of the mouth when the
clenching spasm is over. This affinity can also be seen in forced expiration and in the relief of inspiration. When there is an affinity between these patterns of tension and shape, a feeling of stability gives
structure to changing states of excitement and calm. Lack of control
over these affinities brings on temper tantrums during which the
young child lengthens with high intensity and shortens with low intensity. Once able to stand erect without straining, the child begins to
balance his or her excitement by lowering and heightening it without
loss of control. This is usually achieved by the end of the second year
of life.

Bipolar *hollowing or bulging* (third line of Diagram 5) can be seen
in swallowing and the preceding deepening of the oral cavity. Two-
year-olds bulge, leading with their bellies and breathing by bulging
and hollowing; they will do so more often when they dawdle on the
way to the bathroom to urinate. When they finish urinating, they ac-
centuate the emptiness of the bladder by hollowing. Abdominal and
pelvic fullness go together with bulging and hunger with hollowing.
Abdominal and pelvic pain lead to hollowing in forced expiration,
with relief bringing bulging inspiration. Hollowing by pullling in the

lips in pouting, and bulging by puckering the mouth for kissing are typical facial expressions of the same age. Being full and contented and empty or deserted are the affective expressions that accompany rhythms of bulging and hollowing. When these tendencies are well balanced the child develops a feeling of *confidence*.

There is an affinity between abrupt changes of tension and hollowing, and between gradual changes in tension and bulging. This can be seen during abrupt swallowing of liquids (gulping) which is accompanied by a decrease in the depth of the oral cavity. The filling of the mouth with an increase in its depth is done more gradually. When the affinity between these patterns of tension- and shape-flow is preserved, the child reacts with confidence in the fact of changing states of alertness and leisure.

Bipolar shape-flow changes diminish with age. They become incorporated into ego-controlled patterns of relating to objects through the shaping of space. Their control is established in a heirarchic order. Regulation of narrowing and widening is accomplished in the first year, shortening and lengthening in the second year, and hollowing and bulging in the third year of life. This developmental sequence is colored by individual preferences and influenced by the adjustment of shapes in the imitative interplay between maternal and infantile shape-flow patterns.

Bipolar shape-flow give a psychosomatic base to organ-object-images[117] and to self-object[128] representations. It contributes to the formation of the body image by giving it volume in the three dimensions of the body.

Johnny (Profile 1, Diagram 5) has learned to balance his excessive narrowing with widening and lengthening. In this change, he was greatly helped by his mother who had a natural proclivity for widening. Mother had learned to narrow when she wanted to take Johnny in her arms. They developed mutual trust, but their control over familiarity and unfamiliarity was poorly managed because their horizontal shape-flow by far exceeded their capacity to use even flow or flow adjustment (Diagram 2, upper line). Thus their balance between a desire for sameness and for novelty was not as fully developed as their trust in each other and in themselves.

Johnny's excessive lengthening expressed his feeling of grandiosity. At the age of nine months he stood in his highchair while eating. Although he was not secure in this position and had to be strapped in, he towered over the other members of the highchair brigade and acted like a king. His mother's elation (expressed through lengthening, see Profile 1, Diagram 5, second line left) over his "standing" in the baby community did not nearly match his own. However, the harmony between lengthening and low instensity of tension which she used sometimes kept her at peace with herself, despite her own poor balance between lengthening and shortening. Johnny himself lacked stability and could not structure his occasional states of high excitement by securing his pelvis through shortening. As a result, his temper had a diffuse quality.

Johnny's mother was taught to shorten so that she could stand securely and give support to Johnny. Simultaneously she learned to increase tension in the middle of the body and feel the center of her gravity. This was necessary for her to acquire the strength through which she could exert authority and safeguard Johnny from accidents.

Neither mother nor child had a sufficient shape-flow structure for their frequent abruptness and graduality. When mother moved abruptly, her inability to hollow made her look awkward. Retraining did not succeed in helping her to hollow. Her body image of a wide and bulging maternal figure was too entrenched to be changed.

Unipolar shape-flow (Diagram 6) can be best understood when one compares the human body to an amoeba which extends it pseudopodia and withdraws them. In unipolar shape-flow only that part of the body grows and shrinks which reacts to a real or imaginary attractive or repelling stimulus. Correspondingly, we classify unipolar shape-flow attributes in accordance with specified body areas. As precursors of directions, these attributes can be divided into the following body-sectors:

Lateral	growing to one side—unilateral widening
Medial	shrinking towards the midline—narrowing from one side
Cephalad	growing or shrinking upward—lengthening or shortening
Caudad	shrinking or growing downward—shortening or lengthening
Frontal	growing or shrinking forward—bulging or narrowing
Dorsal	shrinking or growing backward—hollowing or bulging

Lateral widening and medial narrowing can be seen when infants learn to turn from prone to supine and vice versa. Cooling or pinching an arm or a leg or the side of the torso leads to a shrinking from the stimualted side. Stroking or warming these body parts leads to a widening towards the stimulated side. Through the experience of unipolar shape-flow in the horizontal dimension, the infant becomes acquainted with the lateral and medical periphery of his or her limbs and the side of the torso. The infant may also feel a midline which divides the body into two sides.

Cephalad and caudad motions can be either *lengthening or shortening*. If a pleasant stimulus actually occurs or is imagined as occurring on the head or shoulders, lengthening upward occurs. If the stimulus appears unpleasant, we observe a shortening downward. If the fingertips or soles are warmed, the arm or leg lengthens downward. If they are cooled, we observe a shortening upward. These reactions give the child the opportunity to become acquainted with the upper and lower parts of the body. He or she may also feel a series of horizontal lines inside the body which divide it into upper and lower sections. The principal line of demarcation is in the pelvic region.

Frontal and dorsal shape-flow consists in bulging or hollowing in the front or the back of the body respectively. Pleasant stimuli evoke bulging frontward or backward, unpleasant stimuli evoke hollowing frontward or backward. The stimuli can be substituted by real or imaginary attractions or repulsions which do not touch the child's body, but are located near the responding sections of the body. Two-year-old children will sit hollow-bellied when they have nothing to do. However, hollow bellies become potbellies when toddlers bulge frontally in tune with taking in a story read by the teacher. A rhythmic alternation between frontal bulging and hollowing can be seen in young listeners when the teacher shows pictures and withdraws them to look at the book herself. Stroking a child's back may result in his or her bulging it like a cat. Pinching it leads to hollowing towards the front by arching the spine. Frontal and dorsal shape-flow acquaints the child with his or her front and back. The child may become aware of inner sagittal lines which divide the body into its front and its back.

While unipolar shape-flow is coordinated with tension changes in large areas of the periphery of the body and with those in the center of the body, it is also coordinated with tension changes localized in spots and along lines on the periphery of the body and inside the body. Regardless of body direction, unipolar growing is affine with free flow and unipolar shrinking affine with bound flow. Moving towards the side is affine with tension-flow adjustment and towards the middle with even flow. Moving cephalad is frequently accompanied by a low intensity tension, and moving caudad by a high intensity. Moving frontally goes together with a gradual change of tension and moving towards the back, with an abrupt change of tension (Movement Profiles, Diagrams 6 and 2).

Unipolar shape-flow plays a role in the transformation of rhythmic repetition into two-phasic actions. It is a tool used by the child to develop anaclitic relationships. That means that contact is discontinued when the need is satisfied or the stimulus ceases to be attractive. It is also used for withdrawal from aggression and for turning to friendly or loved objects.

In the developmental hierarchy of unipolar shape-flow, a child gains control over lateral and medial shape-changes in the first year, over cephalad and caudad changes in the second year, and over frontal and dorsal shape-changes in the third year of life. Thus, lateral and medial changes facilitate turning (first line of Diagram 6), while cephalad and caudad changes help in climbing and are intrinsic to walking.

At eight months, Johnny's preferred reaction to stimuli was to lengthen and to shorten in the cephalad body directions (second line of Diagram 6 on the left). As preparation for climbing he shortened, bending his legs upward, and then lengthened the upper part of his body to pull himself up. He was also proficient in caudal and frontal and less so in dorsal shape-flow attributes, but had little use for lateral and medial body-directions. His mother disapproved of his climbing and walking on tables, but was not capable at this point of discouraging him in a consistent fashion. Her preference was to narrow on one side and in a sequence of cephalad and caudad body-motions restrain Johnny and put him down on the floor. He responded by freeing himself through bulging frontally or hollowing dorsally to free himself from his mother's arms. His excessive frontal bulging was often done in an abrupt way. Such clashing motions had a startling effect and mother responded to them by abrupt tightening and narrowing of her grip. As soon as he seemed settled in her arm, she would widen again unipolarly or bipolarly.

In designing a retraining program, the staff aimed at increasing Johnny's capacity to move laterally and medially (Profile 2, Diagram 6, first horizontal line), so he could indicate his wish to free himself by a turning motion to which his mother could adapt. Through our direct intervention with him and through our teaching the mother, we hoped to promote Johnny's capacity to increase tension gradually in conjunction with frontal bulging. Mother was taught to bulge frontally in a gradual manner to accommodate to the child and make it attractive for him to settle back in her lap by dorsal bulging into her. This would make him feel more attracted to his mother and would give her an assurance that she need not abruptly lose contact with him. She might have to respond at first with abruptness and only then proceed to gradually bulge into him.

Bipolar and unipolar shape-flow are apparatuses for dealing with the inner and outer environment and for coping with internal and external stimuli. These mechanisms of relatedness come into the service of the ego in the course of development. Dimensions of the body are then projected into space, and body-directions extend outward and eventually become differentiated from spatial dimensions and directions.

SHAPING IN SPATIAL DIRECTIONS AND IN SPATIAL PLANES

Whereas shape-flow is centered on the mover's body, shaping in space is based on the acknowledgement of distances between the self and objects. We have learned how the body develops an inner and outer structure. A similar structure is imposed on space during repeated experimentation with objects.

> The localization of an image or a perception is primarily given with a tendency to arrangements in a system of six primary coordinates: left and right,[12] below and above, before and behind, and that only with the further development of the perception is there elaborated a definite orientation in space concerning directions and localization. Furthermore, a primary impression has to be brought into the system of coordinates. Six positions are particularly outstanding; but primarily the object is given in all possible positions. Careful observation reveals that individuals are continually experimenting with the various positions, until finally, under the influence of forces which are not merely optic, a specific direction and localization is given to a perception of an image (Schilder,[215, p. 51]).

---

[12] Note here that the baby does not distinguish between right and left even when beginning to distinguish the middle from the side. The understanding of the difference between sides evolves from unipolar narrowing and its extension into the direction ''across the body.''

Through the shaping of lines in space, the child creates a relationship between him or herself and the distant object. The child moves:

> Sideways and across the body
> Upward and downward
> Forward and backward (Diagram 8, Movement Profiles)

In one linear movment the child can combine two or three directions. For example, forward and upward or sideways can be combined, and downward and backward. The latter are extensions of the body projected into a cube.[133, 48] All these lines are bridges from the self to the object. Other lines which are not connected to the mover's body connect two or more objects, thus objectifying the localization of objects without reference to the mover.

At first, seeing the mother or hearing her voice substitutes for the immediate satisfaction of nursing and touching while being supported. Fixating an object by channeling one's attention and directing one's gaze towards it is often used in lieu of support. Creating directional lines and discovering clearly localized spatial points and spots creates a simple structure in space, a structure which underlies separation and bridging over separations, through which reaching is superceded by pointing and localizing without motion.

During the first year the child primarily practices moving sideways and across the body; in the second year he or she prefers the upward and downward directions, and in the third, the forward and backward directions.

Having pulled himself into standing very early, Johnny at eight months rarely moved downward and hardly ever across the body and backward (Profiles 1, Diagram 8). His mother preferred not to move across and backward, but had more propensity for moving downward than Johnny. Neither moved in diagonals. Mother and Johnny found each other in directional space by both moving sideways, Johnny moving upward and mother downward. Johnny moved forward a great deal and mother rarely could follow him in this direction (Profile 2, Diagram 8).

Shaping in spatial directions is related to precursors of effort. Both patterns are used for learning new skills which are later automatized. Experimentation with objects entails not only their creation, so they exist for the child, but also protection against them. While precursors of effort are the motor means of defending oneself against drives, directional shaping is used in defending oneself against objects, usually by erecting barriers in space.

Precursors of effort and directional shaping of space have the following affine patterns (Diagrams 3 and 8):

SHAPING IN DIRECTIONS	*PRECURSORS OF EFFORT*
1. Moving across the body	-channeling
2. Moving sideways	-flexible
3. Moving downward	-vehement or straining
4. Moving upward	-gentle
5. Moving backward	-sudden
6. Moving forward	-hesitating

It should be noted that indulging percursors of effort are related to directional shaping which opens up space (2, 4, 6 above) and aggressive precursors of effort are related to directional shaping which restricts space (1, 3, 5 above).

Affine combinations of precursors of effort and directional shaping are used for learning to bar distinctions in order to define issues (1), displace to generalize (2), explain issues in attacking a problem (3), seek explanations from others (4), gain insight from past experience (5) and anticipate consequences in making step-by-step deductions (6). The same combinations are used when defenses against objects and drives act in harmony with one another, as in barring access to the body to support isolation (1), displacing to support avoidance (2), putting down someone to support defensive aggression (3), seeking guidance submissively to support reaction formations (4), escaping in a rush (5), and anticipating another person's actions to justify postponement (6).[124]

At eight months Johnny seemed almost exclusively to use displacement, appeasment, and anticipation to "support" defensive aggression and counterphobic rushing into danger (Diagram 8, all lines on the left, and Diagram 3, middle and bottom line on the right, Profile 2). Retraining was designed to practice patterns which would support the defenses against drive, and attain a lessening of isolation in the mother and its increase in the child.

Interwoven with the network of linear structures, representing the traces of directional movements, are multidimensional configurations, sculpted by *shaping in planes*.

Speaking of childrens' play, Schilder came very close to developing a theory of shaping in planes. He said:

> One sees that emotional problems and formal problems cannot be completely separated. The experimentation of the child with form and configuration is an expression of his tendencies to come to a better handling of objects by action. By trial and error, he develops insight into the structure of objects. . . . The form of the organism and its motor possibilities determine the play of children. . . . Motility adapts itself to the plane on which the play takes place. Play starts with the formation of foreground and background. The child undertakes continuous experimentation concerning the geometrical quality of lines, angles, clusters.[13] In three-dimensional games, the child is particularly interested in whether something can be put into something else. . . . The definite form of play is adaptable to the biological situation.[221, pp. 36, 37]

At first the infant plays with his own body and the body of his mother, then begins to experiment with objects. Bipolar shape-flow is a tool through which he or she learns about dimensions, volume, and mass, and about inside and outside. There is an affinity between bipolar shape-flow and shaping in space. All cavities, but especially the mouth, are a model for the space that surrounds us. We always picture space as finite and livened by objects. The tongue shapes the space of the mouth while at the same time its own shape changes and there is touch contact between the mucous membranes and the tongue. Via the hand which helps the tongue to investigate, the experiences in the mouth are transposed into space. From the experience with breathing, the child derives the feeling that there are vast and small expanses inside his or her body. The shape and the volume of the inside of the body changes and these changes are transposed into the external cavity (space) which envelops us. The child feels the food in the mouth, the air in the lungs and the fecal mass in the abdomen. Sometime later he or she becomes aware of the pelvic cavity and its fullness and emptiness.

There is an infinity between growing in shape and free-flow. When we are free to take in substances into the body, we grow.

---

[13] These qualities are represented under the heading *Shape-Flow-Design,* Diagram 7 of the Movement Profiles.

There is an affinity between shrinking in shape and bound flow. When we expel substances from the body, we tighten in bound flow and shrink. When we are attracted to a stimulus, we are free of anxiety so that we can grow towards it; when we are repelled by a stimulus, we become cautious in bound flow and we shrink away from the unpleasant stimulus.

The transposition of shapes from the inside to the outside is based on the following affinities between shape-flow (Diagram 5) and shaping in planes (Diagram 9):

Shape-flow		*Shaping in Planes*	
Shrinking		concave, closed shaping	
Growing		convex, open shaping	
Narrowing	horizontal	Enclosing	horizontal plane
Widening	dimension	Spreading	
Shortening	vertical	Descending	vertical plane
Lengthening	dimension	Ascending	
Hollowing	sagittal	Retreating	sagittal plane
Bulging	dimension	Advancing	

In the first year, the infant learns to move in all planes, but practices more in the horizontal plane as he or she reaches, grasps, takes, encloses, and explores through spreading in space. In the second year, the toddler tends to confront people in the vertical plane, as he or she climbs, comes down, picks up things and demonstrates them, always either descending or ascending. In the third year, the child practices more advancing and retreating in the sagittal plane as he or she begins to play ball and approaches people or withdraws from them in a much more complex way than before. Throughout experimentations with planes he or she incorporates shape-flow changes into the space-shaping actions. For instance, the child will widen to spread, shorten to descend, and hollow to retreat. Spatial configurations created through shaping of space in planes structure effort. Affine combinations of shaping and effort are:

Shaping in Planes	*Effort*
1. Enclosing in the horizontal plane	—Direct
2. Spreading in the horizontal plane	—Indirect
3. Descending in the vertical plane	—Strong

4. Ascending in the vertical plane   —Light
5. Retreating in the sagittal plane   —Accelerating
6. Advancing in the sagittal plane   —Decelerating

It should be noted that aggressive efforts are structured by closed-shaped forms and indulging efforts by open-shaped forms. Affine sets of effort-shaping combinations are used in communication and investigation when attention combines with exploration (see top lines of Diagrams 4 and 9), in presentation and explanation when intention combines with confrontation (see middle lines in Diagrams 4 and 9), and in operational procedures when decisions combine with anticipations (see bottom lines in Diagrams 4 and 9). These relationships can be noted in Table 3.

SHAPING IN PLANES
COMPARISON OF JOHNNY'S PROFILE TO MOTHER'S

Johnny's predilection for ascending and advancing reflected his premature motor development (Profile 2, Diagram 9, left middle and bottom line). He managed to advance toward his mother or father, and climbed up on them or on furniture by ascending to reach heights. The tendency to ascend was consistent with his lengthening bipolarly and using frequent cephalad motions. It was important to note that his localization of objects upward (Diagram 8, left middle line) did not match his grandiose ascending (Diagram 9, left middle line). As a result, he did not always understand where he was allowed to climb and which lofty objects were forbidden. It was rather frequently that he could not descend from the heights he reached (Profile 2, Diagram 9, right middle line). He would walk on a table as he did on the floor, but his gait was unstable and he propelled himself with acceleration (Diagram 4, right bottom line) without a proper balancing of the retreating motion of one leg when the other was advancing (Diagram 9, right bottom line).

Johnny's load factor in effort (44 percent) was quite high and much less so in shaping of planes (37 percent). This bespoke the high dynamism in his use of adaptive patterns for which he did not have sufficient structure. The lack of matching between effort and shaping was indicative of a conflict in the ego between his incessant goal to conquer the forces of nature and his relationship to people who ordinarily guide the child in his endeavors to adapt and master obstacles. As would be expected from a child overridden by locomotor impulses, Johnny's attentiveness was of a low order. He had no facility to pay indirect attention (Diagram 4, top line on the left), yet he had some need to explore in large areas (Diagram 9, upper line on the left). Sometimes he could pay attention directly (Diagram 4, right upper line), but this was not structured by enclosing of small places (Diagram 9, right upper line). In ordinary language we would have to say that Johnny's attention was severely impaired. Observing him one had the impression that he had no time to pay attention, and he was particulary oblivious of his surroundings when he walked and climbed.

Johnny's mother's shaping was more mature, more highly loaded and more evenly distributed in various planes (Profile 1, Diagram 9). By spreading around in space she could keep track of Johnny's explorations (left upper side of Diagram 9); by advancing and descending she sometimes succeeded in preventing her child from climbing to dangerous heights (right middle and left bottom lines of Diagram 9, Profile 2). However, she could not keep up with the frequency of his advancing and ascending (left middle and bottom lines of Diagram 9, Profile 2). Her own conflicts became evident as she spread to explore without sufficient indirect attention to what was going on (Diagram 9, left upper lines, Profile 1). For instance, she watched out for her child from a distance, without paying sufficient attention to his sudden and accelerating advances. In addition she did not have sufficient ascending elements to match her lightness (Diagram 9 and 4, left middle lines). As a result, her good spirits were not always recognized by the child. To some degree she seemed to emulate Johnny's exaggerated accelerating advance, but she did not retreat enough to structure her own accelerations (Diagram 4 and 9, right bottom lines, Profile 1).

GESTURES AND POSTURES, REFLECTING THE FUNCTIONING OF THE OBJECT-ORIENTED EGO AND EGO-IDEAL

Shaping in planes is used to appeal to other people. The configurations in space, created by shaping, are representations of the self and of objects to whom the mover exposes the self or from whom he or she protects the self. Sequences of shaping actions, in the area of exploration (Diagram 9, line 1, Movement Profiles), of confrontation (line 2) and anticipation (line 3) provide motor phrases for which language has no words.

Postural shaping (shown by dotted lines, Profile 1, Diagrams 4 and 9) encompasses the whole body in the service of one or more shaping patterns. It does not develop before the age of five or six and does not become integrated with gestures until adolescence. Repeated comparisons of the ratio between gesture-posture shaping with clinical observations suggest that shaping in postures reflects the mover's ego-ideal. A discrepancy between postural shaping and that performed in gestures reveals a conflict between the ego and the ego-ideal. The ego-ideal, when incorporated into the superego during latency and increasingly in adolescence, gives guidance to a person's aspirations. It supervises what a person would like to become and checks whether these aspirations have been attained. The consequence of its failure is not punishment, but a loss in self-esteem.

Schilder discussed the ego-ideal and its relation to the superego in several books.[208, 218] The following quotation is pertinent to our thesis:

> Human beings have a very strong wish for perfection . . . .
> It means the capacity to gain love from others. The idea of
> power is, of course, also involved . . . . Perfection has to be
> measured in relation to one's past and in relation to other
> human beings . . . . Freud has shown that the ideal we
> develop of ourselves . . . has a complicated development,
> is in close relation to identification with the parents and
> with other love objects, and has a close relation to self-
> punishing tendencies and feelings of guilt.[218, p. 180]

Movement studies suggest that we can discover conflicts within the superego (between its indulging and punitive components and its encouraging or disparaging components) when we observe a mismatching between postural efforts and postural shaping.[134, 118, 123, 170]

The following quotations from Schilder give us insight into the influence of parent's and educators' ego-ideal upon children:

> Since the child is experienced as part of the parents they
> enjoy a partial fulfillment of their own perfectionistic ideal
> . . . . in the ego ideal there are strong tendencies to go into
> and be imbedded in the future. [218]

> Sooner or later parents have to build up the picture of
> their children according to reality. This process has two
> sides. They have to realize the needs of the personality of
> the child and how far this personality can be reconstructed

by human relations with the child. This process is one of the models of interhuman relations. These same problems are significant to the educator and the leader.(p. 181)[218]

They are equally significant in the assessment of postural shaping in adult profiles.

DISCUSSION OF MOTION FACTORS, REFLECTING HARMONY AND CONFLICTS WITHIN THE SUPEREGO.
(See broken and dotted lines in Diagram 9 and comparison to Diagram 4, Profile 1)

When Johnny's mother was striving for perfection, she would communicate with Johnny by postural and harmonious directing of her attention into a small area of space (Diagram 4, line 1 on right and Diagram 9, line 1 on right, dotted lines). To be able to address him that way, she had to "catch" him and hold him, to which Johnny reacted with attempts to free himself and temper tantrums. At that point, her strength could be invoked more easily (Diagram 4, middle on the right, dotted lines), but she could not face him by coming down to his level (Diagram 9, middle right, dotted lines). When she was ready to make a decision (Diagram 4, right bottom line) she would not retreat (Diagram 9, right bottom dotted lines), giving Johnny no alternatives. When she did not set herself goals dictated by her ego ideal and her punitive conscience, she was able to spread to follow Johnny around (broken left upper line, Diagram 9), but then she would employ strength less often and would accelerate instead (Diagram 4, middle right and bottom right).

RETRAINING TO RESTORE HARMONY IN MOTHER AND CHILD

Our staff has been helping mother to raise her level of aspirations in her role as a mother. Enjoyment of ascending (Diagram 9, left middle dotted line) has been on the increase and we have seen her smiling in admiration of Johnny whose motor feats were a source of awe for all and whose radiant feeling of omnipotence created a contagious feeling of similar quality in others. Mother was helpful when the staff also concentrated on helping Johnny to descend and develop more strength than vehemence (Diagrams 9 and 4, right middle lines, Profile 2). We taught him to come down directionally (Diagram 8, right middle line) rather than by changing his body shape from unipolar shortening to bipolar lengthening (see Diagram 5 and 6, middle line). He learned to go down to the floor rather than grope around and maneuver his body without proper relation to the surroundings. We helped him to experience bipolar shortening by holding his waist and letting him feel a stability there for the short moment he allowed us to do so without escaping. To improve his ability to attend and to explore (Diagram 4 and 9, upper line) we showed him attractive stationary and mobile objects and we walked around with him showing him things on the way. By getting him interested in colors and sounds made by objects, we helped him reduce his precarious indiscriminate walking and climbing.

Relying on data from movement profiles, we are able to outline ranges of harmony and conflict, between parents and children, as well as internal harmony and conflict. This in turn helps to design a training program which can be conducted on a nonverbal level. Through exercises in attunement of tension flow attributes and rhythms and in adjustment of shape-flow attributes, we diminish clashes between mothers and infants. By taking into consideration the distribution of functions, those which foster adaptive aims and those which serve to promote relationships, we can train babies and parents to develop more harmoniously themselves. With inner harmony restored, clashes between them diminish without further aid.

SUMMARY AND CONCLUSIONS

Paul Schilder always maintained that movement cannot be separated from perception and is intrinsically connected with the psyche. Trained as I was in the Viennese tradition of neuropsychiatry, meeting Schilder who had been my teacher in absentia in Vienna was like meeting an old friend. I always knew that his influence on my work directed my thinking even after he died. In reviewing his work for this manuscript, I could trace what seemed a very original creation, the Kestenberg Movement Profile, from Schilder's teachings. I have prefaced not only my whole paper with quotations from Schilder, but I headed each section with some of his thoughts on the subject under discussion.

I have introduced the Movement Profile in a somewhat simplified form and discussed eight types of movement patterns which can be correlated with psychic functions.

Rhythms of tension-flow are expressive of needs and drives, such as oral sucking and biting, anal twisting and straining, urethral "walk-run" and "run-stop-go" rhythms, inner-genital-undulating and inner-genital-swaying as well as phallic-jumping and phallic-leaping rhythms.

Tension-flow attributes reflect emotions concerned with safety versus anxiety and aggressive and indulgent feelings.

Precursors of effort are used for learning and for defenses against drives.

Efforts proper are the adaptive motion factors which deal with space, gravity, and time.

Bipolar shape-flow attributes which account for comfort and discomfort are operative in breathing and in expressive movement.

Unipolar shape-flow attributes are expressive of attraction and repulsion, which underlie anaclitic relations.

Shaping space in directions evolves from unipolar changes in shape-flow and permits the child to form spatial bridges to objects and to localize in space.

Shaping space in planes occurs in one, two, or three planes (horizontal, vertical, and sagittal) and reflects complex relationships to people.

In addition, I have discussed:

Postural efforts which reflect the older child's and the adult's punitive and indulging components of the superego; and

Postural shaping which reflects the older child's or adult's discouraging and encouraging components of the ego-ideal which is part and parcel of the superego at large.

All these patterns develop in an epigenetic sequence, which tension- and shape-flow present at birth and before. Innate preferences for certain patterns may overshadow the orderly development of motion factors. Both mother and child influence one another and modify each other's preferences. By comparing diagrams, representing the relative frequency of motion factors that can be noted in a given observation period of mother and child, we can study the areas of their mutual harmony or clashing. Retraining the mother and/or the child is a method which reduces clashing and prevents pathology, making childcare more enjoyable.

Aside from studying interpersonal relationships by comparing profiles of two people, we search for areas of conflict and clashing within the individual. Certain patterns are affine to others. When there is continuous clashing between patterns in the same person, there is also a lack of psychic harmony in that person. The clash may concern a discrepancy between self-feelings and affects of the safety-danger range, when for instance a grandiosity is combined with anger or anxiety. It may concern learning-patterns or defenses against drives and against objects, when for instance isolation is associated with displacements, an incompatible combination. It may concern a conflict between adaptation to the forces of nature (reality) and adjustment to objects, when for instance strength combines with ascending. This strikes people as comical rather than authoritative or serious. Retraining attempts to eliminate too much clashing or conflict, and tries to restore harmonious patterns in the individual. When this is accomplished by the mother, she, in turn, can help the child to achieve more harmonious, affine movement combinations. However, clashing and conflict is part of life and cannot be avoided. Pathology arises when conflicts cannot be resolved and the individual does not have at his disposal a movement repertoire that would allow for conflict resolution.

In retraining the adult we take into consideration clashes that may exist between ego controlled patterns and those influenced by the superego and we also pay attention to conflicts within the superego, especially those in which punitive or indulging superego components clash with discouraging and encouraging aspects of the ego-ideal.

And last, it should be mentioned that this paper was not concerned with diagnosis in a conventional sense of the term, but rather with a diagnostic, developmental assessment, comparable to that developed by Anna Freud.[70]

Not all aspects of the retraining program are based on profiles. Following in Schilder's footsteps, we have been studying infants' reflexes which are designed to facilitate support and equilibrium. We have observed that many ways of holding the baby do not take the infant's attempts at embracing or clinging to the mother into consideration. Schilder's [221, p. 134] pioneering discovery that clinging through sucking and grasping serves to secure the infant's equilibrium (protection against being dropped) has led us further to the discovery that the tonic neck reflexes are an inborn equipment that help the baby embrace the mother. [175, p.40]

Chapter 13

THE EMOTION OF MOTION[1]

Functions of the Vestibular Apparatus

David G. Hubbard, M.D.
Charles G. Wright, Ph. D.

THE EMOTION OF MOTION[2]

Many contributors to this volume were influenced by Paul Schilder through direct, personal interaction. This paper, however, reflects the great power of Schilder's personality to manifest itself through his writings alone. We hope to represent, in some measure, the many others who have been moved by his written works. It is logical to use the verb move when pointing to the infectiousness of the notions of Dr. Schilder. He appears to be the first psychiatrist to view the human psyche as a physical phenomenon, *suspended in space*, and actively moving through it.

As a gifted neurologist, Schilder returned again and again to the cerebellar and vestibular systems, which are intimately concerned with body motion and spatial orientation. Most investigators have overlooked the role of gravity (as a linear accelerative force which constantly influences vestibular function) in connection with human development and behavior. Paul Schilder did not. His observation of

[1] This article was prepared under the auspices of the Lauretta Bender-Paul Schilder Memorial Project with the support of a grant from the Leland Fikes Foundation to the University of Texas at Dallas, subcontracted through the Aberrant Behavior Center, Dallas, Texas.

[2] As proposed by Herbert C. Haynes, M.D., Assistant Director of Mental Health Services, Department of State, Washington, D.C.

the human ego and its perceptions seems to have prevented him from riding in elevators in an absent-minded way like most of us. Instead, he observed his own reactions and wrote of the ego, the sense of being, as it shifted within (and even outside) his body as the elevator accelerated in relation to gravity.[204] Such observations are classic. We believe they are much more important in pointing the way toward a better understanding of human existence than most of his readers have appreciated.

Stimulated by Schilder's ideas regarding motion and space, the senior author began some time ago to consider the potential influence of gravity in relation to human personality development. Psychoanalysis teaches theories of oral, anal, and genital stages which decisively influence development. On the other hand, Schilder's work seems to suggest an additional psychological stage (gravitational) which is operative over a lengthy period of personality development extending through and beyond the traditionally recognized stages. This gravitational stage appears to be more influential in orderly, sequential development of logic, of neurological reflexes, and of personality function than Freud's classical stages. We must, for example, bear in mind that a human infant spends the first years of life learning to move and orient its physical body against the ever-present force of gravity. The individual then spends much time and effort during the following 10 to 15 years developing motor skills which make possible coordinated movement despite that force. It would seem that this long process must play a part in molding the maturation of personality.

Surprisingly, however, a careful search of the literature both in psychiatry and neurobiology revealed almost no reference to the influence of gravity upon development. Moreover, in the course of this effort it became clear that a great deal remains to be learned concerning the basic structure and physiology of the human vestibular apparatus, which is, of course, the principal receptor organ for the physical forces of linear and angular acceleration.

During the past few years, we have been privileged to work closely with a number of other investigators, (whose research efforts are cited in the body of this article) in a collaboration which has come to be known as the Lauretta Bender and Paul Schilder Memorial Project. Although the project members have widely differing specializations, their overall research effort has been bound by a common interest in vestibular mechanisms and their role in behavior and disease processes.

One of the most active areas of current research concerns

documentation of pathological alterations in the vestibular sensory organs due to the influence of diseases affecting the inner ear. During Paul Schilder's lifetime, laboratory techniques for adequate evaluation of organic changes in the vestibular apparatus were unavailable. Very little was known about the involvement of the peripheral organs in pathological processes involving the labyrinth. Until recently, the vestibular apparatus was generally viewed as completely mature at birth, subject to little variation between individuals, and virtually unchanging throughout the human lifespan. Such limitation of factual knowledge about variation in the end organ tended to limit development of theoretical concepts.

In the last two decades laboratory methods have been developed which permit detailed and reliable morphological studies of the vestibular receptor organs in man and experimental animals. One of the most important of these is the microdissection technique, which was perfected in its modern form by Engstrom and his colleagues in Sweden.[54] The improved method, subsequently brought to the United States by Professor Joseph Hawkins, Jr., has been extensively utilized in human temporal bone studies at the University of Michigan.[96]

The microdissection approach to inner ear anatomy and pathology allows direct, three-dimensional observations of the intact sensory organs. More traditional methods of temporal-bone histology which made use of decalcification, microtome sectioning, and serial reconstruction did not permit such observations and sometimes led to significant error. The microdissection technique permits rapid preparation of specimens. Material may now be examined by either light or electron microscopy without lengthy storage in preservatives or acidic solutions which severely alter the inner ear tissues.

As illustrated in Figure 13-1, the peripheral vestibular apparatus consists of two distinct sets of sensory receptors, the semicicular canals and the otolith organs. Angular acceleration is sensed by the receptors of the three canals. However, information regarding linear acceleration and static head position within the earth's gravitational field is provided by the otolith organs of the saccule and utricle. The otolith apparatus is our topic.

The saccule and utricle are thin-walled membranous sacs, each of which contains a neuroepithelium consisting of sensory and supporting cells aggregated in a patch-line spot, or macula, attached to the membranous wall (see Figure 13-2). Each receptor cell is equipped with a tuft of hairlike processes (stereocilia) which projects

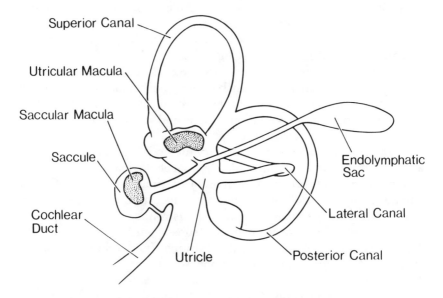

Figure 1. Schematic diagram of human vestibular labyrinth showing location of saccular and unticular maculae. Drawing modified from Schuknecht, 1974.

toward a sheet of gelatinous material covering the entire macular surface. The gelatinous membrane, in turn, is covered by a mass of tiny calcium carbonate crystals—the otoconia, which collectively constitute the otoliths.

In the chemically unfixed state, the otoconial layer has the consistency of lightly packed sand.[109] As generally used, the term "otoconial" membrane refers to the combination of gelatinous and crystalline layers which function as a unit in stimulation of the hair cells. Since the vestibular receptors are tonically active, they project a steady stream of neural impulses to the brain, even when the head is at rest. Changes in head position result in minute displacements of the otoconial membrane which mechanically deforms the stereocilia, thereby modulating the receptor neural discharge.

Figure 13-3 presents surface views of human otoconial membranes lying in place on the utricular and saccular maculae in specimens obtained by microdissection. The rippled contours of the crystalline layers are reminiscent of drifted snow. In fact, a curved ridge which is known as the "snowdrift line"[2] is a prominent surface

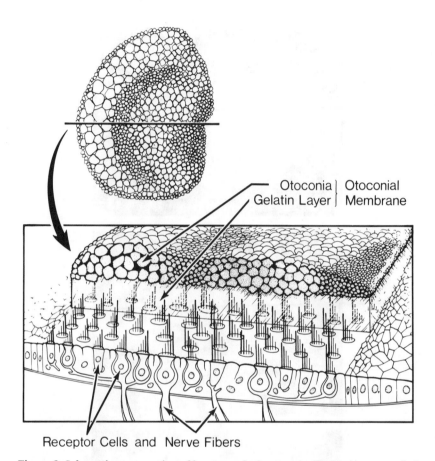

Otoconia | Otoconial
Gelatin Layer | Membrane

Receptor Cells and Nerve Fibers

Figure 2. Schematic cross section of human utricular macula, illustrating anatomical arrangement of sensory cells and otoconial membrane. (Arrow indicates sterocilia.) At upper left a top view of the otoconial membrane is shown. Drawing based on Lindeman, 1969.

feature of both the saccular and utricular otoconial membranes. This thickened band directly overlies a specialized region of the neuroepithelium known as the striola.[141]

In the guinea pig and other species commonly used in the laboratory, the "snowdrift" is also present as a distinct ridge on the saccular membrane. However, the corresponding area of the utricular otoconial membrane is quite thin or even lacking in crystals.[138, 141, 180] As first pointed out by Johnsson and Hawkins,[109] the "snowdrift" is a prominent thickening on both the saccular and

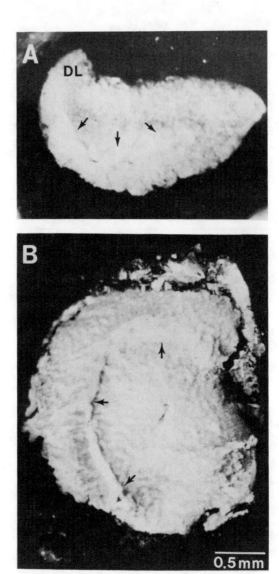

Figure 3. Light micrographs showing whole-mount preparations of saccular (A) and utricular (B) otoconial membranes from a young adult. Arrows indicate position of "snowdrift line" on the surface of the crystalline layer of each specimen. DL, dorsal extension of saccular otoconial membrane. From Wright et al., 1979a.

utricular otoconial membranes in humans. Their observation is in accord with our own findings in fetuses, infants, and adults.[251, 249]

Watanuki and Schuknecht[241] reported a striking increase in the receptor cell populations and surface areas of the human maculae compared to those of laboratory animals. They suggested this enlargement might be correlated with the acquisition of the upright posture during human evolutionary development. In humans, the mass of the utricular otoconial membrane is increased over the striola relative to other species in which this region of the membrane is thin. It seems plausible that this may represent still another specialization in response to the physiological demands of the bipedal posture.

Our observations of human otoconial membranes have revealed considerable variation in overall shape of these structures between individuals. Such variations are particularly striking in saccular specimens, as illustrated in Figure 13-4. Though there are sizable variations between different persons, the otoconial membranes on the two sides of the same head tend to be nearly identical in shape and total weight.

The development of electron microscopy for biomedial studies represents a major technological advance which is now widely used in inner ear research. The great potential for better understanding of vestibular morphology offered by the electron miscroscope has been exploited by investigators, such as D.J. Lim and M.D. Ross, who have combined transmission and scanning electron microscopic methods to explore the ultrastructure of otoconia. Scanning electron microscopy, with its capacity for high magnification and great depth of focus, has been extensively used as an adjunct to light microscopy for study of human material in our own laboratory. Figure 13-5 illustrates the use of both techniques in the examination of a saccular otoconial membrane from a two-year-old child.

Electron microscopic studies of the otoconial membranes have now been carried out in a variety of animal species.[139,102] In mammals, individual otoconia are cylindrical in shape and have pointed ends formed by the intersection of rhombohedral terminal facets. In a study of the guinea pig vestibular system, Lindeman[141] found that otoconia of various sizes (ranging from 0.5 to 30 microns) are distributed across the otoconial membrane in a consistent pattern, as illustrated in the diagram shown in Figure 2.

Consistent differences in size and shape are now known to exist between saccular and utricular otoconia in humans.[179, 249] We have found that saccular crystals are fairly homogenous in size (ranging between approximately 8 and 15 microns in length) and have a

Figure 4. Light micrographs of saccular otoconial membranes illustrating variations in shape between different individuals. (A) Premature infant (twenty-nine gestational age); (B) Newborn infant; (C) six-year-old child; (D) thirteen-year-old child.

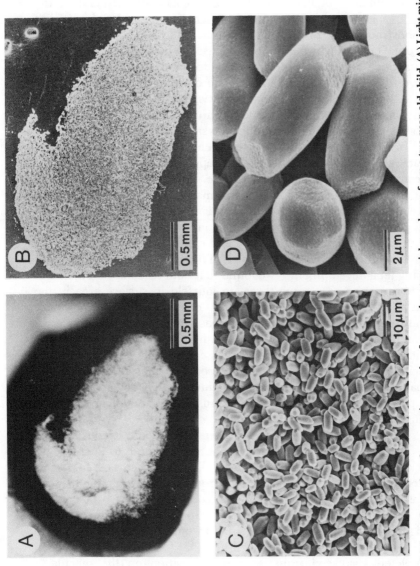

Figure 5. Light and scanning electron micrographs of a saccular otoconial membrane from a two-year-old child. (A) Light micrograph showing the membrane lying in situ in the temporal bone. The otoconial membrane was dissected off the neuroepithelium, dried, and studied by scanning electron microscopy as seen in "B" (36×), "C" (550×), and "D," the morphology of individual otoconial crystals may be easily studied.

uniform cylindrical shape. Utricular otoconia are consistently smaller (one to 10 microns in length) and vary widely from purely rhombohedral to cylindrical.

Mammalian otoconia are composed of calcium carbonate in the form of calcite, which has a specific gravity of 2.71.[42] Lim[138] has demonstrated the presence of organic matrix within individual otoconial crystals which is often condensed in the form of a nucleus or nidus. Such nuclei are widely believed to serve as centers for deposition of calcite during formation of the otoconia. Available data indicate that the organic material comprising the crystal matrix is the same as that in the gelatinous portion of the otoconial membrane, which is rich in sulfated acid mucopolysaccharides.[247]

In their painstaking development studies, Veenhof[240] and Lyon[145, 146] showed that otoconia first appeared on the fourteenth or fifteenth day of gestation in the mouse. Bast and Anson[10] estimated that the first crystals are formed in humans during the tenth week of development. Ross et al.[179] found evidence for continued formation and growth of otoconia during the second and third fetal trimesters, which extended even into infancy and childhood.

In a recent study on the growth of human otoconial membranes during fetal development[250] we found that both saccular and utricular membranes increase some three- to fourfold in surface area in the course of the last two trimesters of pregnancy. Dry-weight measurements showed a steady increase in mass of fetal otoconial membranes up to about the twenty-sixth or twenty-seventh week, by which time they had attained weights comparable to those of adult specimens. Thus, the vestibular sensory organs attain functional capability before birth in man and continue their development into the postnatal period when the infant must first begin to cope with the reality of gravity in the environment.

During the first several weeks after birth, the gelatinous layer of the human otoconial membrane has been found to increase in thickness and become less adherent to the macular surface so that its potential for movement over the neuroepithelium is apparently increased postnatally.[249]

In this connection, we consider it important to recognize that in a significant number (nearly one-half in our studies) of babies who die of sudden infant death syndrome (SIDS) the membrane has been completely displaced from its normal position on the macula.[250] Whether this occurred pre- or postpartum is as yet unsettled.

During the past 10 years, it has become increasingly clear that otoconia are subject to alternation by pathological processes affecting the human inner ear. Perhaps the most thoroughly studied of these abnormalities is the degeneration of crystals which sometimes occurs in association with aging.[110, 111, 179] In most cases, the breakdown and loss of otoconia appears to parallel a generalized sensorineural degeneration which frequently affects the auditory and vestibular receptors in older individuals.[178, 226]

Localized foci of abnormal crystals, similar in appearance to those which may be present in older patients, have been found in portions of otoconial membranes from infants.[179, et al., 1976] Whether this phenomenon represents a remodeling process occurring in the course of normal maturation or is a form of pathology, is not yet clear. However, it emphasizes the highly dynamic nature of the otoconial mass, which is apparently greatly subject ot change throughout its existence from the fetal period to old age. The recent work of Preston et al.[166] demonstrates that there is in fact a continuous turnover of calcium between the otoconia and the body calcium stores. Thus the older notion that mammalian otoconia, once formed, are fixed and unchanging, is quite untenable in the light of present knowledge.

As emphasized by Johnsson and Hawkins,[109] the otoconia are not truly embedded in the gelatinous portion of the otoconial membrane, but they largely rest on the surface of the gelatinous layer, apparently only loosely bound by small amounts of matrix material. It is possible for crystals to be dislodged from the membrane—either experimentally by exposure of animals to centrifugal force,[102] or in accidents involving head trauma in humans.[5] Lim[138] has suggested that a physiological mechanism may exist (at least in the utricle) for removal of dislodged otoconia. He has consistently observed crystals in contact with the so-called dark cells of the utricular wall which appear capable of dissolving displaced otoconia. If dislodged crystals escape from the utricular cavity, they may give rise to troublesome vertiginous symptoms. Schucknecht[227] has published evidence from histological studies indicating that otoconia sometimes enter the ampulla of the posterior semicircular canal and provoke a violent positional vertigo which he terms cupulolithiasis.

More than 2 decades ago, Dix and Hallpike[51] reported a high incidence of otitis media among individuals with the cupulolithiasis syndrome. In our studies, it has been found that pathological alternations of otoconia may occasionally occur in the presence of otitis media.[249] From a total of 26 temporal bones obtained from the infants with otitis media involving severe inflammation of the middle ear mucosa and the presence of effusion, four were found to contain giant, malformed saccular otoconia like those seen in Figure 13-6.

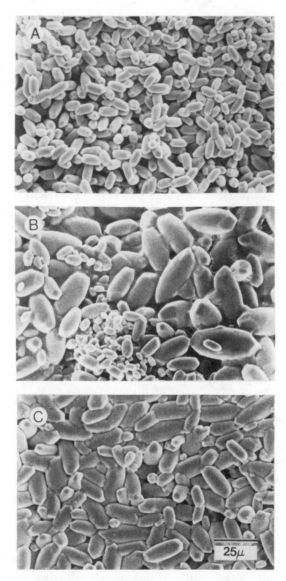

Figure 6. (A) Normal saccular otoconia from a two-year-old child. (B) Giant saccular otoconia from a six-month-old infant with purulent otitis media. The largest crystals seen in this view are approximately 40 microns in length. (C) Very large saccular otoconia from another six-month-old infant with purulent otitis media. Note dense, cobblestone-like packing and peculiar shape of crystals. From Wright & Hubbard, 1978.

The otoconia normally exist in a state of dynamic equilibrium with their fluid environment. Biochemical changes in the inner ear fluids, particularly those involving fluctuations of pH, could readily produce alterations of the otoconia. It is puzzling how scientists can have believed the system is static considering the fact that every detail of the organ's structure loudly suggests the existence of chemical flux rather than fixity. It is suspected that toxic substances produced by middle ear infections may sometimes reach the endolymph and cause changes in ionic balance andor pH great enough to affect the otoconia and hence the vestibular end-organs. This notion seems plausible in light of previous investigations which have demonstrated an increased incidence of sensorineural hearing loss in otitis media cases.[4, 160]

Genetic abnormalities may produce defects in the static receptor apparatus as also occurs in degeneration, mechanical displacement, and infection. Thus far, our knowledge of this type of pathology is based largely on work done with experimental animal models. A number of mutant strains have been discovered in which pigmentation anomalies are associated with defective otolith organs.

The most thoroughly investigated of these animals is the pallid mouse in which coat color is diluted to a pale grey and otoconia fail to develop, even though the macular sensory cells and innervation are normal. Hereditary absence of otocoia in pallid mice was first described by the English geneticist, Mary Lyon.[143, 144, 145] More recently, the pallid mutant has been extensively studied by Dr. Lawrence Erway and his collaborators.[57, 58, 59] In many of the pallid animals, there is a total absence of otoconia as illustrated in Figure 13-7. Associated with the lack of otoconia is a marked reduction in the number of melanocytes in tissues of the inner ear.[140]

It has been discovered that pregnant animals which are deprived of the element manganese in their diets will produce offspring with otoconial defects very similar to those found in pallid mice.[58, 225] On the other hand, supplementation of manganese at the appropriate time during gestation will prevent these defects in pallids, as well as other animals, such as the pastel mink, which have similar genetic abnormalities.[57, 59, 60]

Manganese is apparently required for synthesis of mucopolysaccharides which make up the organic matrix of otoconia.[140] Erway et al.[59] have hypothesized that the melanocytes normally present in the inner ear serve as a reservoir for manganese which can be used in mucopolysaccharide production. Thus there may be insufficient amounts of manganese available for development of otoconia in the

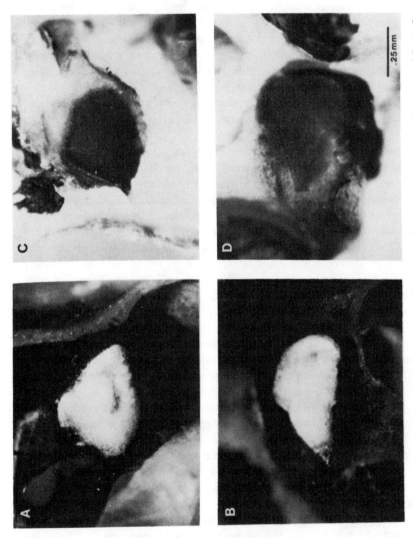

Figure 7. Saccular and utricular maculae from normal and pallid mutant mice. Normal crystalline otoconial membranes lying on the saccular (A) and utricular (B) maculae are shown at left. In "C" and "D" the darkly stained saccular and utricular neuroepithelia of a pallid mouse in which otoconia were entirely absent are illustrated.

genetically defective animals which lack pigment cells—unless dietary supplements of that element are provided in the laboratory.

The highly specific nature of the genetically determined otolith-organ defect has made the pallid mouse a valuable subject for studies of vestibular system anatomy and physiology. In work conducted at the University of Washington, Drs. Robert Douglas and Geoffrey Clark have found that, relative to normal animals, pallid mice show reduced numbers of neurons in those parts of the brain-stem vestibular nuclei which receive neural input from the saccule and utricle. This loss of neurons (which amounts to some 26 percent for the saccular area) is not a general phenomenon due to overall reduction in brain size, but is specifically confined to vestibular regions of the brain stem.[44] The data acquired thus far indicate that the neuronal deficit is due to inadequate vestibular sensory input, in animals lacking otoconia, during critical periods of brain development.

In pallid animals with vestibular system defects, Douglas and Clark have identified a variety of behavioral abnormalities.[52] Such mice show poor vestibular reflex capabilites, so that when deprived of a firm substrate on which to stand they become disoriented. If , for example, a pallid mouse is placed in water it flails about wildly and will quickly drown if not rescued. This behavior is quite in contrast to that of normal mice, which are proficient swimmers. In addition, pallid animals exhibit poor spatial orientation ability, hyperactivity, and high degree of emotionality. Curiously enough, the behavior seen in pallids is much like that observed in animals with hippocampal damage. Riopelle[174] has had some success replicating pallid mouse findings in Rhesus monkeys. Some observers also compare pallids with some of the more obvious characteristics of autistic and schizophrenic children, such as clinging and whirling behavior. Clark et al.[44] hypothesized that this may be due to lack of appropriate input to the hippocampus from the cerebellum, which may itself be impaired because of inadequate vestibular stimulation early in life. Thus in support of Schilder's original postulations, data are now accumulating which indicate that vestibular system defects are capable of adversely affecting widespread regions of the brain.

It is of interest to note that a human infant with a vestibular abnormality strikingly similar to the defect present in the mutant mouse was recently studied in our laboratory.[251] This was a six-week-old victim of sudden infant death syndrome in whom otoconia were congenitally absent. At the time of temporal bone fixation, it was clearly determined that all four vestibular maculae were entirely devoid of otoconia. Figure 13-8 shows a light micrograph of the right utricular macula from this infant compared to a specimen from another individual with normal otoconia. Although the otoconial crystals were absent, the gelatinous layer of the otoconial membrane was intact and in place over each of the saccular and utricular neuroepithelia. Figure 13-9 presents a series of scanning electron micrographs of the gelatinous membrane covering the utricular macula upon which the crystals would normally have rested. As is also true in the mutant mice, all other inner ear structures were found to be anatomically normal. This case demonstrates that a vestibular end-organ defect exactly paralleling that present in the experimental animal model may also occur in man.

VIEWPOINT

We believe that an article honoring Schilder should not be limited to conclusions which may be drawn from concrete and clearly established data, but should provide a happy, or celebrant, occasion for exercise of a measure of the freedom and speculation which characterized the man. Accordingly, leave will now be taken to play upon a few of the ideas suggested by the studies outlined above.

Let us first recall the history of the vestibular system in relationship to vertebrate evolution. The lateral line receptor, often regarded as one of the earliest complex sensory end-organs, probably had its beginnings in the armored fishes of the Silurian period over 400 million years ago.[49] However, it is striking to note that a well-differentiated labyrinth was already present in these ancient creatures whose survival was eminently dependent upon a reliable source of equilibratory input.

During subsequent evolutionary development, the lateral line and labyrinth (collectively termed the acoustico-lateralis system) appear to have established commissural brain-stem projections which represent the structural foundation for the organ we now know as the cerebellum. Thus, as Larsell[137] has observed, the primitive cerebellum may rightly be viewed as an outgrowth of the acoustico-lateralis system. The marvelously elaborated cerebellum of modern vertebrates which plays such a dominant role in sensory-motor integration and coordination is still heavily dependent upon reciprocal interaction with vestibular centers. Though the cerebellum operates outside the sphere of consciousness, it nonetheless precisely complements the synergistic needs of the conscious motor system in the programming of voluntary motor behavior. We use such words as

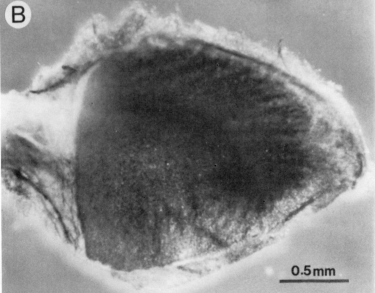

Figure 8. (A) Light micrograph of normal crystalline otoconial membrane covering right utricular macula of a twelve-week-old infant. (B) Right utricular macula from a six-week-old infant in whom otoconia were congenitally absent. From Wright et al., 1979b.

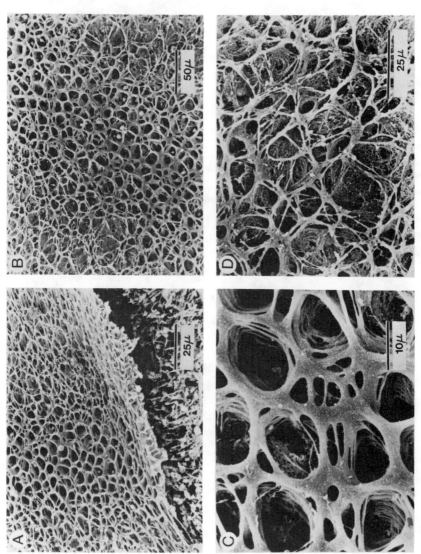

Figure 9. Scanning electron micrographs showing gelatinous layer of right utricular otoconial membrane from infant in whom otoconia were absent. (A) Low-power view near anterior aspect of macula; note surface of neuroepithelium at lower right. (B) Central area of gelatinous membrane in striola region. (C) Higher-magnification view of openings in gelatinous layer over the striola. (D) Surface of gelatinous layer in the lateral portion of the membrane. From Wright et al., 1979b.

poise and balance as physical expressions denoting this cooperative interaction of cerebrum and cerebellum. One must note that these words have common neurologic and psychologic meanings and reflect development not by chance. Language is surely a reflection of mental development, function and activity. It is replete with a special hidden language form designated by Hubbard[100] as the "Crypto-vestibular" language in which the relationship of body image and motion endlessly reflects changes in the social, moral, professional, and personal life of an individual. Vestibulo-cerebellar mechanisms *must* play a significant role in personal image formation and evaluation.

In addition to the cerebellum, the vestibular nuclei have of course established a multiplicity of central projections including the oculomotor centers, the reticular formation, the thalamus, and the spinal cord. It is likely that no other sensory system maintains such widespread and diverse interconnections with other brain centers. This fact demands that we add to our thinking the possibility that functional alterations of the end-organ which supplies input to these systems may well be reflected in complex alterations in sensation and function.[100]

For some time, the vestibular system has been recognized as an essential mechanism for the integration of oculomotor and postural reflexes. Paul Schilder's careful clinical observations and perceptive insight pointed toward a broader role for the vestibular apparatus in neurological development and behavior. Indeed, it was his contention that organic changes in the vestibular apparatus might be highly significant in the etiology of certain neuroses and psychoses.[204] We feel that participation of the vestibular system in the most fundamental sensorimotor processes speaks strongly in favor of this view. New observations concerning variations in morphology open wide areas for reconsideration.

Unlike the auditory ear and the eye, which have quite limited function prior to birth, the vestibular apparatus begins early in development to send impulses to the developing brain.[252, 101] The brain's orderly progressive maturation is directly enhanced when vestibular input is adequate, but may be seriously retarded or limited in the event of irregularities of that end-organ. A newborn infant's body-tone, its fear of falling, the Moro Reflex and the neck-righting reflex may all be expressions of this sequential development of the central nervous system and its relative normalcy or pathology. Arnold Gesell[88] found significant variations in these functions among infants whom he believed were doomed from the moment of birth to involvement in autism and childhood schizophrenia. Primary intrauterine neurological aplasia of the vestibular nuclei and secondary failure of development of higher centers might well cause these phenomena. The mere fact that a patient does not have vertigo or nystagmus does not exclude vestibular pathology. Adaptation by the brain will conceal most evidence of anomalous vestibular development in children by the age of eight or nine years.[50] Testing in such cases within hours of birth demonstrates that development and function in these individuals will be abnormal throughout life, even though adaptation will have concealed evidence of vestibular pathology.

The importance of the otolith organs in baby chicks for orientation inside the egg prior to hatching is directly related to the chick's survival and must be genetically programmed.[47, 130] (Chicks pecking downward fail to escape from the shell. It has been noted immediately prior to hatching that most chicks orient themselves to peck upward). Hence, at least for the lower phylogenetic levels, an image of body and space exists prior to birth and is vital to survival. Conceivably, this might also be true of human infants and their characteristic placement in the pelvis prior to birth. Ablation of the vestibular receptors in baby chicks produces death. Is this a consequence of their inability to orient themselves in space? Or, does it represent a lack of motor tonus to maintain vital life function? Is it possible that detachment of otoconia or slippage of otoconial membranes may have a direct relationship to some number of those infant deaths referred to as sudden infant death syndrom (SIDS)? It seems possible that SIDS might be related to vestibular pathology as a consequence of maturational deficits so grave as to render an infant unable to maintain normal physiology. The observations that some infants are born without otoconia and that the otoconial membrane may become detached leads to the speculation that their deaths may have been linked to these pathologies. Such infants, deprived of input from the macular receptor during intrauterine life (or perhaps later in the early postpartum period), would be less capable of maintaining muscle tone and life-sustaining functions than normal infants.

The fact of alteration of otoconia by pathological processes requires increased logical thinking about the nature of the system. These crystalline structures are far more nearly designed to be part of a system subject to a "red hot flux" rather than to static stability. Had nature intended true "ear stones" of unchanging characteristics, a single large crystal with maximum mass and smallest surface area might have been designed. Exactly the opposite structure and possibilities exist, with a system comprised of millions of small crystals offering a large total surface area for chemical interaction. Moreover, had the system been designed to be static, the crystals would have been deeply buried behind an impermeable barrier rather than surrounded by membranes containing active ion pumps operating in a fluid of nearly neutral pH. (We should remember that calcite is readily soluble in solutions of pH less than 7.)

Most scientists are startled by the possibility that conscious sensation and affect might arise not only from motion but from loss or gain in otoconial mass. We must consider it seriously. The suggestion is made in terms of the degree of sensitivity that can exist in such systems, as for example, the acuity of the "hearing ear" which is accurate in terms of one one-millionth of a second in the localization of a sound source. It is conceivable that the phylogenetically older vestibular system could have equal or greater sensitivity in the perception of stimulus variations? If, as Schilder observed, there is a slight modification of mood from brief vigorous stimulation of the ear in the movement of an elevator, what would be the consequences of a substantial chronic loss or gain of vestibular input over an extended period of time? Might the cumulative effect be translated into emotional sensation akin to elation or despair? The cryptovestibular language strongly suggests this possibility.

In a highly stimulating article, A. Peto[164] suggested that the vestibular system is the precursor of those mental functions which are grouped together as superego: "This vestibular forerunner includes imagery and fantasies which develop in the course of those traumatic experiences of the child that are part of normal maturational and developmental conflicts." Indeed, no person ever excapes these experiences in childhood. This evaluation system is at first physical in kind but later has a moral or ethical system superimposed upon it. Freud once said, "Where id was, ego shall be." One might add to this "and its perpetual antagonist is gravity, which speaks through its own organ."[100]

The tiny crystals of the inner ear are physical particles which symbolically represent the outer world. W.H. Auden once suggested that "a poet is the man who tries to understand the world through a grain of sand." Does this mean then, that we have within our ear the grist of poetry? And are those grains of sand our first (physical) introject, and do they provide the prototypical physical experience from which subsequent mental introjects derive their absolute quality?

In connection with space and motion having both physical and psychic connections one is reminded of clinical material. Consider the patient who just came to my office, gravida IV, age thirty-two at term. She stated, "I have reached a *turning* point. I am trying to figure out my *position—where* I'm at. I don't seem to know which end is *up*. I'm so afraid I will *let my husband down* but I'm so tired of *supporting* him. I don't know whether to be *distant or close* to him in my relationship or whether or *stand up or lie down*. I'm generally ready to *bend over* and let him have his own way."

THE BODY IMAGE

Chapter 14

PAUL SCHILDER'S WORK ON THE BODY IMAGE[1]

Lauretta Bender, M.D

The body image is based on the structural organization of the human organism. But though it is based on physiological data, these receive their final synthesis from the personality. All the life experiences, the inner life history, take part in the elaboration of the body image. Our inner life history is also the history of our relation to our fellow human beings and the community in its broadest sense. [220, 327]

Paul Schilder came to New York University and Bellevue Hospital in April 1930 from the Johns Hopkins University where he had been an Acting Professor at the Henry Phipps Clinic of the Johns Hopkins Hospital for 3 months at the invitation of Adolf Meyer.

He was forty-four years of age and had been born, raised, and educated in Vienna, Austria. He left there because of the persecution of Jews by the Nazi regime.

His first interest was philophy. He obtained a Doctor's degree in Philosophy from the University of Vienna while serving in the Austrian Army at the front and in base hospitals. He obtained his medical degree in 1909. He chose medicine as a profession "to be closer to human beings," as he said, and through psychiatry he felt he might approach the fundamentals of human life. (See Paul Schilder, *Vita,* published in this volume).

Before the war he studied the basic neurological sciences at Leipzig and Halle, Germany where he was much influenced by the teachings of Wernicke[245] who based his system of psychiatry on brain

[1]Presented by Lauretta Bender at The Paul Schilder Memorial Lecture, New York University School of Medicine, Department of Psychiatry, September 15, 1977.

pathology. Wernicke was the first to speak of "somato-psyche" which Schilder saw as the beginning of insight into the body image. Schilder spoke of this in his *Vita*.[216]

> However, these basic insights of Wernicke needed a deeper psychological study. This followed in Schilder's *Selbstbewusstsein und Personlichkeitbewusstsein* (1914) before Schilder was thirty. It considered the problem of self-awareness and depersonalization from many angles which were basic to insight in the body image. The central idea of this book was that the individual cannot be happy unless he directs himself towards the outer world and displays his various tendencies in experience.

Schilder spoke of a "structural psychology" which needs to be understood in his work. It means that each individual structures one's own psychology, one's own life processes, one's own body image, from one's inherent capacities and life experiences. A person is goal-directed toward the future. By such structuring,

> psychological processes are directed towards the real world in a process of continuous trail and error. This constructive process leads to comparatively stabilized configurations which represent not only the possibility for knowlege but also for action.[216]

Schilder clearly perceived this constructive process at work as the person built up the experience of the body into the body image. The body image was based on Wernicke's idea of the somatopsyche and Sir Henry Head's ideas of the postural model of the body.

Studies on the body image which he started in 1923 when he first published a treatise *Koerperschema* (Body Scheme) occupied him until his death.

Part I

THE IMAGE AND APPEARANCE OF THE HUMAN BODY: STUDIES IN THE CONSTRUCTIVE ENERGIES OF THE PSYCHE

This book was written in English by Paul Schilder during his first 3 years in New York at New York University and Bellevue

Hospital. It records case histories from Bellevue through 1932 as well as earlier case histories from Vienna, and quotes the literature through the period. It was published in 1935 in the *Psyche Monograph Series* in London. He always considered this his most original contribution. I want to review this book and also note his work with the body image until his death 5 years later. I also include a discussion of contributions to the body image by his colleagues.

The first paragraphs of Schilder's Preface to *The Image and Appearance of the Human Body* are quoted:

> The problems with which this book deals have for many years attracted my attention. Clinical observations on brain lesions which provoked difficulties in the differentiation between left and right started my interest. These researches came to a preliminary conclusion in a little study on the *Koerperschema*. I tried there to study those mechanisms of the central nervous system which are of importance for the building up of the spatial image which everybody has about himself. It was clear to me at that time that such a study must be based not only on physiology and neuropathology, but also on psychology. I wrote: "It would be erroneous to suppose that phenomenology and psychoanalysis should or could be separated from brain pathology. It seems to me that the theory of organism could and should be incorporated in a psychological doctrine which sees life and personality as a unit.
>
> I therefore used the insight psychoanalysis has given to us with its psychic mechanisms for the elucidation of problems of brain pathology. The study of the mechanisms of the brain in perception and action helped to a deeper understanding of psychological attitudes. I have always believed that there is no gap between the organic and the functional. Mind and personality are efficient entities as well as the organism. Psychic processes have common roots with other processes going on in the organism.
>
> I found out later that this attitude corresponds closely with the best traditions of American psychiatry, as they appear in the work of Adolph Meyer, William A. White, and Smith Ely Jelliffe. The same attitude is also inherent in the

doctrine of psychoanalysis. Psychology under such an aspect is necessarily psychobiology (Adolph Meyer's term) and can also be termed *naturwissenschaftliche Psychologie*. It seems to me also that the basic position of the Gestalt psychologists is a similar one. For the Gestalt psychologist, the gestalt is the outside world, and is also in the physiochemical processes, which are correlated to the psychic processes in which the gestalt principles appear.[208, p. 7]

In another place, Paul Schilder[215] said that the German word *Gestalt* referred originally to the shape and construction of the human body and its derivation came to refer to forms or configurations seen in the outer world. He also expressed the idea[214] that *Gestalt* and especially *Gestaltung* was more than a perceptual experience, but that there was always an ongoing process of construction of perceptions. In a similar view, he said that the body image was never static but is a process of constant change and reconstruction dependent on neurological functions, libido problems, and social experience in relation to other human beings and the objective world.

In the introduction to *The Image and Appearance of the Human Body*, Schilder defines the image of the body as "the picture of our own body which we form in our own mind, that is to say, the way our body appears to ourselves." It is the Body Schema or the postural model of the body. The latter term was Sir Henry Head's. It was often used by Paul Schilder as nearly interchangeable with body image until his later writings refer only to the body image. Head seemed to have had a more neurological concept based on visual, tactile, and kinesthetic sensations, immediately perceived or remembered, which located the position of one's body in space and the parts of the body, the limbs especially, in relationship to the body as a whole. Paul Schilder enlarged the concept by adding the libidinal and social factors.

The Image and Appearance of the Human Body is divided into three parts: 1) the physiological neurological basis of the body image, 2), the libidinous structure of the body image, and 3) the sociology of the body image. There is also a conclusion with philosophical discussions and an appendix with several detailed case histories and a brief description of the anatomy and physiology of the central nervous system.

In Part I, the physiological or neurological basis of the body image, he discusses the sensory experiences, visual, tactile, and kinesthetic constructs of the postural model, and the localization of these sensations both on the surface of the body and their origin in the cortex. He quotes Head often and discusses case materials extensively. He gives a detailed report of Head's experiment on himself in which he had the sensory nerve of his arm surgically intercepted, demonstrating the acute loss of function and more chronic recovery, with signs and symptoms. Localization of sensation was selectively disrupted and returned at different rates of time for different types of stimuli, i.e., epicritic or protopathic (terms created by Head at this time), touch, pain, kinesthesia, and temperature.

Using case material and frequent references to the literature, he discusses the following conditions due to brain pathology and which throw light on the basic postural model body or body image.

1)   Alloesthesia or allochiria occurs in cases where paralysis of one side of the body is associated with stimuli to the skin of the healthy side (especially the left) being referred to or felt on the paralyzed side (usually the right). This was first observed by Obersteiner (1832), but Sir Henry Head related it to the postural body.

2)   In other cases of paralysis the patient can localize a stimulus to the paralyzed arm but not locate the arm in space. The lesions in these cases were localized in the parietal lobe or the central posterious gyrus. In these cases the visual image was intact and Schilder referred this phenomenon to the optic perception which corrected the body image from its failure to perceive on one side of the body, referring the sensation to the opposite side.

3)   In cases of optic agnosia or mind-blindness, even though the patients disclaim visual perception they were better able to use their limbs if they watched them. Optic perception of the body image seemed to be necessary for the beginning of any movement or action. It was concluded that spinal mechanisms connect the two symmetrical parts of the body, especially for the most primitive types of sensation such as movement and pain in contrast to a tactile pattern or Gestalt.

4) Body image imperception was associated with a failure in perception or impairment in certain functions of they body such as paralysis, blindness, or deafness. Babinski[3] first used the term ''anasognosia'' and noted that left-sided hemiplegias are most likely to demonstrate this condition. The patients ignored their deficits and if asked, denied them and tried to function, i.e., walk as though there was no paralysis. They might say that the paralyzed side belonged to somebody else, that it was a dead snake someone had put in their bed. They tended to turn and look away from the paralyzed side. Schilder

called attention to psychic factors in these cases, that the individual did not want to accept his disability and defect. Some of these patients also had Korsakoff-like syndromes where recent memory was at fault. Schilder spoke of an "organic unconscious repression" in contrast to Freud's "system unconscious." A euphoria often accompanied this condition as also was seen in sensory aphasia or the postencephalitic hyperkineses. Schilder had the opportunity to observe encephalitis lethargica and postencephalitis problems in the 1918 or post-World War I epidemic at which time he was associated with von Economo in Vienna.

He always emphasized the close relation between perception and action in the body image. He said "Every perception is connected with an attitude and every perception has its motility."[208, p. 34]

In studies during this period (the 1920s) it was observed that perceptual problems, with right-left disorientation or "imperception" occurred most often when the pathology was in the right brain, even in cases with left brain dominance or left anosognosia. Considerable discussion did not resolve the problem at that time.

5) Agnosia concerning the body image of "autotopagnosia" was found to occur in patients with diffuse lesions of the brain, especially on the dominant side. Such patients could not orient themselves to stimuli to any part of the body. There were special problems with right-left orientation. There was also difficulty in motor action towards the outside world, for example, in locating and grasping for a desired object even when vision was intact, or to move in a desired direction.

The syndrome of Gerstman was described as finger agnosia, right-left orientation problem, agraphia and acalcula. Such patients have difficulties in actions such as writing because of finger and orientation imperception, although there are no problems in perception of other parts of the body. Lesions were reported located in the temporal lobe. Schilder found considerable evidence for the body image concept in patients with this syndrome which he studied and those Gerstman reported. He noted for example that patients who had imperception problems in specific areas of their body such as the finger agnosia and left-right disorientation, also had similar imperception difficulties in the same areas of the bodies of other persons.

Also, he noted that when there was an apraxia or agnosia, or the knowledge of the body image was incomplete or faulty, all actions from that part of the body would be disturbed. Thus the agraphia and acalcula are problems in Gerstman's syndrome. Primitive calculations were done by the use of the ten fingers, giving rise to the decimal system.

Apraxia was seen as a difficulty in action when there was imperception or disturbed perception of a plan of action. The condition demonstrated a body-image problem since a plan of action usually brings the body in closer relationship with an outside object or other parts of the body.

Schilder emphasized that in the postural model of the body the middle line played a specific part, especially of the head. Apraxic patients were often unable to cross the midline, that is, they could not find the left ear with the right hand. The midline of the body is extended into the space around the body so that to grasp an object to the left of the body with the right hand was impossible. This also emphasizes that the body image extends outside the body into space. Also apraxic patients could not reach with their own left hand or the left hand of the examiner facing them, which indicated difficulties in the interrelationship of body images.

The phantom of an amputated limb was recognized first by Ambroise Paree in the sixteenth century, according to Lawrence Kolb[129] who contributed a great deal to understanding of the body image in later years. Paul Schilder ascribes its first recognition and its first report to Weir Mitchell in 1871.

The phantom is the image of the amputated limb that is retained long after the amputation and by which movement and pain is felt even to the farthest extent of the limb. It tends to be obliterated by time or a cortical lesion.

Paul Schilder describes his own phantom of the third and fourth fingers of his left hand which he lost in 1930 while he tried to drive a Ford down Broadway. He experienced vivid pain and tactile impressions as though the fingers were bent painfully at the first interphalangle joint. The phantom persisted after the pain was relieved, but the phantom was straight at the joints. With variations, it became shorter and thinner. Eventually there was no pain and he forgot that he had lost his fingers.

Sometimes the phantom of an amputated leg, for instance, is felt as moving in concert with the normal leg. Directing the patient to move the phantom leg may result in movement in the normal leg.

Motor components are also important in building up the image of the body. The various tonic neck attitudes and postures were first studied by Hans Hoff and Paul Schilder in Vienna.[99] The "phenomenon of persistence of tone" was demonstrated by the inability of subjects, standing with their eyes closed and hands held forward in the horizontal plane, to bring an arm that had been passively displaced back to position parallel with the other arm. Subjects are not aware of "persistence in tone" and the experiment indicated that the postural model is dependent on the pull of tone. It belongs to the group of postural reflexes, also demonstrated by Magnus and de-Kleijn[148] in animals that had upper spinal transection or decorticalization and are of importance in the posture and locomotion of the body. Every movement changes the posture of the body. Pathological material has shown that vestibular irritation, cerebellar lesions and parietooccipital lesions contribute to disturbances in muscular tone.

Sam Parker was a Bellevue physician for many years in the 1920s and 1930s and is due the credit for actually arranging Paul Schilder's move from Vienna to the New York University and Bellevue and also wrote the first review of Schilder's work in the English language published in 1926.(exerpts published in this book) He worked with Paul Schilder in Vienna on the effects on the body image of going up and down in an elevator: the sense of weight of the body and center of gravity changes, and the postural model of the body, like a phantom, continues to rise or fall in relation to the body when the rising or descending elevator stops.

Paul Schilder emphasized that our awareness of our own body is very incomplete. Parts of the body can only be seen with mirrors, but we can see all parts of the bodies of other individuals. The surface or skin is "felt" especially in places under tension or in contact with outside objects. Pain is felt as just below the surface of the skin. The insides are felt as a heavy mass. Children believe they only have the food they have eaten inside the body.[207] The openings of the body are felt only a short way inside the body. Although physicians study medicine, anatomy, and physiology and have some pictorial-like awareness of the insides of our body, they still retain the primitive image of the body.

In a few remarks about the development of the body image Paul Schilder commented on the limited perception of pain and of motor control of the limbs in infancy, both of which are important in building a concept of the body image. The libidinous structures are also necessary and are still incompletely developed. On the other hand, every sensation contributes to the building up of the body image and "every sensation has its motility or motor answer." The development of the body image runs to a great extent parallel with the sensory motor development.

Schilder took special interest in children's drawings of the body which earlier scholars claimed as inadequate representation. He noted that children are completely satisfied with their drawings and believed that the way children drew human figures truly reflected their knowledge and sensory experience of the body image. He did not at this time refer to such drawings as projections of the body which we later recognized at Bellevue Hospital. I believe we were the first to make that observation.[221]

Schilder cited the value of Piaget's work[165] especially in the development of left and right connotation in children. Piaget connected this development with judgment and reasoning while Paul Schilder related it to the development of the body image.

Part II

Part II of *The Image and Appearance of the Human Body* deals with the libidinous structure of the body image and is largely concerned with psychoanalytic concepts. Schilder began with the narcissistic love of one's own body and referred to Freud's statement[77] that we are interested in the integrity of our own body. "Freud states that the libido is first given to the body as a whole. We call this the stage of narcissism and we suppose that only the embryo and newborn child have only narcissistic libido." Secondary narcissism is the auto-erotic state which concentrates on the erogenic areas.

In the oral stage the child is said to be cannibalistic, desiring to incorporate the whole of the outer world, especially the mother. Paul Schilder emphasized that the infant also enjoys his own muscular activity, skin sensation, and the genital sensations as well as those from the anus and urethra. Later the baby gradually becomes aware of the outer world and the satisfactions it can give.

Sadistic impulses arise from the desire for power over the love object. By identification with the love object, the sadistic impulse for power is turned back on the self and becomes a masochistic desire to come under its power. In the Oedipal state, the child develops an interest in the love object and wishes its well-being, while sadism persists as the impulse to overpower the love object or destroy a rival.

In Freud's later writing, *Beyond the Pleasure Principle*,[74] he developed the concept of a primary death instinct which proposed that an individual has a tendency to self-destruction and needs a great deal of libido for self-preservation. He also identified aggression with the death instinct. Paul Schilder did not accept this theory. Rather, he adhered to the former psychoanalytic theory of primary interest in self-preservation and the preservation of all individuals. For him, the impulse for growth and action toward the world and other human beings and their reconstruction and preservation was primary. This became the foundation for his belief in a constructive psychology.

Schilder saw grasping, groping, and sucking as the most primitive functions of the ego. These behaviors return with regressive forms of injury to the human brain. Individuals will then seek the use of the outer world in self-preservation. Thus, the world and the self always coexist within the human capacity for projection and introjection. As the image of the body is built up, the narcissistic libido will be attached to different parts and a continuous change in the body image will occur with further elaboration of the libido.

The erogenic zones of the body image, the body openings, are important because they bring the body closest to the world, either by ingesting or excreting. These include eyes, ears, and mouth, and genitals, anus, and urethra. There is a need for the child to touch all parts and have his care giver do so, also.

Paul Schilder stated:[208, p. 127] "Pain, dysaesthesias, erogenic zones, actions of our hands on the body, and the action of others towards our body, and sensations arising from the function of our body are important in final construction of the body image."

Neurasthenia and hypochondria are neuroses in which particular parts of the body act as if they were autonomous and as though they were genitals. At such times, there is an increase in libido in these parts of the body. This has been shown by Freud[73] and Ferenczi[64] and Paul Schilder.[198]

Early in his career, Paul Schilder studied depersonalization from a philosophical point of view.[186] This condition occurs frequently in the early stages of psychoses and alone as neuroses. It is characterized by a person whose ego functions are intact, yet who feels entirely changed and feels the outer world and his or her relationship to it altered as well. The patient especially cannot "see" himself in the same way, especially those parts of the body most highly valued. *The body image is no longer apparent.* Libido is withdrawn from the outer world, the body image, and the ego.

Paul Schilder's earlier and more detailed studies in depersonalization led to the conclusion that "depersonalization is a sadomasochistic negation of the patient's own body—and is connected with the vestibular mechanism."[223, p.48] Perception of one's own body is dependent on muscle tone. Vestibular action is connected with changes in muscle tone.

Hysteria also has its own body-image problem. From Schilder's point of view, it was essentially a change in the body image in which other parts of the body came to symbolize the genitals.

Organic diseases that progress to abnormal sensations will change libidinal investment in body parts as well as the body image. Schilder commented that symptoms are psychological problems in the body image arising in connection with organic signs. He stated:

> The processes which construct the body image not only go on in the field of perception but also contribute to the building up of the libidinous and emotional life. The fear of castration is ultimately a fear of being dismembered or the body image being disrupted or of a loss of integrity of the body—this applies to both sexes and is not limited to loss of penis.[186, p.174]

He believed that the nucleus of the body image is present in the oral zone at the beginning of life and the images of the head, arms, hands, legs, and feet develop sequentially.

In discussing the libidinal development of the body image, he refers to the early work of Bernfield[34] and Preyer[168] who observed that children have practically no knowledge of their bodies and must distinguish them from other objects by kinesthetic, motor, and visual data and by the coordination of optic, tactile, and other experiences with kinesthetic, visceral, and pain experiences.

The details of early development of the body image are uncertain but probably at first there is an inner maturation in all psychic abilities and, later, a dependency on individual experiences for final expression. The early work of Gesell[87] when he attempted differential training of identical twin infants was quoted. Thus the primary body image evolves as a factor of inner maturation but its final development and its tempo are determined by individual experiences and activity. There is a phylogenetic as well as ontogenetic development. The body image of each individual is forever recreating or restructuring itself.

Schilder stated, "Every desire and libidinous tendency changes the structure of the image of the body and gets its real meaning out of this change."[208, p.201] All clothing and personal adornments change the body image as well as our relationship with others. Gymnastics and dancing also change the body image.

PART III

THE SOCIOLOGY OF THE BODY IMAGE

The previous discussion of the libidinous factors in the body image and the relation of clothing and dancing, for instance, have already suggested the importance of other human beings and of social factors in the image of the body. This is perhaps one of Paul Schilder's most original contributions. The body image extends to a space beyond the body surface. Everything that enter or that leaves the body is part of the image—the voice, the breath, odors, excreta. Some schizophrenics experience the flying away of parts of their body. Case histories of Bellevue patients are used here for illustration.

Genital sexuality is always directed towards the body image of another. The development of one's own image of the body is dependent on visual experiences of other persons and on other forms of contact. Libidinous tendencies are necessarily a social phenomena. There is always curiosity concerning our own appearance and the appearance of others. Pathological extremes lead to exhibitionism and voyeurism.

Social neuroses[223] are discussed as problems in body image and libido. Fear of blushing is an example, as are anxiety and perspiring hands in social situations.

From the beginning there are connecting lines between body images of other persons. The distance in space may determine the amount of interplay, but libidinous factors may bring even a distant body image closer or increase our desire for nearness.

Imitation occurs in various situations as a social factor in the body image but creativity in the structuring of the ever-changing social body image is more significant. Paul Schilder said the social body image is a *Gestaltung*, not fixed or static, but a creative construction of the social image. Imitation is not a xerox copy, but an effort to experience the life of the other person. In the same way identification enriches the experience of the identifier in a relationship to another.

Beauty we regard as primarily connected with the beauty of the human body. Some patients suffer because they believe themselves unlovable for lack of beauty. The body image remains variable because of the many factors that go into its construction. Schilder has brought in anthropological data to discuss this.

Finally there is a deep connection between our interest and action towards ourselves and others. The preservation of integrity of the body image of others is an ethical value. However, *there is a paradox here*. Whatever tendencies there are to destroy our own or other's body images can also lead to the possibility of renewed construction which is, after all, the meaning of life.

I close with the conclusion written by Paul Schilder in *The Image and Appearance of the Human Body*:

> A discussion of a body image as an isolated entity is necessarily incomplete. A body is always the expression of an ego and of a personality, and is in the world. Even a preliminary answer to the problem of the body cannot be given unless we attempt a preliminary answer about personality and the world. [208, p. 304]

Schilder's Later Contributions

Schilder continued working on the body image after he completed the writing of *The Image and Appearance of the* Human Body. In 1932, he presented a paper on the localization of the body image before the Association for Research in Neuroses and Mental Diseases. He emphasized that the body image was more than Sir Henry Head's postural model or body schema, since it was more than the sum of the sensory experiences of the position of the body in space and its parts in relation to each other. Its development depends also on libidinal and social factors. However, an intact body image requires the integrity of the cortical centers for the sensory functions. Pathology in the lower parietal lobes and the adjacent occipital areas and the angular gyrus lead to the various body-image syndromes. He again emphasized that localization of cortial pathology was related to disturbances in functions but not the localization of the functions themselves. All of the peripheral sensory nerves need to be intact for the integrity of the body image.

The experiencing of the body image is primary to all action. Pain is an important factor in disrupting the body image. Any localized cortical pathology that modifies the recognition of pain interferes with the body image. Vestibular functions are important in the perception of the body image as well as the experience of space. Schilder developed both topics further in 1934 and 1935.

Schilder emphasized the importance of the vestibular apparatus in *The Image and Appearance of the Human Body* when he said, ''The vestibular apparatus plays an enormous part in the integration of our sensual experiences and consequently in the construction of the body image'' [208, p. 118]. He continued his studies with the vestibular apparatus[204] and summarized by saying: ''The vestibular apparatus has a special position as a uniting factor among the senses and as a general organ of tone and motility.''[219]

Schilder wrote in the *Psychoanalysis of Space*, ''There is not only a space outside of the body but also a space which is filled by the body. The image of the body extends into space and implies space perception.'' [208, p. 189] The individual in every action must start with an orientation towards his own body and the body of others. Every action is based on the body image. Body image experiences are socialized since they take place in space and in the world of objects and other human beings. [219, pp. 83, 189]

In a 1934 paper,[206] Schilder emphasized that the body image is different from the perception of the body itself. It extends beyond the body boundaries. It is constructed slowly throughout a lifetime and belongs to the community. *It is a social construct and not a physical one.* It is constructed from all of our life experiences and our inner life and social relations. Schilder's term ''construction'' best describes this fundamental psychological process based on the constructive energies of the psyche which he called the ''constructive psychology.''

In 1934, in several papers on depression[222] he spoke of the aggressivity in depressive psychoses that tends to disrupt the body image and the relationship with other people and threatens the integrity of the body image of the others.

Pain also disrupts the body image but leads again to its reconstruction. Depersonalization, which is often present in depression as well as in schizophrenia and neuroses, denies the individual the capacity to experience visual images of the body image and the relationship to other people in the objective world.

In 1938 in a paper on *Psychoanalytic Remarks on Alice in Wonderland*[212] which attracted wide attention, he commented on the anxiety that these stories must have produced in children. He referred to the frequent destruction of the body image and the changes in size so that the body was often too large or too small for the space available to it, or the parts of the body such as the feet were too far away. Food was denied to Alice, and the Queen frequently ordered, ''Off with her head!'' Time stopped and went in the opposite direction.

In 1939 in a paper on schizophrenia,[215] Schilder discussed distortions of perception in the outside world and also of the body image. He believed that these problems pointed to an interparietal syndrome in schizophrenia, comparing it to Wernicke's somato-psychic disorders. These changes occur also in mescaline and hashish intoxication.

In an article titled, *The Art of Children and the Problems of Modern Art*, written in 1939 (and reprinted elsewhere in this volume as *On Art*), he again emphasizes the development of the body image in children, its instability and the influence of social experiences in its construction. He discusses the way in which the body image is distorted by various artists such as Pablo Picasso, Georges Braque, Max Ernst, Amedeo Modigliani. He noted that schizophrenic children also drew distorted forms of the body image, experimenting with space and gravity and integrity of the body image. It was also recognized that the drawings of the human form or portraits are largely self-portraits or projections of one's own body image.

Also written in 1939 and published in 1942 after Schilder's death is a paper on *The Body Image in Dreams*.[217] The body image is again defined and Freud's contribution to symbols and their interpretation in dreams is discussed. By the analysis of several dreams, Schilder calls attention to the importance of the body image in dreams. He concludes that "a part of the difficulties in dream interpretation can be alleviated by keeping constantly in mind the relation of the dream to the body image. In a great number of dreams the body image appears in an infantile form and symbolically disguised even when the body image appears also in the manifest content of the dream." [217, p. 125]

CONTRIBUTIONS OF COLLEAGUES

Many other authors have written about the body image. Several have already been mentioned. Paul Schilder had started the Society for Psychopathology and Psychotherapy in New York in 1935. After his death, in 1940, it was renamed the Schilder Society of Psychopathology and Psychotherapy. An annual meeting was then given over to one speaker as a memorial meeting for Paul Schilder. These memorial addresses frequently discussed the body image.

Heinz Hartmann, who had co-authored papers on the body image with Paul Schilder in Vienna (1927), gave the 1933 address on the *The Psychiatric Work of Paul Schilder*. He spoke of the dialectical quality of Schilder's way of thinking, and that he was not a systematizer and was not fond of classification, but had a great gift for synthesizing. Hartmann emphasized Schilder's psychoanalytic contribution, especially in the areas of neurological and psychiatric illnesses. In regard to body image he noted that Paul Schilder had been influenced by Wernicke and Head but that he had deepened and widened these ideas "to a degree that had been unknown before his time so that they could become the center of a psychology of the human personality." Hartmann linked these ideas with Freud's doctrine of the body ego, with Freud's libido theory, and especially with the theory of narcissism.

David Rapaport was never associated with Paul Schilder but translated several of his writings from German. He gave the 1951 address before the Schilder Society on *Paul Schilder's Contributions to the Theories of Thought Processes*. Rapaport spoke of two basic concepts of Schilder's:

1. Human thinking is based on the existing world of objects,

and

2. that socialization, just like reality, directs people in a basic implication of thinking and human psychological life. These are the two factors, in addition to organic functioning or pathology, that Paul Schilder emphasized in the structure of the body image. In fact Schilder had said that the concept of the body image and the processes of thinking summed up the two human psychic functions or ego functions.

Rapaport also said that Paul Schilder was an "unsystematized genius," the psychiatric polyhistor of his time, with an encyclopediac mind.

If Paul Schilder was unsystematic, and I think review of his work shows this, Joseph Gerstmann compensated for him. Paul Schilder and Joseph Gerstmann were colleagues and co-authors, especially in their studies on motility, for many years in Vienna. Paul Schilder accepted Gerstmann's work (1927) on the so-called Gerstmann's syndrome: finger agnosia, right-left confusion, and acalcula as pertinent to his concept of the body image. Gerstmann (1958) gave the 1957 memorial address on *Psychological and Phenomenological Aspects of Disorders of the Body Image*. He classified the disorders of the body image in six categories by causation:

1. Disorders of the body image in casual connection to lower parietal or parietal-occipital lesions in the dominant

hemisphere, including Gerstmann's syndrome of finger agnosia, and left-right disorientation, etc.

2.   Disorders of body image in connection with the nondomi-nant parietal and parietal-occipital lesions. Here he in-cludes the anosagnosias or imperceptions of or amnesias for paralysis, etc., on the left side of the body.

3.   Disorders of body image in relation to sudden loss of a limb or the phantom.

4.   Disorders of body image occurring in connection with the neuropsychopathological mechanisms of controversial nature, "products or organically induced projections into outer space, or objectification of the body image."

5.   Alternation in body image in psychoneurotic patients with abnormal sensations and perceptions.

6.   Disorders in the body image experienced in the hyp-nogogic state, in dreams, and induced by certain drugs such as mescaline and LSD and in schizophrenia.

This classification may contribute something to the thinking of those who like categories. It would seem to me (and I think to Paul Schilder) much too rigid to apply such a classification to quite complex human behavior.

M. Ralph Kaufman gave the 1962 memorial address on *Schilder's Application of Psychoanalytic Psychiatry*.[114] Kaufman had psychoanalytic and clinical psychiatric training with him during the last year that Schilder was in Vienna. Kaufman reviewed the development of the concept of body image emphasizing Schilder's psychoanalytic point of view. He also said that "working in a general hospital (Mt. Sinai, New York) as I do, I was particularly interested in his presentation of the problem of organic disease from this stand-point. Organic disease and psychogenic disturbance lead in the same way to suffering. Suffering expresses itself necessarily in the postural model of the body. Mental suffering finds its way into a somatic ex-pression and somatic disease leads to mental suffering."

Postscript: The Bellevue School of Body Image

To give the reader a sense of history and a perspective on the development of Paul Schilder's concept, the following section has been added by Lauretta Bender. (The Editors)

Warren Gorman has written a book on *Body Image and the Image of the Brain*.[90] The book has two parts, the first being an historical review of the literature, definitions, and what the body image is and what it is not. The second part seeks to describe the image of the brain, which does not here concern us.

This book is essentially based on Paul Schilder's *The Image and Appearance of the Human Body*. Gorman begins by saying, "Similar to sex... the body image is an intimate and personal possession which is constantly in a state of exposure and revelation... and also exists in the mind as a concept that affects every bodily action. It is a conception rather than a perception."

Gorman spoke of Morris Bender's work with "double simultaneous stimulation." I do not know that Morris Bender would want to be identified with the Paul Schilder body image group, but his work was allied to it, being more neurological and very important. Morris Bender's studies showed that the face was dominant and the hands in turn were dominant over lower parts of the body.

Gorman also spoke of Harry Teitelbaum's study in which he made the post-hypnotic suggestion to forget the names of various parts of the body. Indeed, a patient forgot the names but also developed right-left disorientation, finger angosia, agraphia, and dyscalcula, or Gerstmann's syndrome. But the condition of these patients resembled a Ganser's syndrome rather than a neurological syndrome. Thus it appeared to Teitelbaum that psychological factors could have almost as much effect as brain lesions.

Gorman speaks of the French School of body image, the British School, and Vienna School when he discussed Schilder's work, and finally the "Bellevue School." He speaks of my work on the body image in 1) patients with somatic disease that distorts the body image, such as dwarfism and Paget's Disease[13] and 2) in children who had had encephalitis lethargica[16] and schizophrenic children. [18, 30, 31]

However, the number of workers at Bellevue who were influenced by Paul Schilder's body image concept were far greater than Gorman apparently knew. The following are but a few of those influenced.

Karen Machover, as a result of her contacts with Paul Schilder, wrote a deservedly popular book, *Personality Projection in the Drawing of the Human Figure*,[147] dwelling on body image problems.

On the Children's Service at Bellevue there were many studies of the body image both before Paul Schilder's death and since.

David Wechsler, working with Paul Schilder, explored children's attitudes toward death and what they thought was inside the body.[205, 207] These investigations indicated that for children not influenced by religious training the body and its image is intact but merely temporarily immobile after death, and that the insides of the body are an undifferentiated mass consisting of the food last eaten.

A. G. Woltmann, known as "Casper the Puppeteer" on the Children's Service of Bellevue Hospital, contributed much to the understanding of children's concepts of their body image through puppetry[14] and especially clay modelling[23] which proved to be nearly specific for active investigations into the body image or postural model. It dealt especially with body function of the genital and anal areas, sex validity, motility and aggression[21] (Chapters 14 and 15).

In 1941 Francizka Boas used a creative form of dance on the children's ward, both as therapy and as a means of investigating the body image in movement and dance. Many others have since developed it further.[43]

A. A. Fabian made an important contribution to the body image and gestalt maturation in children when he observed[61] that with the visual motor gestalt test the child's spatial orientation coincided with the change from the horizontal to the vertical in the postural model and their gestalt or human figure drawing revealed this.

J. A. Montague[153] studied the art of schizophrenic children and together with Bender[18] reported on the use of art in therapy of children, revealing the significance of body image problems in these disturbed children, as expressed both in their art and in their dreams.

H. Caplan,[41] after he returned to Montreal, considered the body image in the development of children and in the brain-damaged child. He pointed out that the brain-damaged child may indicate the pathology sometimes most definitively through a drawing of a man because it reveals equilibrium problems and tonus pulls, perceptual and integrative difficulties, and social inadequacies.

Katrina de Hirsch[98] includes a drawing of a man as a body image projection test in her study of maturational lags in her book, *Predicting Reading Failure*.

A. A. Silver with L. Bender[27] wrote a paper on *Body Image Problems of the Brain-Damaged Child* in which Schilder's concepts of the development of the body image in children were elaborated, and disturbances in this development, which often handicapped the brain-damaged child as much as the neurological disability. The need to recognize and deal with both disabilities was emphasized.

A similar paper written by Gloria Faretra with L. Bender[29] dealt with disturbed children having a variety of developing disabilities including schizophrenia, and emphasized that body image disturbances occur with every childhood illness or developmental disturbance, and require recognition and therapy that will help the child accept the problem. In both of these papers, the use of the child's drawing of the human figure in evaluation of the body image of the child is discussed.

W. R. Keller with L. Bender[20] explored the body image of schizophrenic children with electric shock. Human figure drawings by schizophrenic children were studied before, during, and after a course of electric shock therapy. At first, there was a dissolution of the body image to a primitive amorphous stage, due, apparently, to the organic impact. Then an immediate reconstruction occurs, giving rise in some cases to a more integrated body image gestalt.

F. J. Curran and J. Frosch[45] published a paper on the *Body Image in Adolescent Boys from Bellevue Hospital*. They studied the attitude of boys through questionnaires. It was observed that the boys most often were preoccupied with their neuro-muscular apparatus in relation to problems in interpersonal relations. F. J. Curran and M. Levine[46] also did a survey on the body image of prostitutes on the prison ward of Bellevue with similar findings.

Chapter 15

THE INFLUENCE OF PRIMITIVE POSTURAL RESPONSES ON THE BODY IMAGE OF CHILDREN WITH SCHIZOPHRENIA[1]

Archie A. Silver, M.D.

Paul Schilder's concern with the interrelationship between mind in its physical parameters and thought and behavior in their psychological aspects is reflected in his concept of body image. He believed the development of body image is genetically determined by physical laws of growth and maturation but that its final form is determined by the action of the environment upon that physiological substrate. Neither exists in isolation; damage to either may distort the outcome.

As one example of this principle, Schilder described a twenty-five-year-old patient, McL, who "suddenly developed a state of excitement" in which he would spontaneously rotate on his longitudinal axis and at the same time would feel that such motion has great influence on the world, that he can turn the world by his own movement. This rotary movement could also be induced by passive turning of the patient's head which would then cause his body to turn on its own axis in the same direction. Schilder described McL as follows: "Sometimes he turned by himself round his own axis. By this, he said, a change takes place in the world and he turns the world upside down. . . . When one turned his head to one side he very often turned his body in the same direction and he came into this movement turning around his own axis, and his movements grew quicker and quicker. Sometimes he resisted a passive movement in a given direction, turned his head in the opposite direction and began to turn in the opposite direction from that in which the experimenter tried to turn his head." [201, p. 92]

[1] The author acknowledges with gratitude and fondness the many years of his training in child psychiatry and association with Lauretta Bender.

Schilder states further:

One can, of course, say when one observes such a phenomenon that we deal with a patient who has some delusions and is acting according to this delusional thinking. . . . I do not believe that these hyperkinetic states can be interpreted merely as reactions to delusions. This type of motility belongs to a more primitive level. Of course I do not believe that there is any motility which has nothing to do with psychic elements, but the psychic elements of a conscious delusion belong to a rather high level, and this impulse of turning around his own axis belongs to a rather deep level, a level which we can understand better from a physiological point of view. . . . The turning around the longitudinal axis is based on the centers of the righting reflexes. . . . (Here there is a) hyperexcitability of the postural and righting reflexes, a special state in the motor apparatus at a lower level'' (i.e. subcortical) and. . . The patient's idea that he can turn the world upside down is in connection with changes in his righting reflexes. [201, pp. 93, 94, 103]

In short, the motility has determined the expression of the delusion.

In this patient McL, the cause of the hyperexcitability of the postural and righting reflexes is related by Schilder to regression to the narcissistic level. In other patients there is clear evidence of organic damage to the central nervous system (as in the patients with von Economo type encephalitis with whom Paul Schilder had much experience) which sets the state for the emergence of primitive reflexes and primitive postural and righting responses.

This paper will explore the relationship between primitive postural responses and psychological function particularly in teenage adolescent boys hospitalized with the diagnosis of schizophrenia. It will focus on the neck-righting responses. The neck-righting response is the rotation of the trunk and arms to follow rotation of the head, so as to maintain the alignment of head, neck, and body. To elicit this response, the patient stands, his feet together, his eyes closed, and his hands extended forward and pronated, parallel to each other, while the head is passively but gently and slowly turned to the right and the to the left. In young children three to six years of age, the body will not only rotate along with the head to maintain the head-neck-body alignment, but it will also continue to rotate with passive movement of the head. In normal three- and four-year-olds, the body will continue to rotate even though rotational pressure is no longer applied to the head. Certainly, the tendency of normal three- and four-year-olds to rotate spontaneously with their arms outstretched has been repeatedly observed.

adolescent boys hospitalized with the diagnosis of schizophrenia. It will focus on the neck-righting responses. The neck-righting response is the rotation of the trunk and arms to follow rotation of the head, so as to maintain the alignment of head, neck, and body. To elicit this response, the patient stands, his feet together, his eyes closed, and his hands extended forward and pronated, parallel to each other, while the head is passively but gently and slowly turned to the right and the to the left. In young children three to six years of age, the body will not only rotate along with the head to maintain the head-neck-body alignment, but it will also continue to rotate with passive movement of the head. In normal three- and four-year-olds, the body will continue to rotate even though rotational pressure is no longer applied to the head. Certainly, the tendency of normal three- and four-year-olds to rotate spontaneously with their arms outstretched has been repeatedly observed.

The physiology of this maneuver in the experimental animal[148] suggests that vestibular-red nucleus integrity is needed for its expression. In the intact human, pyramidal and extra-pyramidal influences modify vestibular-red nucleus responses, so that by the age of six years to nine years the neck-righting response normally is not elicited. It does not disappear from the central nervous system however. Just as the emergence of a Babinski response will follow disruption of the pyramidal tract, so will disruption of supranuclear pathways, or interference with their maturation, permit the reappearance of neck-righting responses.

As suggested above, modified neck-righting responses may be seen in normal six-year-olds. Between the ages of six and nine years, the appearance of a neck-righting response suggests mild delay in the maturation of supranuclear pathways. Above the age of nine years, its appearance appears to be abnormal and will be found in conditions which have interfered with maturation of the supranuclear pathways and in those in which the vestibular influences are not adequately modulated.[232] Schizophrenia is one such condition.[233]

With consideration only of descriptive phenomena, we find within the wide spectrum of schizophrenic and schizophreniform disorders, one group of children which may be identified by a traid of symptoms: 1) profound anxiety, 2) dysidentity characterized by problems with body image and ego boundary and 3) plasticity: the capacity for extreme, variable, uneven response to stimuli, and an extremely variable, uneven maturational profile with retardation in some functions side by side with acceleration in others. Speech and verbal language, for example, may be markedly retarded while visual-motor function may be excellent; object relations may be distant and impaired yet occasionally manifest a capacity for close and intense emotional relationship.

According to Lauretta Bender,[22, 24] these symptoms may in turn be related to the retention within the organism of a primitive physiological organization reminiscent of that of the fetal infant as described by Arnold Gesell.[88] This primitive organization is characterized by immaturity in the homeostatic apparatus, in fluctuating states of consciousness, in doughy muscle tone, in motility based on tonic-neck and neck-righting responses and in difficulty with the synchrony between respiration and speech. There are now many studies to substantiate the existence of a group of children characterized by the physiological organization postulated by L. Bender.[66, 68] There is, however, a question as to the nosological significance of these physiological symptoms—a question which will not be discussed here. Nevertheless, clinically, the persistence of motility based on neck-righting responses is one aspect of the immature neurophysiological organization seen in children described as suffering from schizophrenia.

I here propose that many of the distortions in thought and perception as seen in schizophrenia relate to the fundamental immaturity in motility, particularly to the persistence of neck-righting responses, found in children with schizophrenia. This suggestion is consitent with Paul Schilder's concept that thought, behavior, and psychological maturation are inextricably and reciprocally tied to neurophysiological organization, and that mind and body are but two ways of examining the same phenomena.

What influence, then can the retention of primitive postural responses have on thought and behavior?

Consider Leonard. He was fifteen years old when first seen on the inpatient adolescent service. He was referred because he had become increasingly aggressive and disruptive in the special residential school which he had been attending, setting off fire alarms, exposing himself to the female teachers, giving vent to impulsive and unpredictable violent behavior. He had always had school difficulties, not only academically, where his achievement fell far below his intellectual ability as measured by standard intelligence tests, but also in impulse control, with aggressive outbursts. A sturdy black youngster, he came into the examination room eating a jelly sandwich which he consumed in three or four immense bites. His affect was extremely labile, ranging from giggling and laughing, mostly inappropriate, through sadness in which he sat quietly with tears streaming down his face, to depths of depression in which he talked about killing himself. He was verbal, describing in very specific terms what pills and how many he would need to kill himself.

He had major symptoms relating to body image. He exhibited a feeling that one hand was growing longer than the other, that even as he was sitting in the examination room, he could actually feel his hands and his feet growing. He was concerned about who he was. He would look in the mirror wondering who it was in the mirror, who was making his reflection move, what person was behind the mirror doing all these things. Then, as he would watch, the image in the mirror would slowly shrink until it was no bigger than so high (demonstrating with his hands, about 12 inches apart). He was very concerned that when this happened, he would never get back to his own real size. Sometimes when he would talk to people they too would shrink in size. Sometimes he thought his body had changed and he was his cousin Thomas, a boy his own age who had recently drowned. When he lay down to sleep he had feelings of levitation, that his body was rising from the bed, and sometimes he felt that his body was "mushing together." He distorted time. At the beginning of the examination, for example, he spoke of his father as though he had just died. He described the funeral in minute detail, the grave and the smell of the flowers and how he could smell the flowers even now when he talked of his father. In reality his father had died 10 years ago, when Len was five years old. He had auditory hallucinations. He talked with his father and with his dead cousin Thomas and was not sure whether or not this was his imagination.

Leonard showed many other symptoms. His thinking was dereistic, i.e. not directed towards reality or characterized by logic. He was concerned about his brother, who was born 1 year after his father's death. He felt his mother had betrayed his father and now as a result he had very mixed feelings about his mother. He was paranoid. He felt that other people "pester him," talked about him, and that he must strike at them when they did so. He felt that much of his problem was due to the fact that he was "born the wrong way," an elaboration of some comments his mother had made about his birth. He remembered, however, when he was a "couple of minutes'' old, looking at faucets in the room.

Neurological examination was within normal limits except that he had markedly immature praxic ability, impaired finger-gnosis and made many errors in right-left discrimination. Synkinesis was marked, with visual-motor immaturity and difficulty with auditory rote sequencing. In addtion, a neck-righting reflex was easily elicited with the patient rotating his body fluidly on the longitudinal axis to maintain a head-neck-body alignment. This rotation would persist even though pressure was no longer applied to the head.

What is the relationship between the symptoms Leonard presents and persistently immature neck-righting response?

Clinical observation by Bergman and Escalona[33] have implicated perceptual distortion and perceptual sensitivity in a group of severely disturbed children. Preoccupation with spinning objects and abnormal reactions to changes in spatial relationships or to vestibular stimuli has been shown in schizophrenic children by Bender and Freedman.[22] Induction of vestibular stimulation by ''whirling'', (i.e. persistent rotation of the body on the longitudinal axis) and excessive head swaying and body swaying suggesting vestibular dysfunction has been demostrated in autistic children by Ornitz [158]. Also, experimental studies suggesting disturbed vestibular function in schizophrenic children have been summarized by Ornitz.

Physiologically, the persistence of the neck-righting response into adolescence and the persistence of the ''whirling'' tendency seen in younger autistic children means these patients retain a drive to vortical and gyrating motion. This kind of motion tends to emphasize centrifugal forces. Bodily sensations are driven away from the center of gravity into the periphery. There periphery appears heavier, the fingers and toes seem to enlarge, the hair flies about, clothing appears separated from the body, the very physical limits of the body-image are distorted. In younger children the body may seem to fly off into space. This may persist into adolescence and in severely disturbed children, the body may even seem to explode in space. These feelings may be brought out by situations where gravity is upset as in a high speed elevator. Adolescents may feel that the elevator will not stop but will fly off into space or, when the elevator is descending, that their neck is elongating. These physical sensations emphasizing the periphery of the body may be interpreted as abnormal sensations of growth in the extremities and, because of the distortion of the physical boundary of the body, a blurring of the ego-boundary with subsequent dysidentity may result.

With patients whose sensations are driven into the periphery, one can understand their need to restore their body image by attempts to pull back into themselves. Younger children may attempt to use the dimensions of the adult's body as a limiting force to counteract the forces of dissolution within themselves. Symbiotic behavior may be interpreted in this way: an attempt to use the body of an adult to delimit one's own body. The soft doughy muscle tone of the young child with the pervasive immaturity syndrome contributes to the symbiotic behavior.

When a child is not certain of the physical limits of his body, as when the neck-righting response persists, he or she has difficulty orienting and stabilizing him or herself in space. Looking into a mirror is one way these feelings may be mobilized. In adolescence, the contrast between image perceived and sensations experienced is sharp. The adolescent perceives in the mirror an individual with definite limits in dimension and in orientation. This is not congruent with his or her own centrifugal bodily sensations which create indefinite body limits and dimensions. The mirrored image then becomes a stranger, who may resemble the adolescent, but is not actually him or herself.

The frequency of micropsia, a condition in which objects appear smaller than they are, may be, in part, an attempt to control the centrifugal tendency evoked by the neck-righting response, by imposing the opposite force, namely a centripetal one. This may represent a tendency to pull him or herself together and may be the physiological matrix to a symptom such as micropsia which obviously may be interpreted only in psychological terms.

It has been indicated above that the persistence of the neck-righting response suggests immaturity in the supranuclear apparatus impinging upon lower vestibular and red-nucleus pathways. It may also, however, involve inadequate modulation of vestibular stimuli. There is evidence that nystagmus in response to vestibular stimulation is reduced in children with schizophrenia.[158, 68] The vestibular apparatus is concerned with orientation in space[68] and with the regulation of muscle tone. Vestibular tone influences also autonomic response as seen in the dizziness and vomiting which may be induced by excessive vestibular stimulation. Inappropriate or inadequate vestibular function therefore may also contribute to disorientation in space, to inadequate muscle tone and to inadequate autonomic homeostasis. Whereas the neck-righting response is concerned with stimuli from the periphery of the body, stimuli from the vestibular apparatus is concerned with sensation from within the body. In the latter case, a feeling of heaviness within the body, or conversely a feeling of emptiness or nothingness within the center of the body, may ensue.

Immaturity in homeostasis however may have its own repercussion into thinking and feeling. With an immature homeostatic apparatus the organism cannot readily adapt to stress. A person does not have what Cannon has called "the wisdom of the body." Stimuli, which the normal child will easily assimilate, becomes for the child with inadequate autonomic response a thing of persistent increased heart rate, excessive or inadequate sweating, poor temperature control, inappropriate vascular tones, and gastrointestinal motility. Further, although this has not been proven, there may be abnormal response of the adrenal cortex to stress. Anxiety may well be the psychological parameter of homestatic dysequilibrium.

Let us view Leonard's symptoms in the light of the above considerations. He manifested marked concern with the periphery of his body, had sensations of expansion of his hands and feet, showed evidence of fluid identity, was not certain of his own body limits, not certain even of who he was, sometimes felt he was shrinking, had micropsia, had feelings of levitation, had disturbed sensations within his body ("mushing together") and of course had a persistent neck-righting response. These symptoms may be the way Lenny interprets the sensations induced by persistent neck-righting response. These sensations relate to the vortical motion of persistent neck-righting, motion which intensifies centrifugal forces and shifts sensation to the periphery of the body. Psychologically, these sensations may be interpreted as a fluidity in ego-boundary, uncertainty in its limits and uncertainty in identity. The persistent neck-righting response becomes the physiological force which the child with schizophrenia attempts to understand and which emerges in symptoms of body-image distortion.

Another patient, Robert, was fourteen years old and felt that he was "going crazy." He felt his body was changing and that he was being rejected by his mother and stepfather. On three occasions prior to his admission to the hospital, he attempted suicide by ingestion of pills. On examination he was anxious and depressed. However, he formed an immediate relationship with the examiner, clinging psychologically and physically. A major symptom was in body image. He had a feeling of emptiness and dissolution within himself. He had a sensation of his body changing, his hands growing as he looked at them, the nails particularly growing very fast. He felt his body was twisted and distorted and he had hypnagogic sensations during which he felt so light that he was flying around the room. He was hypochondriacal and believed that the peculiar sensations in his abdomen meant he had cancer. His reality testing was tenuous and impulse control poor. In contrast to Leonard, Robert appeared much more intact. His depression and suicide attempts of course were important symptoms yet the depth of his disturbance was not apparent until his body image was explored, where the nature of his illness was seen to be more than depression.

In adolescents a systematic approach to the study of their body image is needed.

1. Suggested lines of inquiry concerning the periphery of the body may include the following: Can you feel your body changing, getting smaller or larger? Can you feel your fingers or toes or nose growing? Is one side changing faster than the other? Can you feel the changes even as I talk to you? Can I see the changes too? Are parts of your body getting heavier or lighter? Do people seem to change in size as you look at them? Do you feel that sometimes part of you may just explode, or fly off into space?

2. Possible questions concerning the ego-boundary may include the following: When you look in the mirror, do you sometimes wonder who it is that is looking at you? Do you ever think there is someone behind the mirror looking at you, imitating your movements, making you move the same way he does? Are you sure who you are? Do you sometimes feel that you are outside your body looking at yourself? Does you voice sound strange as though you can hear your words even though you stop talking? Do you sometimes feel you are another person?

3. Queries concerning vestibular sensations may include: Do you frequently feel dizzy? Do you ever have a sensation that you can fly? Sometimes do you feel your body is rising off the bed as though it were light? Do you feel your body is just an empty shell? Are there unpleasant feelings inside your body? Can you feel the inside of your body getting heavier or lighter as though to rise in the air or sink into a chair? Do your insides work right? Are things inside of

you twisted or bent? Can you hear your own thoughts in
your head, are there voices, or people inside your head?
How large are they? How did they get in, how did they get
out? Do you feel something in your chest or abdomen tell-
ing you what to do?

Such questions become part of a routine protocol in the examination of body image. Dean, another patient, was twelve years
old when he was seen in consultation at a residential treatment center
and had made little progress in 10 months of treatment there. His
past history revealed bizarre, aggressive, hyperactive behavior along
with significant language delay since he was three years of age. The
family history was disturbed. The father, who left Dean and his
mother when Dean was six years old, had been an alcoholic and
abusive. Through the years Dean's neurological examination was
repeatedly described as normal with normal EEG's. In our examination, Dean was thin and wiry with no gross ectodermal defects.
There were occasional gross tics in which the eyes turned to the right
and upward and the left side of the face contracted. There were no
respiratory grunts or coprolalia. The tics were accentuated by tension and were relieved as the patient relaxed during the examination.
Primitive posture responses were noted. Gentle turning of the head
to either side caused fluid rotation of the body on its longitudinal
axis. Autonomic lability was noted in marked sweating of palms and
feet and in marked perioral pallor. He could not clearly distinguish
bilateral asymmetric stimuli on testing finger-gnosis. His voice had a
peculiar monotonous tone quality. The remainder of the classical
neurological examination was within normal limits. Perceptual examination revealed poor visual-motor function, marked immaturity
in auditory rote sequencing, and extinction of the hand stimulus on
the face-hand test.

Dean's body-image was markedly disturbed, as seen in the
draw-a-person test. His drawing appeared to be whirling about with
the arms in a tonic neck posture and with the peripheral aspects of
the arms (forearms and hands) wider and heavier than the chest and
trunk. The hair also seemed to be flying off the head.

Dean appeared depressed and his responses occasionally
dereistic. His most prominent emotion, however, was that of anxiety, with loudly expressed fears of ghosts, monsters, dark and light.
He sometimes felt there was a ghost behind him. He would hear his
footsteps but when he turned, the ghost was a whirling shadow, spin-

ning around. This evoked intense anxiety. Sometimes he felt his arms were so heavy that he could not lift them. He was afraid to look in the mirror because the image was "like a ghost, turning." He obeyed voices inside his head which told him to hit people. There were times when he did "magic" which consisted of his spinning about and turning his body with his arms outstretched. He believed that when he did this he could make the world stop and time go back to when he was happy.

His distorted body-image suggests centrifugal forces. The persistent drive for rotation of the body on its longitudinal axis is a source of anxiety when it cannot be controlled. He attempted however, to utilize the persistent rotational tendency in a defensive maneuver to make his own "magic." It seemed clear that unless one understood the persistence of the neck-righting response in this child, one could not understand his bizarre symptomatology.

SUMMARY

This paper has attempted to illustrate the influence of primitive postural responses on the kinds of symptoms seen in adolescent schizophrenics. A persistent neck-righting response drives the organism into tonic rotatory motion with a tendency for sensation to flow from centrifugal forces, emphasizing the periphery of the body and creating problems in the awareness of the physical limits of the body. Concerns with the periphery of the body, sensations of elongation of the periphery, or fears of parts of the periphery flying away from the remainder of the body are experienced. In addition, the lack of stability in space adds to problems of dysidentity, and creates confusion as to the position of one's body in space. It is possible that vestibular dysfunction, which contributes to the persistence of primitive postural responses, may set the stage for distorted sensation withing the body. All of these distortions are incorporated into the emerging picture of body-image delusions seen in many children with schizophrenia.

SELECTED WRITINGS OF
PAUL SCHILDER

Chapter 16

BODY IMAGE AND SOCIAL PSYCHOLOGY[1]

Paul Schilder, M.D., Ph.D.

Social psychology concerns itself with the psychological processes of the group structure. It poses the task of exploring the psychological course and pattern which the individual experiences as a member within a group. Above that it seeks to establish to what extent the individual group member exhibits specific traits. Also of great interest are the actions and motivations of the group as such. Is the group greater than the sum of the psychological process of the individuals? Does a mass soul exist with characteristics different from those of the individual? What form of expression do emotions take, and how do the emotions of one individual influence those of another? These are important problems. Yet social psychology so far as failed to take sufficiently into account that individuals are not only mental entities but possess physical bodies as well.[2] The fellow creature, to us, is not

---

[1] *Das Korperbild und die Sozialpsychologie* originally published in *Imago* 19: 367-376, 1933, Vienna. New Translation by Hilda Giorlando, 1977. New York.

[2] Three assumptions illustrate Schilder's break with the conceptual framework of classical psychology. His thoughts parallel the ideas of Edmund Husserl's phenomenology (*The Idea of Phenomenology,* 1907), especially his critique of cognition. Schilder no longer maintained the clearcut distinction between ''impression'' and ''expression'' in the human psyche as regards perception and action. The two modes are wedded in a fundamental way and experienced as one process by the human body.

Complementing his refusal to divide cognition and action, Schilder embraced an intersubjective theory of human communication in which the strict dichotomy between the sender of a message and the receiver of a message is broken down.

merely a mental unit but also a physical entity. As individuals we not
only experience ourselves mentally but the awareness of our own
body and physical reality as well. To pursue social psychology, we
will have to know how this experience of our body is assembled, and
how we gain insight into the bodies of others. The relationship
between knowledge of one's body and knowledge of other persons'
bodies is a fundamental problem of social psychology which thus far
has not received satisfactory attention. Whenever we take any action,
our own body as well as those of other individuals is taken into consideration. Individualities without bodies do not make sense. In the
excellent *Social Psychologies* by McDougall, Bogardus, Folsom et al.,
this aspect has been neglected. It might be explained that despite the
works of Head and Pick, psychology showed little interest in the problems of the body image. The consciousness of corporality has been
taken for granted, requiring no further description and explanation.
Again and again, the materialistic philosophy expressed the opinion
that the body is the original experience. Psychology as well took the
point of view that to the newborn child, the body solely is contributed
while I repeatedly stressed that body and environment are correlated.
A body without a world is just as unthinkable as a world without
bodies. The consciousness of our corporality, the three-dimensional

---

[2]Instead, a dialectical interplay occurs in which the receiver is not passively waiting for
impressions (as a blank page awaiting print) but actively giving himself/herself to the
speaker, intuiting, inviting, discouraging, and influencing the other in the very act of
listening. Schilder defined the body image by this power of nonverbal communication. The body image is an incarnate organizing ability which is evidence that the acts
of perception and motor response are parts of a unitary process. At one level, the
body image is the picture we generally have of our own body. At another level, it is
the means by which we experience the world and is itself changed by contact with
other human beings and body images.

With Schilder's psychology, the psyche has returned to its embodied source.
As neurologist and clinician, he sought the origins of consciousness within the
tissues, grey and white matter, nerve processes, reflect arcs, and muscle fibers. But
he never lost sight of the organisms as a whole — nor retreated into mechanistic explanations. The origins of human behavior are manifold, not simplistic. Human
motivations, both physiological and psychological are equiprimordial in their appearance and often undistinguishable. Knowledge of a body awakened to consciousness must be obtained by several methods, observation and speculation,
careful gathering of evidence and special attention to intuitive clues. Schilder step-
ped beyond the psychology of pragmatism, which assumed the body as a given and
thereby ignored its importance as a source of immediate knowledge.

concept of our self which we carry in us, must be the knowledge of the outside world. It is constantly being constructed and expanded from the tactile, kinesthetic, and optic raw materials. These materials are utilized to suit the overall situation. Early impressions and later experiences lead to a definite design. The total conditions of our motor adjustments have a deciding influence on the final formation of the body image. The body image is filled with a heavy mass. We evaluate this heaviness in different ways depending on the state of excitation of the equilibrium and the condition of the muscular system. The sensations originating in the body centrum are being pushed up to the body surface without ever quite reaching there. Construction and design of body image by no means take place under the guidance of the intellect and the merely cognitive interests. They result in expressions of ambitions and needs. We desire the integrity and uniqueness of our bodily self: narcissism. Corresponding to the respective instinctive attitudes, certain parts of the body image will emerge stronger than others. The sex organs and the genital zone are particularly pronounced in the body image. The erogenous zones play a singular role. The individual character of the basic drives will manifest itself in the body image. Where anality is dominate in instinctual life, there the anal part of the body scheme is noticeably accentuated. Thus the experienced body image becomes the mark of the instinctive impulses. When disturbances in the instinctive system occur, a change in the body image will immediately set in. Sadistic impulses endanger the unity of the body image.

> I observe a case in which a female patient felt her body falling apart. She complained of parts of her body flying about. It was a question of a compulsive neurosis with hysterical properties.

If the hypochondriac grants certain elements of his body too much libido, then these same elements project from the body image. The hysteric relinquishes simultaneously with the genital sensation other parts of his body: hysterical anesthesia. Federn has demostrated that the body image shows, before falling asleep and while dreaming, extensive changes which run parallel to libidinal processes. Therefore the body image is based on impressions of the senses and built up and constructed from them. It is a process under the guidance of the outside world, a constantly renewed experiment aiming to find that which fits the momentary life situation. Yet the final form of the body image is not only dependent on sensory impressions but primary instincts as well.[3]

Lesions of the brain, especially those of the lower parietal lobe, cause extensive changes in the body pattern. The patients are unable to orient themselves about their own bodies; they cannot locate their particular body parts. Especially important in this respect is the finger agnosia (described by Gerstmann), where the patients are not able to differentiate among individual fingers. They also make errors in distinguishing between their right and left extremeties. The location of this disorder is well known. It involves foci at the borderline of the left lower parietel lobe and the second occipital fissure. Of greater interest is the fact that such patients have not only lost orientation of left and right and of their own finger, but of that in other persons as well. Other cases of parietel lesions cannot, in their actions, distinguish between their own body and that of a person facing them. When asked to point to their own nose they are likely to reach for the nose of the analyst.[4] Thus the body images of different people are already closely connected with the perceptual physiological sphere. But the link between the body image of different people finds an even clearer expression in the emotional and libidinal spheres. However, a few preliminary remarks are necessary before we turn to this problem.

The body image by no means coincides with limits of the physical body. It grows beyond it. A walking cane, a hat, clothing of all sorts become properties of the body image. The closer and more stable the link between a piece of jewelry or clothing, the more intimate the fusion with the body image. Objects which once were in close contact with the body will permanently retain some of the characteristics of the body image. Voice, breath, smell, and body emissions remain part of the body image, even when separated in space from the body. Space surrounding the body image differs from space in physics.

A schizophrenic female patient imagined the breath of another person to be her very own. When other people shrugged their

[3] Here Schilder appears to say the body image mediates instinctual drives and social responses within the individual.

[4] These cases are presented as clinical evidence that body images are interdependent on each other; that is, my consciousness of your body is somehow related to my consciousness of my own body. The precepts of classical psychology cannot account for such clinical phenomena.

shoulders, she felt the motions as her own: body images crept into hers. Distance in space between the body images is cancelled out. Watching a man walking along the street is stepping on her. One may say that her libido draws others close to herself. A boy living on the floor below hers has intercourse with her "through electricity."

In general, magic acts influence the body image without consideration of the true distance. The genitalia are the center of influence, and not in this case alone. The psychological space around the sex organs has a distinctive structure.

A compulsive neurotic felt his penis and his bladder lying in the street. An automobile ran across and squashed these organs far removed from himself.

Therefore, the space surrounding the body image has its special pecularities; the distance from object to body is determined by the instinctual life.

Libidinal impulses are, of necessity, social phenomena. They are directed at body images in the outside world. Even in the narcissistic stage, the direction of consciousness towards the outside world exists.[5] Vision which leads to the construction of one's own body also forms the body images of other people. However, we do not merely see, we also have a desire to see. Any separation of perceptual processes and affective processes is artificial. Obeying an impulse, the eye wanders. There are voluntary and impulsive processes which form part of perception as such: they are the limits of the personality and are very similar in different individuals. Yet they blend constantly with the deeper factors of the personality, with that emotional life which is less typical and which expresses the deeper aspirations of the personality. The aspect of the human body is above all a physiological problem.

However, it also arouses immediate sexual curiosity. This curiosity extends not only to the strange body but especially to one's own. We not only desire to satisfy our own curiosity but also that of others. Freud, in *Drei Abhandlungen zur Sexualtheorie (Three Dissertations on Sexual Theory)*, comes to the conclusions that the exhibitionist exposes his body and sex organs to induce the other person to exhibitionism also. He expects in turn as his reward satisfaction of his own curiosity. However, I believe that the desire to be seen is as primitive

[5]This is a restaurant of a principle which Husserl borrowed from Brentano: that consciousness is always consciousness of something else and is directed toward a world of objects or other beings. This belief underlies Schilder's concluding statement that, " 'I' and 'You' mutually presuppose one another. p. 211

as the desire to see. [6] A profound association exists between one's own body image and the body image of the next person. Over and over again we construct our body image and we test that which could be absorbed into our body. We are no less curious regarding our own body than we are inquisitive about those around us. As soon as the eye is gratified the pleasures of touch are desired. We explore every orifice of our body with fingers. Voyeurism and exhibitionism have the same root. Body image is a social phenomenon. But human bodies are never inactive, they are continuously in motion. Movement of the body is either expression or action; it is the body of a person with passions and motives. Sexual curiosity is not only curiosity as to genital organs and sexual acts but it is also curiosity probing into the sexuality of a person. Intuition, in the meaning of Lipps, T. does not exist. We don't have to imitate and create experiences to know what occurs within other people. Again and again, our knowledge of our own body has been overrated, and the knowledge about the body of the next person underrated.

I have observed a journalist who, since early childhood, showed a great interest in other people's affairs. At age twenty he was a volunteer detective in a murder case. Some time later he investigated the extent of homosexuality among navy personnel. His own sexual life was limited to intercourse with prostitutes. He considers all other sexual activities to be immmoral. He is a heavy drinker. While he imbibes, his desires don't plague him. He developed an alcohol hallucinosis during which, in the foreground, stood an illusion that other people could read his thoughts and interpret his gestures. Persons surrounding him are stirring forbidden thoughts in him. His free associations are resulting in perverse ideas. He expresses these through mouth and hand movements readily recognizable to everybody. He comprehends the body and the motions of other people and they in turn understand him. Their gestures and his gestures, their thoughts and his thoughts are closely interconnected.

Therefore, expressive motions signify communciation with other persons.

Children frequently show particular interest in their bodies, especially in such parts of the body which do not fully satisfy esthetic and functional demands. Very often the interest in one's own body

---

[6]Here, Schilder challenges the notion that social motives are but epiphenomena of physiological drives. For example, the desire to be seen would be present in the earliest strivings of an infant. Indeed, Schilder consistently states that all drives are social from their very beginning.

will be aroused by conversations and comments. What is discussed in the family is of particular importance. Once the interest in function or form of one's body is awakened, then the corresponding elements and operations of other persons are also observed. The individual and social interests in the body run parallel to each other.

Fear of blushing is often termed a social neurosis (see, e.g., Fenichel). It is indeed remarkable how much some patients avoid contact with other people and how far they isolate themselves from their fellow men.

Over a long period of time I have analyzed a patient of this type. From early childhood, he felt insecure. He was tall for his age, and was afraid to be asked why he was playing with smaller children. His difficulties increased when, at age thirteen, he began to masturbate. He felt masturbation stimulated facial hair growth, which other people would notice. He was terrified that his erections could be observed. He also suffered from obsessive impulses to strangle other people and, above all, to hurt his wife and child. Since his early years he had stood in great fear of his father. He had at once both anxiety and a desire to be castrated by his stern father, as well as to be sexually used, as the father was an example of unusually strong masculinity. Analysis made it plausible that he was referring to his father's extraordinarily large penis. When about four years old the patient showed an abnormal fear of being watched while defecating. The threat of genital castration by the father probably had intensified strong pregential-anal and passive traits. A masturbation fantasy, in this connection, takes on a special significance. He imagined a physician taking the rectal temperature of a woman, and sniffing on the thermometer. The patient imitated the process by wetting his finger with saliva and smelling it. Later, however, he put a thermometer into his anus and took his penis between his legs, pictured himself as a woman. At the same time he imagined himself lying next to a woman and inserting his penis into her genital organ. In all his fantasies he rather often used the image of the wife of his father's business partner. A long time before the beginning of the masturbation period the patient had observed how the doctor had taken his brother's rectal temperature.

The psychological situation during his anal masturbation is characteristic and complicated. The patient is, above all, himself. But, he is the doctor as well. Again, he is also the woman in whose rectum the doctor puts the thermometer. Likewise, he is the woman who has intercourse, and is the person who had sexual intercourse with this same woman as well.

No better example can be given to point out the fact that strange body images are contained in one's own body image. However, these must already have been perceived by the patient before he can fuse them into his own body image. He lives simultaneously within and outside his body. His own and the other body images together are presented to us. The body image is not the appersonation of other body images, although elements of them are absorbed. Neither is it a product of identification, although such identifications may enrich our own body image. At the same time we don't gain information of other bodies through projecting our own into the outside world. There is no question that a steady interaction occurs between our own body image and that of other persons. This exchange is either an exchange of parts or of entities. All body images are interconnected. The closer they are in space the tighter they are linked together. A spatial distance between bodies is a fundamental factor in the exchange interplay of bodies. Contact facilitates this in considerable measure. The optical assessment of the scene diminishes as two bodies come very near each other; the blending of body images proceeds more easily and the reconstruction of one's own and the other body image is made possible.

Besides the spatial distance the affective relations of persons among one another have to be considered. Affectivity brings body images nearer to us. Language expresses this very clearly: we say a person "is close to us." The metaphoric distance between body images of different persons is by no means equal for all parts of the body. Elements which a rouse erotic interests are closer to one another than those which do not. Erogenous zones are particularly close. Communication between body images is made through the erogenous zones. Perhaps, it is not an accident that the German *Verkehr,* and the English "intercourse" are both used in the sexual sense. During coitus the body images fuse together extensively. If at some time we should arrive at a psychology of coitus (we are, at present, rather far from it), then the relationship of body images during coitus will have to be the basis.

The masturbation fantasy of the above-mentioned patient connects the body images through the anal zone. It is the expression of the sexual attitude of our patient. However, in this fantasy, his five body images do not constitute a whole but a sum. Perhaps we have here a significant psychological problem. The patient shifts his genital interest from below upwards to the face: growing of hair, blushing. Body images cannot exist in isolation. We demand the union of our body image and we insist on this close link, especially as

regards sexuality and its expression in the body image. Even masturbation can be social sexual activity, and the face gains special importance. In the face, the secondary sex characteristics are manifested in
the growth of hair. Persons who masturbate often are concerned that
their habit is revealed to others in their eyes. Thus, the wish for
belonging turns into fear. One's own and the other's eye develop into
tools of social association. Not only masturbation but erection is a
social phenomenon and concerns the body image of other people as
well as one's own. Our patient strives eagerly to hide his erection (a
phenomenon that is quite frequent among neurotics). Blushing
transfers erection to the face. This time the relocation occurs also in
the physical sphere. His face, now, becomes the center of the body
image. It evokes the attention of his fellow-men and brings them
closer to himself. Originally, he wanted this attention for defecation
and erection. So, we arrive not only at psychology of blushing but
also at a psychology of expressive movements.[7] The face gains unique
importance, since it is not only expressive but visible to all. From this
point of view the mouth becomes a principal organ in social respects.
The blushing of our patient says, "Look at my erection and defecation, share my excitement and come closer to me." Thus the patient
stands in a more intimate relationship to other humans. Blushing
diminishes social distance; but the superego does not condone this
unauthorized satisfaction, so he begins to shun other people. Yet the
patient has the goal to have as many friends as possible.[8]

   This patient attaches special importance to his clothing. He
wishes to be the center of attention; he would like to be an actor and
public speaker. The actor is the center of emotional interests. His
body image attracts crowds; he is separated from them by an invisible wall. We can define the actor and the patient as narcissistic, yet
both have a close relationship with other people except that their individuality is of no consequence any longer. They are merely human
beings—body images.

   Body images are never isolated, they are always surrounded by

[7]Schilder speaks of the "psychology of blushing" and the psychology of expressive
movements" but one could also say he is doing a phenomenology of these events,
giving attention to their detailed description as an interpersonal experience.

[8]Always the astute clinician, Schilder points out that a patient's beliefs and actions
can be incongruent with the appearance of his body image, a concept which Gestalt
psychotherapists (Perls, et al.) later developed into a technique of intervention with
their patients.

body images of other persons. Changes in the body image are always social phenomena and alter the body images of other people. One's own body image and the body image of others are equal one to another, and one cannot be explained through the other. A continual exchange between one's own body image and those of other persons occurs. Nevertheless, the total body image of others can also be absorbed, and one's own body can be projected as a whole. In the precepts of identification one should consider, more than has been the case, that identification between bodies occurs, or better yet, between persons whose bodies are inherent in their character. The body images of other people, and parts thereof, together with one's body image, can form an inner unity, or they can merely be added and joined with one's own body image. The body image is not static. It changes according to the life situation. It is a creative construction. It is erected, dissolved, and built up again. In this process of construction, reconstruction, and dissolution, the courses of identification, appersonation, and projection are present.

These processes which take place between individuals seem to make them resemble one another; they even appear, to some extent, to be similar. Yet body images always belong to individuals and personalities. Once an individual has socially adapted his body image it still remains his body image. There is no body image of the group or the "We." Indeed, in this respect, social psychology is the psychology of individuals, conditional on life of the community. Social life generates the tendency to identify with another person. Imitation also belongs within this range of psychological phenomena. Yet community life is not only based on identification but also on actions which presuppose that other individuals are persons with their own bodies. There exist two conflicting tendencies. The first absorbs, by identification and related processes, his fellow creature into his own ego. The second, no less strong and primitive, classifies and accepts the other person as an independent unit. This social antinomy[9] is of great consequence. Beauty, as well, falls into the realm of social phenomena which are based on the body image. The human body, the body image, is the main object of the fine arts. A beautiful body arouses sexual desire without gratification. Still beauty is common property, belonging to all people. Delayed action is part of the essence of beauty. One understands that the classic ideal rejects the expression of strong affects and violent motions. While we admiringly recognize beauty as such, we renounce our own claims in the in-

[9] (Kant: Paradox)

terest of the community. However, beauty is originally the beauty of a person which is reflected in the body image.

Likewise is ethics not only based on assessing the intrinsic value of the next person but also on acknowledging the body image and body unity of other people. Even the rules of ethics rest on the relation of body and body images one to another, and on the tendency for identification and projection. It is of great inner urgency to the individual that his fellow-man exists, and moreover that he is satisifed, that he constitutes an entity to build up and to ruin our own body image and we have the same tendencies towards other body images. Construction and destruction of a body image are fundamental processes in social living. We exist in a group where other personalities and other bodies have the same basic significance as we ourselves. "I" and "You" mutually presuppose one another, "I" and "You" are persons, and a person has a body and a body image.

Chapter 17

PAUL SCHILDER ON ART[1]

Theories of Art and Its Relation to the Psychology and Psychopathology of Childhood

As a preface to Paul Schilder's essays on art, we present the comments of Charles Wentinck in discussing the theories of G.C. Argan in *Modern and Primitive Art.* [244, pp. 11-13]

. . . . The discovery of primitive art by the moderns arises from much more profound motives than the simple realization of a relationship acting as a catalyst between artistic conceptions of the world. It cannot be denied the the concentration of the artist's vision on more austere, starker forms, independent of the subject depicted, went hand in hand with an ever increasing knowledge of primitive art. The artist in the modern world is interested in the most diverse sculptures, whenever they coincide with his own ideas about form: his concern is to solve the problem of integrating volume and space without having recourse to the usual method of perspective. His way of understanding the purely artistic data—that is, through the imagination rather than simply visually—apparently corresponds to what might be called the intellectual realism of primitive art. For those artists too created a form of art which first and foremost transcribes what the mind knows, and not what the eye sees. They sifted out those elements which seemed to lack interest even though they might catch the eye first, and instead depicted invisible things that they regarded as essential . . . Both modern and primitive artist were seeking to understand space logically, according to its simplest laws. . . .

[1] Exerpts and Figures A-E taken from *Child Psychiatric Techniques*, 21 under references.
Reprinted with permission.

In 1908 Wilhelm Worringer's book *Abstraction and Empathy* . . . set out the following principle: the less mankind is able to understand the phenomena of the external world and, consequently, the less kinship he feels with them, the stronger is the impulse which drives him to create a powerful and abstract beauty. It is not that primitive man is searching for laws in nature, nor that he feels them more keenly than another; on the contrary, he experiences an even greater desire to free these phenomena from arbitrariness and chaos, because he feels lost and overpowered by them. So he endows them with the urgency and value of law.

Children and animals play, but they also take their activities very seriously. For instance, when you watch a kitten it seems to be in continual movement, but there also appears to be an element of playfulness in its motion. Karl Groos developed a theory that the play of animals serves as a preparation for later biological functions, but he was merely expressing the point of view of the observer who already knows what the later development of the animal will be. From the point of view of the kitten its play does not represent preparation for the future. The kitten takes life and the world seriously. Its actions bring it into contact with the world, and with every new action new qualities of the world merge into the kitten's experience. The emergence of new qualities of the object is, obviously, but one of its immediate psychological aims, but the animal also wants an inner relation to the object. It wants to get hold of it and sooner or later to incorporate it into itself. In addition, it gets pleasure from its muscular activity and not only learns about the object but also learns about itself when acting. Parallel with this development, control over its own movements increases. External world, body and muscular control merge in this active process, guided by the urge towards the world and towards satisfaction of biological needs. It may be said that there is no immediate evidence for the assumption of certain psychological processes in the kitten. In the development of the child, more evidences of psychological processes can be offered. In its play the child learns something about the world, satisfies its needs and gains control over the mechanics of its actions.

This play is, of course, primarily a process of maturation and development. However, the psychological adaptations connected with motility give final shape to the developmental process. The aim of every activity is mastery of the object. This can be attained only by continous experimentation which does not stop even when the object is removed, because it remains in the child's mind. Objects and situations are revived in the memory, either wholly or in part. With this revival of the actual world, processes of experimentation continue. Parts of experiences of the past are put together in new sequences until finally a satisfactory unit of imagination and memory is reached which furnishes a suitable basis for new action and experimentation. Such units may be called gestalten or configurations.

These configurations are parts of the world and emerge during action, but they may also be reached by the processes of imagination and memory. They are "good" configurations, or *gute Gestalten* as they have been called by Max Wertheimer, only when they fit into and are part of the world. The process of imagination and remembering contains elements of action as well. There is no picture in the mind which is not connected with a set of motor attitudes and small movements, carrying on the process of experimentation which took place in the perception and action. There has been a controversy as to whether the process of thinking can go on without optic imagery pictures. It is known however that thinking can proceed when mental image are indistinct and incomplete. It is, further, of importance that the path from thought to action should be a very direct one. Thinking is an efficient preparation for action, and Freud has justly called it trial action performed with small amounts of energy. Human beings, especially children, are continually experimenting with perception, imagination, memory, and thinking, all of which are based on and interrelated with motor attitudes and actions. Human experience cannot be separated from activity which builds itself up in a sequence of levels by a continuous process of trial and error. It is a continuous construction.

Where does art fit into this scheme? Art does not lead to immediate action. Even when art is used for propaganda it is different from an immediate call for action. A Soviet novel or drama is more than a mere call to direct political action and propaganda. Even when a Diego Rivera or a Jose Clemente Orozco creates revolutionary murals, the message of such morals can hardly be adequately expressed by a political program.

The misfortunes of friends and of those whom we love may be called tragedies; still, the emotions experienced on such occasions are different from those we may experience when we see a performance of Eugene O'Neill's *Mourning Becomes Electra*, in spite of the fact that it would be difficult to imagine that human beings could be harder hit by fate. A storm is an esthetic object only so long as human beings are not threatened with disaster. The emotions experienced in a love affair are obviously more direct than those aroused by any piece of art. One is doubtful about persons who experience their strongest emotions in relation to art and is inclined to object to their estheticism. The conclusion may be drawn that art provides emotions of a quality which is not equal in fullness to those experienced in everday life. The world of art, music, and fiction is not one of direct emotion and action.

Some objects of art and esthetic enjoyment seem to be present in nature without man's activity. They are not created by man. It almost seems as though they were received as a gift. If the active character of human perception is considered, it is realized that the person enjoying a landscape creates this landscape and has something of the artist in him. It is interesting from this point of view that almost every century, nay, almost every generation, has a landscape of its own. The ruins of Nicolas Poussin, the color orgies of Joseph M. W. Turner, and the landscapes of Claude Monet are different worlds. It is well to keep in mind that the creator of a piece of art and the person who is in a state of esthetic enjoyment have much in common with each other.

However, the artist seems to change reality in a much higher degree than does the person who merely enjoys the beauty of a landscape or picture. Leonardo da Vinci has often been quoted advising his disciples to get their inspiration from the chance forms of a crumbling wall. This shows that the objects of art are not merely created from eerie imagination, but portray features of the objective world. Great sculptors have often spoken of the pattern coming from the materials, as if the statue was contained in the marble before it was hewn out. The creative artist does not invent something outside of reality but helps reality to its own creation.

Actions have aims. They are directed by the desires and needs of the individual. The artist obviously wants to show that he has discovered something which nobody else was able to discover before him. He promises enjoyment and a new approach to action. He wants to be praised for it and to gain something in everyday life by discovering esthetic realities. Whether the art manifests itself as music, painting, sculpture, poetry, or drama, the fundamental principle remains the same. Since the world of art does not lead to ultimate emotions and actions, the esthetic enjoyment must of necessity have something to do with the preparation to action, and is related to play. The question remains, why should it be valued in spite of the fact that no direct satisfaction of biological needs comes out of it.

Sigmund Freud has shown that one of the central experiences in human life is the so-called Oedipus complex, by which he means the wish of the child (especially between the ages of three and five) to have sexual relations with the parent of the opposite sex, and to remove and kill the parent of the same sex. The name for this fundamental desire is taken from a tragedy of Sophocles. The classical tragedy leads man back to one of the essential biological and psychological conflicts of human existence, to the solution of which it contributes but vaguely. The great tragedy was created for the community and was the concern of the community. The origin of tragedies lies in religion. The first tragedy was obviously a ritual ceremony which promised the individual an actual solution of his conflicts. Insofar as this conflict was psychological the primitive rites fulfilled a part of their aims.

For primitive man, religion was beyond doubt a serious business. It was an attempt to act by magic. We owe to K. T. Preuss the insight that primitive art and religion had as their core magic wishes and ceremonies.[167]

Magic is based upon strong wishes and urges which demand fulfillment in reality, even when the actual tools are insufficient or when the nature of the wish makes fulfillment impossible. With this insight into the close relation between magic and art, a further step is taken in the understanding of the fundamental functions of art. Whereas the original Dionysian cult, and for that matter also the holy Mass of Catholicism, promise immediate psychological satisfaction to the community, the art production and the artist do not attempt such direct satisfaction but imply that it might be finally derived from art.

In the child, experimentation and play, although serious in intent, are further away from final completion and final mastery of the world. On the other hand, for the child, play is reality and is in some way comparable to the magic intentions of the ritual. The esthetic character of the behavior and actions of the child and the great esthetic enjoyment which can be derived from observation of the child are closely connected with the preliminary character of the activities of children. It might furthermore be expected that the child when untrammeled by conventional education may produce objects of art with comparative ease. It is very doubtful whether for the child its art production actually means mere play in the adult sense. Its drawing and painting may be expected to denote a serious attempt to do something with reality, perhaps in a magical way.

In studying the art of children it must be realized that the child has only limited technical capacities. Its motility prescribes comparatively simple forms. As has already been outlined in previous chapters, this motility is so arranged that primitive loops and whirling movements are dominant at first. In the drawings of small children these primitive units are repeated again and again, and are the units prescribed by the child's motility. There is reason to believe, however, that this primitive unit is also of paramount importance in perception. Knowledge and activity of the child develop step by step until more complicated configurations can be mastered.

The human figure is drawn by the young child in primitive loops more or less round or oblong. This is not the perceived world of the child, but the child's motility in response to his perceptions. The child is satisfied with its product and recognizes it as a part of the world. Perhaps, though, it means even more to the child, who probably has discovered that some geometrical patterns are also present in the human figure, and has learned that by its own movements it can reproduce forms which have at least some relation to what it perceives. The child has thereby conquered a part of the world in its drawing. There is no reason to believe that the child at this stage of development interprets its attempt as a magical act. However, sooner or later the picture drawn becomes more than a mere picture; it may contain a promise of that reality which the child desires. Magic procedures in the strict sense are obviously a great step beyond this.

The art of the child leads us back to the primitive forms which mankind has almost forgotten. The fascinating impression of children's drawing is based on the fact that they reopen to adults a reality which has long since been obliterated. At the same time it inspires the hope that man may be able to start this process of experimentation all over again. It is possible that in this way deeper insight can be gained into what art in general means to man. At any rate, the play of children and their creative art are not so different from each other—both are serious endeavors.

In the art of the children two fundamental principles can be differentiated—the tendency to draw what is seen, and the tendency to draw what is known about the object. Both tendencies are decidedly realistic although the technical capacity to express them is often incomplete. In the first few years of life the child struggles with elementary forms, and therefore simple form principles dominate its efforts.

Even the human figure is drawn as merely a configuration of simple loops. Arms and legs appear as simple lines, and hands and feet are hardly emphasized as distinct entities. For the child, however, such a drawing signifies the human figure, and the objective incompleteness of the drawing does not hinder him from seeing in the figure a complete representation of what he wants to draw. At this stage of development the child is not aware which part of his image of the object is given to him by visual perception and which part comes from memory and previous knowledge. Both are used indiscriminately in the drawing. Full face productions prevail; profiles appear only later on. Perspective is in general a later achievement and is attained early only by gifted children. In no phase of this early development does the child attempt to symbolize. He may find pleasure in simple geometrical form principles and ornamental designs. However, his chief desire is to draw reality as it is. Even if the result of his striving has little similarity to the object from the adult point of view, the young artist offers his production as a full presentation of the object.

It is interesting in this respect that the oldest documents of prehistoric art are decidedly realistic in intent. In the caves of Southern France and Spain there is a monumental and realisitc art of animal portraiture. These paintings, termed Franco-Cantabrian art, are polychrome and of considerable size. The Eastern Spanish or Levantine style shows shadow silhouettes in monochrome in which men and animals are usually depicted in active movement. In general the figures are smaller than in the Franco-Cantabrian style. However by the time of the Bronze Age art ceased to be realisitc and sought its ultimate goal in static geometrical patterns.

There is reason to believe that for the child as well as for primitive peoples the picture does not always merely represent the object but *is* the object. The individual is so intent on attaining the object, that everything which can be used as its symbol, though in completely differentiated form, actually becomes the object itself. The relation between primitive art and magic and ceremony thus becomes obvious. One understands also that primitive art is often part of a ceremonial, although this is not invariably true. At any rate, the child has not given up experimentation. In the long run the child cannot be deceived. He differentiates the object very decisively from the drawn or painted picture of the object, when the experimentation is not prematurely interrupted. The primitive individual also will not be forever satisfied with pictures which represent the object. Bound by his customs and institutions, he may remain in the sphere of magic and refrain from differentiating between magical causality and sequences in reality. The art of primitives and of children opens the way to reality, but one cannot always be certain that they will follow all the way through to this end.

The fascination of the attempts of both the primitive artist and child is due partially to the fact that they represent an effort which has not yet led to definite results. In many respects modern art has gone back to the perception of the essentials of form. In the art of Pablo Picasso, Fernand Leger, and Georges Braque, form patterns are rediscovered which the adult had tended to forget. The principle of seeing simple geometrical forms at first appeared in the so-called analytical cubism in which the abstract form is seen merely as a part of the fully developed form. In abstract cubism and in synthetic cubism, the interest in form of primitive type again dominates. The relation to some of the drawings of children in which the child struggles with the principles is obvious.

Primitive form principles have in no way disappeared from man's perception, but he has turned to a reality which is more or less finished and crystallized. Levels of human existence may come into the foreground which belong to more primitive stages of development. Psychoanalysis emphasizes the tendency to regression in the diverse neuroses and psychoses. Experiences emerge which belong to the different levels of childhood. Primitive form principles which appear in the drawings of children and in some ways also in the art of primitives may be expected to reappear in the art of psychotic individuals. This expectation is indeed fulfilled in the drawings of schizophrenic individuals, which have been collected by Hans Prinzhorn, R.A. Pfeifer, and others. It seems that the schizophrenic person has access in his art to primitive form principles which so-called normal persons have lost.

Prinzhorn's material contains the work of many schizophrenic artists who had no training before they started to draw or to sculpture. They drew ornamental designs in which more lively structures which suggest organic forms suddenly appear. Primitive drawings of the human figure occur but they are combined with rhythmical priniciples which give artistic qualities to the whole picture.

For example, in the drawings and paintings of a psychotic house painter (reproduced by Prinzhorn) dots or flowers in the garden are repeated in a rhythmical way like the faces in a group of saints. It may be said, accordingly, that rhythmical principles are used by the schizophrenic in a much freer way than by other untrained artists. In these pictures one also notices that even artists who are in better command of the techniques and would seem to be capable of drawing the human figure in correct proportions, handle the problem with great independence and freely change the proportions. They experiment with organic forms in general, much more fully than most normal persons would dare. This may be called the principle of free experimentation with the organic form and especially with the human form. The average artist feels rather closely bound to the forms of space as he perceives them.

Primitive artists do not appear to recognize perspective, and add figures to each other without attempting to indicate a perspective relationship. It is well known that the knowledge of perspective is an achievement which comes late in the development of art and is incomplete even in Japanese woodcuts which in other respects reach such a high degree of perfection. Obviously, perspective is a convention, and drawings and paintings which do not use the principle of perspective may yet be of very great value. The schizophrenic artist does not feel bound by this convention and achieves effects which the more conventional individual does not attempt. At the same time the schizophrenic artist is not impressed by the ordinary laws of gravitation, and liberates the individual from its bonds. The figures may be placed anywhere, without close relation to the earth. They may float lightly in space, no longer bound to the earth. One of the most astonishing effects in art is accomplished when the artist attempts to experiment with spatial relations. Often the liberation from the rigidities of space and gravitation also gives a greater freedom concerning the problem of numbers. Objects are multiplied and various faces may be united into one composite figure.

Schizophrenic art might be characterized by the following principles:

1. Primitive form principles make their reappearance. They are used to characterize the forms of the inanimate as well as of the animate world.
2. Geometrical and organic principles are often used in an indiscriminate way.
3. There is a naive pleasure in rhythmicity and multiplicity. Rhythm and multiplication are applied to the organic as well as to the inanimate world.
4. The proportions of the human figure are changed in an experimental way.
5. The problems of space, size, number, and perspective are dealt with in an experimental way.

6. The laws of gravitation are disregarded.

It is undeniable that freedom from convention helps the schizophrenic artist to the possibility of almost unlimited experimentation. This is a condition which may lead even the untrained person to achieve artistic creations. It is obvious that such a release from the conventions of everyday life will have an effect on the content as well as the form of the artistic creation. The schizophrenic often will choose his subject matter from the sphere of the cruel, or the weird, and especially from the field of frank sexuality. He will overemphasize the lower part of the body at the expense of the upper part, as for example in the drawings of Joseph Sell in Prinzhorn's book. The motif of the face may be transferred to the genitals or to the kneecaps. Freedom from conventional form principles creates a mythical word in which the human body blends with the animal body and with the limbs or other parts of other human bodies. On the whole it cannot be denied that the artistic capacities of the individual are increased by the psychosis. This idea may be formulated by stating that the artistic process consists partially of reversal to a stage of free experimentation with the body and the world.

However, neither the schizophrenic patient nor the child are artists simply because they use primitive principles. Obviously something else is required. When one examines the artistic productions of a number of schizophrenic patients, one sees immediately that the severity of the schizophrenic process and the artistic value of their productions do not parallel each other. It is clear that a production is artistic only if it shows primitive form and in addition uses experimentation in order to approach the mastery of reality. Modern psychiatry is of the opinion that the schizophrenic is an individual who cannot master the intricate situations of a complicated world and under stress and danger reverts to more primitive modes of experience. Such a world within may offer security and enjoyment when the differentiated external world has become a threat against which defense is not possible. However, the schizophrenic is not satisfied with a limited world. As a living human being, he is fascinated by the world and wants to go back to the more complicated external forms again. He may cling to those parts of reality which he is still able to master. Primitive form principles and modes of experience which make their appearance in the schizophrenic may represent stages in his retreat from reality, or they may represent stages in his new attempt to return to reality or to try to recover it. The schizophrenic artist reveals problems which are important for art in general. Ernst Kris surmised that in this process of recovery and in his efforts to regain the world, the schizophrenic's earliest concern is with the human face. The human face is one of the first objects with which the child comes into close personal relation. Paradoxically enough, relations between human beings are to a great extent inter-facial ones. One is perhaps justified in drawing the conclusion that the artist has not merely the task of bringing to light the experimental stages of human existence, but also the possibility of advancing beyond this experimental stage to a fuller experience of the world. Schizophrenic art is often lacking in this respect, and even when the first step is taken, the variability of such endeavors is limited. Ernst Kris has further noted that the schizophrenic artist frequently re-mains monotonous in his themes and patterns. However, it is better not to be too severe in setting this criterion, since the successful artist, too, often becomes rigid, using again and again the same pattern which once had a meaning. Of course, the successful normal artist who has become rigid has not necessarily also become a schizophrenic. However, he shares with the schizophrenic artist the impossibility of varying his experimentation in his approach to the world.

So far schizophrenic art has been referred to as one instance of the art of persons who are mentally ill. There are many types of men-tal disease. The mentally ill person has an approach to reality which is different from that of the normal person. Also, the severe psychopathic personality, in his art productions, may use specific form principles in connection with emotional disturbances. The change which has taken place in the world of the depressive or elated (manic) patient will also be reflected in his artistic endeavors. An underdevelopment of the brain which expresses itself clinically in mental deficiency or an organic lesion of the brain which has caused deterioration may give the individual access to primitive form prin-ciples which are unavailable to the normal individual. The emergence of such forms of expression is by no means without artistic significance.

Artistic talents are obviously much more widespread than has thus far been surmised, but by most human beings they are never developed. Human beings show great differences in their artistic ability. It is probably that almost anyone has some capacity to ex-press himself in music, poetry, painting, or building, but the degree of ability varies widely. In the art of singing, physiological differences can be the basis for the variation in expressive ability. The fate of the individual in early childhood is another factor to be considered; in

the schizophrenic artist, endowment is naturally also a factor determining artistic capacity.

From this point of view it is interesting to study the life history of
artists who have been psychotic. The psychiatric diagnosis of Vincent
van Gogh is still a matter of controversy. Some believe that he suffered from a certain form of epilepsy; others, that he was a
schizophrenic. However, the problem of diagnosis is of no special importance here. In all his letters he appears as an individual who
wanted reality and nothing but reality. He was interested in forms
and colors and wanted to get hold of them. Such a thirst for reality
can be found in individuals who have been insecure and are full of
fear that they may lose their access to reality. In the first phase of his
artistic career, van Gogh painted realistically but without much imagination. However, the *Potato Eaters* shows decided distortions in the
faces. The caricaturist clings to one trait of the human face when he is
not capable of approaching the subject as a whole.

Figure 1. Vincent van Gogh, *The Potato Eaters.*

In his most fertile painting period van Gogh painted objects with a direct approach that was almost uncanny. *The Chair* is a characteristic masterpiece of this period, in which the reality of color

Figure 2. Vincent van Gogh, *The Chair.*

and form is striking. The chair is almost more than real. Its colors have become more glowing. There are many pictures of a similar type. On the other hand, the arrangement of the chair in his picture shows a decided tendency to rigidity of form. When an individual clings very fast to reality it becomes overdistinct, and form principles which are almost geometrical immediately appear. In the landscapes which van Gogh painted during this time, formal principles become more and more paramount. Clouds are drawn in more or less primitive vortices which repeat themselves. The principle of parallelism of lines is often used to the neglect of other structural qualities of reality. The colors of his sunflowers are so intense that they look more like suns than flowers, and their forms come nearer to geometrical than organic patterns. Towards the end of this period, formalistic principles are overwhelming and the rhythm of lines based on primitive principles almost destroys the pattern of the object. There are pictures of haystacks and gorges in which vortices and curves, partially in parallel arrangements, extend over the whole picture and destroy the "object."

Van Gogh's portraits, too, are of intense from this point of view. It is worth noting that in the majority of landscapes which he painted, human figures are absent. Parallel lines are predominant, although they are often waved. In the picture *Doctor Gachet,* the composition is dominated by inclined planes. Other pictures are strongly symmetrical. *L'Arlesienne* is dominated by triangular form principles; the colors are schematic. It is worth while comparing the copies he made of Jean Francois Millet and Eugene Delacroix with the originals. The great fascination of the work of van Gogh lies partially in its striving for reality and partially in its renewed attempt to experience reality in primitive geometrical and color principles. It is a valuable human document of an individual who strove with great power toward optic reality. It would be different to explain van Gogh's achievement without recourse to the specific gifts for optic perception which developed in his emotional battle for optic reality.

Thus far children's efforts to use drawing as an attempt to approach reality more closely by experimentation and repetition have been considered. As in children's play in general, there has been seen in this a preparation for action which is based upon an insight into structure. It has been found that in their search for reality children use primitive form principles such as the loop, the vortex, the wave, and the simple geometrical forms. It has also been found that the simple geometrical forms and primitive patterns are used in

Figure 3. Vincent van Gogh, *Doctor Gachet*.

Figure 4. Vincent van Gogh, *L'Arlesienne*.

children's approach to both the animate world and the inanimate world, especially to the human figure.

In the most primitive documents of art in prehistoric times has been found the urge to reality which approached specifically the animate form, either at rest or in motion. In these primitive stages of development space is not seen as a distinct problem but more or less in terms of the sum of objects to be included. Since the effort to attain reality is incomplete it has to be repeated over and over again. Repetition and rhythm are closely connected with the basic organization of human motility. In schizophrenic art there was found regression into primitive form principles, rhythm and formal patterns extending into the animate forms, as well as condensations of the various parts of reality into one, and free experimentation with the principles of space.

In all these various experiences an unquenchable thirst for experimentation was noted, and the wish to master parts of reality and reality as a whole; however, the experimentation of the schizophrenic, the child, and the artist is incomplete. The child needs its growth to complete it. The schizophrenic artist reverts to primitive forms under the onslaught of a reality which he cannot master, but he does not completely give up the struggle for the richer world which he finds threatening him. The so-called normal artist points again and again toward new structures of reality although he never reaches a definite end or takes a definite action. The less he is bound to convention the freer he is in his experimentation and the greater is his chance for new discoveries. A psychosis may help him to get rid of banal everyday attitudes and open up the way to new experiences. He may be a real artist, with or without a psychosis, if his descent to the primitive layers of experience contains at least a hope for a new adaptation to a world which can be shared by the community. The art of prehistoric times may in part have had magical and ceremonial implications. The moment art becomes ceremonial it sets itself definite aims and becomes a tool, and not a reliable one, at that. This definiteness of purpose implies an irreversibility and a loss of freedom which transgresses the realm of art as it is today understood. Religious and magic ceremonies are indeed devious methods of conquering the world.

Human beings have to live with other human beings. Their emotions and actions take place in a community. Even the lonely thinker is not isolated from his social group. In this sense all experiences are social ones. The imagination of the dreamer becomes meaningless unless he can experience his imaginary thoughts and ideas in the life of the community. Charles Hartshorne has called attention to the social character of every perception.

Even when man turns to the inanimate world he does so with the unformulated but definite knowledge that it is also the world of other human beings. Art is a highly social phenomenon. The child who draws does not do so merely for himself but he also draws for the adult who encourages him. The social attitudes of the child, his individual history and the history of his experiences of love and hate will be reflected in every line.

The schizophrenic has sometimes been called autistic and narcissistic, meaning that he withdraws his interest (libido) from the world and diverts it to his own personality However, this conception is not entirely valid. The schizophrenic merely gives up his interest or relationship with objects outside of himself which have become too dangerous and too complicated for him to master. For the complicated human relations he substitutes simpler ones by which he can better protect himself. It is obvious that the artist directs his art to his fellow human beings. Through his art he wants to excite another individual the same attitude which he has experienced in himself. He communicates his vision so that the other individual may know what is going on in him and also to excite the same vision in his fellow human beings. Whatever his gains may be, they are for the benefit of the community and he expects praise and compensation from the community. The communal character of art was more obvious in previous stages of history; it is however never absent although it may be veiled in the most sterile periods of art. Art is, therefore, not only an experiment of a single person but one which the community tries to reach through art to higher forms of life.

Psychic processes similar to those found in schizophrenia form the background of everybody's life experiences. Man's earliest childhood with all its strivings, yearnings, and uncertainties, with all its difficulties in grasping the world and getting in closer touch with other human beings, is still alive in every human being, and it is possible that man has to go back to it whenever he wants to create. Human beings who have access to the deepest layers of human experience have a better possibility of seeing new visions of this world. They may not always find the way back to the world of their fellow men; they may seclude themselves in preoccupation with their inner conflicts. They may feel misunderstood and attacked and may answer with aggression. This is the stuff of which philosophers, poets, and artists are made. Sometimes they do not seem to be able to distinguish between the creations of their own fantasy and the real world. It often seems as if they have forgotten to check their fantasies against reality and against the experiences of other human beings. Such individuals have been called schizothymic, or schizoid, or even schizoid psychopaths. The indiscrimate use of these terms, however, is not advisable.

The genius, even if he appears schizoid, is characterized by a deep respect for the community and for reality, and he merely has reverted to the creative sphere of primitive existence in order to utilize it for a better mastery of the world. This separates him from the schizoid personality and schizoid psychopaths who, in spite of their efforts, do not find the way back to the world as it is generally known.

In our study of the art of abnormal children it may be expected that form principles will appear which are enlightening because they represent the early phases of development and also because they emphasize certain aspects in relation to the psychopathology. From the newer developments of psychology it has been learned that the so-called "pathological" is merely a particular aspect of the so-called "normal." In psychopathology, new facets of fundamental problems of psyche make their appearance. However, nothing extraneous is ever added to the psyche and the variation allows a deeper insight into the fundamental problem.

It has been emphasized that the problems of personality form the fundamental basis for every product of human endeavor, and especially for art productions. In order to understand the art of abnormal children the life history of the child and its emotional problems must be studied. After an insight has been gained into the psychological problems of the child, the basic form principles appearing in his drawings must be examined. The question must be asked whether the primitive perceptual units such as the loop and vortex, or curved lines and geometrical forms which belong to a later development are more prominent. Attention must be paid to how often the same motif is repeated and whether it is repeated in the same form or is varied. It must also be considered whether the forms are geometrical in the narrower sense or whether they approximate the forms which one finds in nature, as in the formation of a river or a hill, which may be regarded as organic forms. It will be particularly interesting to note whether attention is given to the specific form of animate objects, i.e., of animals and human beings. In modern art human and animal forms often have been approached under the impact of geometry, and cubism has emphasized particularly the geometrical principle in the human figure. When an attempt is made to analyze the drawings of children, the question to be asked again and again is whether they are more interested in geometrical or in organic forms. It must also be noted whether they use geometrical form principles in the drawings of human figures.

The human figure has always been the outstanding subject of the arts. In every art production it is of fundamental importance to analyze the way in which the problem of the human form is handled. In primitive experience the human body has no definite form. Even the concept human beings have about their own bodies, the body image, is not fully differentiated. Primitive perception and the dream change the relations of the different parts of the body freely, and qualities which belong to one part of the body image may be transposed to other parts. Children like to hear stories about dwarfs and giants. It is important to know whether greater attention is given to the face or to the other parts of the body. What attitude toward the genitals is reflected in the pictures? When distortions in the body image take place they are bound to have a close relation to the specific human problems of the child. When the body is seen merely from a geometric viewpoint, there is justification for believing that such an attitude shows either a particular primitivity and form perception or a particular aversion to the full perception of the human body.

Many drawings have more than one object, and even when there is only one it often has several parts. These parts may retain their natural arrangement or may be handled more or less arbitrarily. One may want to show one's power by changing and transposing parts of an object or the relation of different objects to each other. One may attempt to organize the parts or the different objects into a unit, or may be satisfied merely to juxtapose one object on another without any attempt to organize them. The question will also arise as to how well the parts of an object are organized into the whole, essentially a spatial problem, and there may be a question as to the degree of insight into spatial relations displayed in the picture. Some artists, whether they are children or adults, psychotic or not psychotic, respect the relations of the three dimensions of space. Others arbitrarily contract or expand one dimension at the expense of the others. In the drawings of Du Maurier, for instance, human figures are not only elongated beyond their measure but the lower parts of their bodies are too large in proportion to the upper parts. Some sculptors see their figures almost flat, others exaggerate the dimensions of depth.

Human beings, whatever they may be otherwise, are bodies with heavy masses subject to the laws of gravitation. Although psychologists have often neglected the question, human psychology cannot be understood unless problems are considered in relation to gravitation. German poets speak of *Erdenschwere* (literally, the heaviness of the earth) pointed to the subjection of human beings to gravitation, which immediately becomes the symbol of libidinous constellations. The wish to fly is one of the oldest wishes of humanity. In art, gravitation and firm relation of objects to the earth may be taken for granted, or one may prefer to experiment with gravitation, have things standing on their heads, and have objects floating in the air although they do not usually do so because of their physical quality. It is interesting to note how freely an artist experiments with gravitation, and it is equally interesting to inquire into the significance of such experimentation. An artist may experiment with spatial relations and gravitation. He may also experiment with the number of objects. He may like to draw hundreds or thousands of people or apples or chairs or houses. He may attempt to draw realistically thousands of houses in New York, or he may use the picture of of one object and its repetition as merely a form principle.

In general, one might ask whether an art production reveals more interest in form principles, or in objects seen as real objects. Conclusions concerning personal and emotional problems can be made from art productions, but it is more significant to recognize that the understanding of the form of a picture will be possible only on the basis of knowledge of the personal and emotional problem of the individual and especially of the emotionally disturbed child. It is obvious that not only the form principles have to be understood in this connection, but also the more or less realistic choice of colors. However, one should not forget that an individual may use well-developed form principles and may attempt to draw a fully differentiated reality, but still may choose scenes and colors with specific personal value as an object for his endeavors. When an individual prefers to draw scenes of cruelty in which the red of the blood or the red of fire become paramount, some inference may be made in regard to his emotional life. Whatever the form principles may be, the choice of subject matter has to be studied carefully; and it is a problem of no mean importance whether an individual prefers to draw landscapes or circus people. The content, the chosen color and form principles can only artificially be isolated from the life problems of the individual. Every art production has to be studied from the point of view of whether it expresses the desire for a fully developed reality, whether it is an attempt to escape from reality, whether it is an overcompensation, or a magic gesture.

Finally, the social significance of these art productions must be evaluated. Does the child want to gain the love and admiration of adults or does he merely reluctantly obey the request from a teacher for an art production? Is the art product a token of good will, or an attempt to bribe? In what way does it express the competition between this child and other children? Does the child suspect that the adult seeks his art production for specific reasons? The problems of the adult artist who is not psychotic do not differ fundamentally in this respect from the problems of our neurotic and psychotic children.

The various questions posed in the above paragraphs represent an ambitious program. We cannot hope to answer them completely. However, we may arrive at some understanding of the art of the abnormal child and may open the way for a deeper understanding of art in relation to human life and its problems.

The Art of Children and the Problems of Modern Art

The study of the art of children and especially of problem children helps in the understanding of modern art and the problems of modern life. Indeed, the problems of human life and of human art find such a clear expression in these children that their consideration leads to the discussion of problems of general concern, as well as to an approach to the problems of modern art.

The Form of the Human Body in Relation to Geometrical Forms

The human body has always been one of the main concerns of art. Human beings are inclined to think that the human body is familiar to them and that they have a clear picture of their own bodies and of the bodies of others. Many schools of psychology are even inclined to believe that the child from the beginning has a clear-cut knowledge and experience of its own body and sees the world in comparison to its own body. However, it has been shown clearly in my own writings and our experience with the graphic and plastic art of children that the child has to gain the knowledge of its own body in the same way that it learns to know the world. Franziska Boas has considered this problem also in relation to dance.

In the gradual constructive processes the child builds up the knowledge of its own body as the body image. This body image is in no way an experience which is stabilized. It undergoes continuous change. If human beings were able to have a clear conception of their own bodies there would be no need for mirrors. Persons learn about their bodies by their continuous contact with the outer world. The bodies of others have to be seen, human beings have to look at themselves and at others. The body image continually changes its shape. It is built, dissolved, remodeled, and reconstructed. One is never sure; one has to gain this knowledge by continuous effort. This is the basis for the continuous curiosity mankind has concerning the body. Naked or covered, it is mysterious and incomplete. One's own body is more familiar to one than that of others. The human form is seen everywhere, the body images of other human beings are perceived but animals and even plants are also graced with the dignity of body images. One might even go so far as to see such images in stones and in the forms of inanimate nature.

This is a world not only of curves, circles, ellipses, and straight lines; it is also one of the human organic forms which are strictly incomparable with geometry. Wherein the actual difference between these human forms and geometrical forms lines is the great riddle. After all, the soft curves of the breasts and buttocks are also geometrical lines. One is not sure where the borderline lies between geometry and the body image. Sometimes the body image is seen everywhere and seems to substitute for geometry. On other occasions geometry progresses into the body. Inanimate and animate nature retains, at first, something of the appearance of human forms in the struggle against geometrical tendencies, but finally triangles, circles, rectangles, curves, angles, and straight lines invade and substitute for the body image. In *Cubism and Abstract Art* there is quoted the letter written by Paul Cézanne to Emile Bernard which reads: "You must see in nature the cylinder, the sphere, the cone." Pablo Picasso's *Head of a Woman* is symmetrically broken in facets like a cut diamond but the form is still sculptural. The paintings and bronzes of this period of cubism are closely related to Negro sculptures. But this so-called "analytical cubism" of Picasso and Georges Braque is soon replaced by so-called "synthetic cubism," in which the tendency to an extreme, almost geometrical severity is outstanding. Similar tendencies can be found in the work of Fernand Léger. In one of the early works of Picasso, *The Studio* (1928), geometry is dominant. From this point of view it is stimulating to study Theo Van Doesburg's *Aesthetic Transformation of the Object* in which a cow and a person are finally transformed into a rectangular pattern. These painters and sculptors reveal the geometry both in nature and in the human body.

Figure 5. Pablo Picasso, *Woman's Head*.

Body image and geometry are eternal enemies. The body image can be pushed aside but it still remains, and it tries to come back. In the later work of Picasso, organic forms crept back; and some of his pictures of the latest period as far as they are not strictly classical in

Figure A. Aeroplane, by Francine.

style, are bonelike, and show forms which are of "organic type."
One picture by Max Ernst in which embryonic forms prevail is titled
*The gramineous bicycle garnished with bells, the pilfered graybears and the
echinoderms bending the spine to look for caresses.* One of the pictures of
Yves Tanguy is titled *Heredity of Acquired Characteristics.*

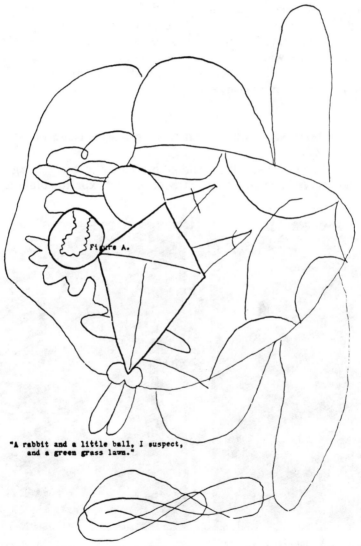

"A rabbit and a little ball, I suspect,
   and a green grass lawn."

Figure B. A Rabbit and a Little Ball, I Suspect, and a Green Glass Lawn, by
Francine.

It is interesting to compare these developments with the work of children who at first draw the human body as an incomplete circle supported on two lines; at about three years vertical configurations replace horizontal ones. The drawings of defective children often consist mostly of geometrical patterns and the relation of these geometrical patterns to the human form is not always obvious. Our most valuable material in the respect is offered in the drawings and paintings by Francine (Figures A, B and C) who drew figures with studied symmetry, reminiscent of some of the work of Henri Rousseau. Afterwards she descended to completely abstract patterns similar in many respects to Orphism, and to designs in which there are only vague hints of organic form (Figure D).

THE MEANING OF THE DISTORTION OF THE BODY IMAGE IN ART

We have stressed the relation between the body image and geometry. We have seen similar trends toward experimentation with

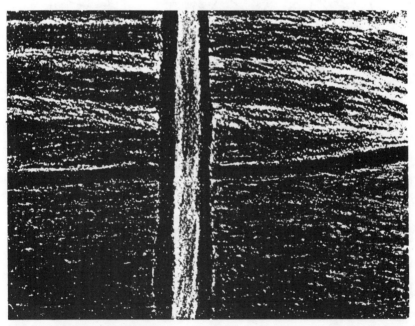

Figure C. A Flag, by Francine.

body images and geometry in modern art and in the drawings of our patients. The body image can also be changed in very different ways. In some of the pictures of Amedeo Modigliani (in the collection of George Gershwin, 1937), not only are the necks elongated but other parts of the body as well. The curves of the cheek in a man's portrait are exaggerated and in a woman's portrait the curves of the breasts and the buttocks are emphasized. In the picture *Anna de Zoorowska* the face is not only slanted but also distorted in the direction of the slant. In Georges Rouault's pictures the figures are often sturdy and quadrangular, as if they had been artificially shortened and compressed from head to foot so that they are broadened. It is remarkable that this painter so frequently chooses to draw dwarf clowns. It is as if he had a particular pleasure in experimenting with the space of the body image and changing it almost arbitrarily.

In plastic art the possibilities for distortions of the space of the body are still greater. One sculptor arranges mother and child in nearly cubic form. Other sculptors prefer to shorten the third dimension so that the figures almost resemble a bas-relief, as, for example,

Figure D. A Bulka, by Francine.

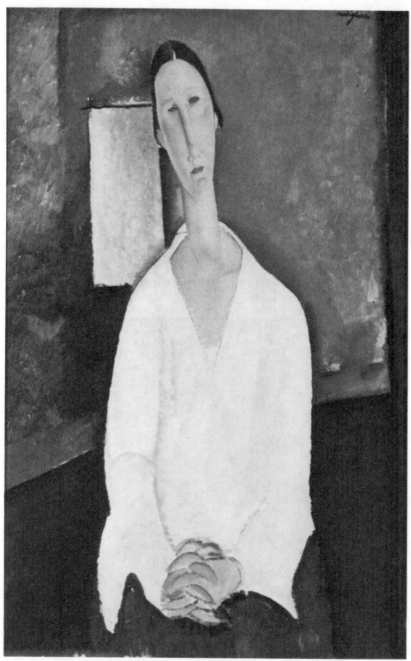

Figure 6. Amedeo Modigliani, *Anna de Zoorowksa*.

in many of the sculptures of Isamu Noguchi. If the depth deminsion is decreased, the figures are elongated; the postures especially of the neck stiffen out and the front view of the figure gains paramount importance. One might say that it is almost as if the human figure had been exposed to a definite pull in one direction or in the other, or as if in some of these pictures the influence of the gravitational forces on the body had been decreased or increased. Similar distortions are indeed subjectively experienced in individuals in whom the organs of equilibrium are affected as if by the vestibular apparatus and its central connections.

Also with Francine, the far-reaching distortions of figures merely served her need to cling to at least one outstanding part of reality as in the facial distortions of "Bender" (Figure E). In both cases caricature is an expression of helplessness concering reality, and an attempt to keep to reality by seeing its single features in distortion.

Figure E. Bender, by Francine.

The schizophrenic child may draw an eye or a face separately outside of the head. In their drawings, pieces of bodies are strewn all over the world. This is true not only of schizophrenic patients but also of some patients with organic damage to the brain. Everyone, as a child, is confronted with the problem of building up the image of his own body. These patients have returned to the primitive mode of experience.

The modern painter, the schizophrenic artist, and the child who draws, go back to the fundamental problem of gaining knowledge of their own body. In order to know it, they have to experiment again and again, and one has no right to say that the seemingly finished product which classic art and conventional drawing offer is a final solution. When one sees that famous picture of Duchamp, *Nude Descending a Staircase*, one wonders which is the staircase and which is the nude. The nude has become almost a geometrical motif. Is this arbitrary? Indeed human beings have to learn about themselves. This is only one of the many phases of the experimental approach of human beings to their own bodies. Accepted and conventional forms make one forget that the organism and human life are in a continuous process of construction and reconstruction. The immense value of modern art lies in its renewed approach to these fundamental form problems. Schizophrenic artists may handle these problems in a way which allows a deeper understanding of them.

EXPERIMENTATION WITH SPACE AND GRAVITATION

The child obviously struggles to bring objects into the proper spatial relation. Modern artists, however, experiment in a much more energetic way with the distortions of space. In the picture by Man Ray, *Observatory Time—the Lovers*, an object in the form of a vulva or a pair of lips of gigantic size is suspended in the air. These artists attempt energetically to overcome the fetters of gravitation. The whole problem of the vertical line and the vertical direction in general is a problem which is of the greatest importance of physiology. It is very probable that a vertical line is perceived as such, not merely by the eye, but also the vestibular influences and by the whole apparatus for equilibrium. Paul Cézanne, for instance, in some of his landscapes stresses the perpendicular line, thereby exaggerating the importance of gravitation. In other pictures he reverts to a compository form which already played an important part in the work of Leonardo da Vinci and of Nicholas Poussin. It is a tendency

Figure 7. Marcel Duchamp, *Nude Descending a Staircase.*

to use the triangle as a scheme for the organization of human hopes. However, Dominiko Theotokopoulous (El Greco) was much more radical in this respect. The faces of his figures are oblique, asymmetrical, and distorted. Pseudophysiological reasoning has been employed by some critics who surmised that the man was astigmatic and therefore distorted the world. This reasoning is preposterous, since one would have to see the canvas astigmatically also, and the picture drawn after nature therefore would not show any distortions. If El Greco was astigmatic in one eye he must have had a reason for choosing the so-called distortion.

Faces and objects which have been brought from the vertical into the oblique line indeed have another meaning. A new symmetry and asymmetry has to be invented and the pictures, less earth-bound than before, acquire a new spiritual meaning. Max Weber's picture *Invocation* is an example of this principle. The fight against gravity has become a religious struggle. The oblique line is in some way more appropriate to the ascetic than the perpendicular line.

Boccioni's *Unique Forms of Continuity in Space*, in the Museum of Modern Art (New York), is an attempt to catch movement in space with rather abstract forms. Modern art is fundamentally interested in problems of space, movement, and gravitation. In some pictures of Chagall, figures float in the air head down. The individual is no longer earth-bound. Objects and persons fly and float. The individual is liberated from the laws of gravitation. Our patients, too, seek escape from these laws. All human beings feel that they are too closely bound to the earth. It is one of the oldest dreams of humankind to get rid of this constraint.

In early childhood we all learn that we have a great enemy. This is the force that makes us fall down and hurt ourselves. By our standing upright gravitation is overcome. The vertical is a direction of fundamental importance. The vertical is not merely an optical experience but one's whole body participates in determining what it is. Such biologically important experiences inevitably affect painters and artists. When orientation is changed from a vertical to an inclined plane some measure of freedom from gravitation is gained. This can be seen in some pictures of Weber and Picasso. In various pictures of Cézanne which treat the motif of the bathers, the human body is seen on an inclined plane and no doubt the deep impression which is received from these pictures is due in part to the freedom from gravitaion which the artist has gained.

So art comes into close relation with the dreams of flying which belong to the deepest inheritance of humankind. Both the child and the artist want to fly. So does the primitive human. Human dreams, the day dreams of the child, the artist, and the primitive come first. Second comes the inventor, the engineer who translates these dreams into some sort of reality. Artists are forever experimenting with space, with gravity, with inclined and vertical lines. Superman and many of the figures in the comics deal with the same problem. Similarly, people who have lost contact with everyday life or who are confronted with difficult situations can no longer be satisfied with small conventional concepts. The value of our patients' pictures lies in the fact that they are the expression not of people who are satisfied but of human beings who strive anew. They have been thrown back to a more primitive world and now have to experiment and build up a new world all over again.

Art should be seen as one of the experimental and constructive drives of human life. Whenever new principles in art occur, whether it be surrealism, dadaism, or cubism, they will in some way be connected with the spiritual movements of the times. The fundamental problems of form which are of importance to the modern artist are also the problem of the primitive man, of the child, and of the mentally sick. In order to handle a new problem in the complex world of today, one has to go back and reduce the problem to its simplest, most primitive terms. Then one can determine its true significance. If one wants to know whether a new movement in art has a definite value one should go back to the art of the psychiatric patient and find out whether the patient tries to solve similar problems. If he does, then we may be sure that the new art tendency deals with fundamental experiences. The art of the patient and the creative artist will always be a disturbing element. In creative art one is forced to go back to primitive experiences and wage again the fight for the conquest of the world. In the art of the mentally ill is thus found the germ from which richer experiences can originate. The creative artist attempts the fulfillment of the deep urge to form and order which manifests itself also in the pictures of our patients.

OTHER APPROACHES TO REALITY

The drawings of almost all of our children indicate that even somewhat complicated proportions in the outer world are comparatively well perceived. It would be easy to relate any apparent distortions to the technical difficulties involved. It is at least probable that the emotional attitude of intense interest towards the human body is a factor in the perception of both the human form and the outer world.

Children in their drawings mostly refrain from distorting reality in such a far-reaching way as Gino Severini, for instance, does when he mixes the different parts of reality together so that they look like pieces of a jigsaw puzzle which are not brought into the proper order. In an artist like Severini, reality is not merely a structure consisting of units and wholes but is also one of parts. Obviously there is a great satisfaction in seeing those parts as such, with the knowledge that by renewed effort the jigsaw puzzle of reality can be put together again. Such principles indeed are to be found in free imagination and it is characteristic that in one of the pictures by Severini the life of a dancer appears in different sectors emanating from the eye. Such experimentation is not generally found in children. They cling more to what they can reach and to what can be expressed in comparatively primitive form. Only when there is a severe dissociation, as in schizophrenic children, may reality be seen in pieces or the inner relation of the body may be distorted completely.

On the whole, children also want to reach reality in their drawings. Nothing is so false to the child as the impressionistic way of drawing, if impressionism is considered as the basic theory that the world consists of single sensual impressions and that reality is built up of single impressions which are called sensations. In some way the impressionists believe implicitly in the theory of Condorcet, that at first there is nothing in the mind and that the sensations enter, one after another, until a picture of the world appears. Newer psychology shows conclusively that sensations are far from being primitive units of experience, but are rather products of a complicated process of abstraction.

THE EMERGENCE OF FORM PRINCIPLES

For children and adults, mentally balanced or unbalanced, art is a preliminary approach to reality. These persons try to master the primitive form principles of the circle, the wave and the straight line. They are interested in ellipses, rectangles, and loops. They want to explore symmetry and assymmetry, rhythm, repetition, and number. Furthermore, they want to approach the objects of nature, animate and inanimate. They are interested not only in hills and stones and rivers, but also in trees, flowers, animals, and human beings. The problem of form for them is closely related to that of color.

Forms extend in space. All of the problems mentioned are more or less specifically connected with problems of space. The fundamental problem of which way the primitive form principles and primitive color principles are integrated into more complicated forms, especially animate forms, appears in hundreds and hundreds of variations. In the transition from primitive to developed forms the whole cycle of human experience is gone through and all the contents of human life make their appearance. All the solutions given by art either in the normal or abnormal individual are preliminary. The lack of definiteness of final action is characteristic for art as is also the fact that one level reached may be given up again for renewed play with primitive forms and experiences.

It is the great merit of modern art that it has taken up the spirit of free experimentation which has been far too long submerged. The final aim of art is the preparation for a definite approach to reality. But to find this approach one often has to give up the preliminary gain, the crystallization of form which appears to be definite. In order to make any approach really progressive one has to regress from time to time and go back to the basic primitive approach. This is the deepest meaning of impressionism, futurism, cubism, constructivism, dadaism, and surrealism.

The abnormal child and the abnormal artist have an easier access to the primitive forms. Also they are often driven by their pathology back to the primitive experience (regression) and then strive more or less earnestly to regain full reality. There is a continuous striving to reach from the primitive experience to the well-developed one and no regression is definite even in the psychotic case. There is always the allure of reality. This is a dynamic process. The art of disturbed children and the psychotic adult brings phases of this gigantic struggle more clearly into evidence. Therefore they represent the same basic human qualities which appear in every fact of art production and in its history. The dynamic approach to reality is an interplay between regression and progression in which the creative forces finally prevail. Since these creative forces are biologically determined by the urge to reality, they conquer reality.

Chapter 18

VITA OF PAUL SCHILDER[1]

Paul Schilder, born February 15, 1886, a son of Bertha Fuerth and Ferdinand Schilder, became interested in philosophical problems at the early age of thirteen. His first inspiration came from the materialist Buechner's *Draft und Stoff* (*Energy and Matter*). From this he progressed slowly to Schopenhauer, Nietzsche, and Kant. He contemplated studying classical philology and philosophy, but finally chose medicine because he wanted to be in closer relation to human beings. He always retained his interest in philosophical problems and the relation of human beings to the world, and through psychiatry he felt he might help approach the fundamentals of human life.

The choice of medicine as a profession was also partially due to the wish of his mother. She had always given him a feeling of security and self-confidence which never left him, even in the most difficult circumstances. He still believes in the world and has a basically op-timistic outlook. His early memories point to some sort of rebellion against his father, and he has never bowed to authority willingly. Nevertheless he still recalls with admiration and gratitude his teachers at the University of Vienna, among whom the philosopher Laurenz Mueller and the physiologist Sigmund Exner remain outstanding.

He believed in and dreamed of the use of experiments in psychology and psychopathology. As a student he worked in the laboratory of Exner. He got his training in pathology with

[1]Reprinted from The *Journal of Criminal Psychopathology (216).*

Weichselbaum, and especially with Froheim. During the last two years of his medical studies his interest in pathology was in the foreground. He also worked in the laboratory of Obersteiner, but this period was less fruitful. He attended Freud's lectures occasionally at this time, but was refractory to his ideas. His first close contact with psychiatry came after his graduation from Halle an der Saale, under Gabriel Anton, who had been a favorite pupil of Meynert. Anton, who had a fascinating personality, showed a deep understanding of the problems of aphasia and agnosia, and imparted his enthusiasm to his assistants. Meynert, although basically a brain anatomist, had had astonishing glimpses into the function of the brain, and had made a grandiose attempt to understand psychiatry from the point of view of brain function. The idea of regression, for instance, can be found in Meynert's writings. In Halle the teachings of Wernicke were still dominant. Some of Wernike's pupils were still there, and the books of Kleist and Liepmann circulated freely. Wernicke, who had based his system of psychiatry on brain pathology, had come to the fundamental insight that there were three basic spheres of experience: the auto-,somato-,and allopsyche. He brought these psychological systems into connections with specific brain mechanisms.

However, these basic insights of Wernicke needed a deeper psychological study. This followed in Schilder's *Selbstbewusstsein und Persönlichkeitsbewusstein* (*Consciousness of One's Self and One's Personality*,) in which the problem of depersonalization was considered from many different angles. In this, Husserl's phenomenology offered invaluable help. Every unprejudiced approach showed that many psychological forces acted without the definite knowledge of the individual. The central idea in this book was that the individual cannot be happy unless he directs himself towards the outer world and displays his various tendencies in experience.

Through this study Schilder was led to a closer approach to Freudian ideas. A study on schizophrenia served to further increase his belief in the validity of Freudian symbolism. During this time he continued his studies in pathology. These led to his classical description of encephalitis periaxialis diffusa. With Neuman and Krueger, pupils of Wundt, he studied experimental and primitive psychology. In his book *Wahn und Erkenntnis* (*Delusion and Knowledge*), he studied the basic similarities between the thought of primitives and schizophrenics, but he remained keenly aware of the fundamental differences in the social settings of the schizophrenic and the primitive.

He volunteered in the War of 1914-1918, spending these years in part at the front and in part in service at base hospitals. During the war years he studied philosophy intensively, sometimes under heavy gunfire. During this intense period he clarified two fundamental trends of thought: first, that the laws of the psyche and the laws of the organism are identical, i.e., that ideas, thoughts, and imagination can be studied with methods similar to those used in the study of perception; second, that this biological process is a process of development which is clearly reflected in the development of each single thought, i.e., that thoughts develop from primitive stages through continuous contact with the motives of experience, passing from a protozoanlike stage to more and more complicated organic forms. In the process of this development the different parts of reality come into focus. Individuals strive towards the world, and through a constructive process arrive at configurations in perception and action. This leads not only to increased insight into the structure of the world, but also to a more satisfactory experience in the unified personality.

Following the war these ideas were deepened and expanded. Schilder was able to work under rather favorable circumstances in the clinic of Wagner von Jauregg. Von Jauregg was an individual with great strength of character, and with unlimited patience for the individual patient for whom he showed a deep sympathy. Although he did not believe in psychoanalysis he permitted psychoanalytic work to be done in his clinic. Although the brilliant Poetzel tried early to combine psychoanalysis and brain pathology, the chief orientation of the clinic was towards the somatic therapies, and the chief interest at that time was in the malarial therapy of general paresis. Interesting biological and physiological problems presented themselves to everyone in the clinic and Schilder participated fully in this part of the work.

In addition, this period brought Schilder into personal contact with Freud, and to closer association with the psychoanalytic society. No unbiased observer could afford to neglect the data which Freud had brought forward concerning human drives and structure of the psychic apparatus. The fundamentals of dream interpretation and of the libido theory seemed to be beyond doubt, and indeed have proved to be of lasting value for the understanding of the organism. However, Schilder differed in one fundamental respect with the tenets of psychoanalysis, in that he could never accept its regressive character. To him it seemed senseless to believe that life should intend merely to return to prior stages of satisfaction and to rest.

Similarly, he was never able to accept Freud's ideas concerning the death instinct. He became more and more convinced that life is not directed towards the past, but rather towards the future; that psychological processes are directed towards the real world in a process of continuous trial and error. This constructive process leads to comparatively stabilized configurations which represent not only the possibilities for knowledge but also for action.

These psychoanalytical insights helped Schilder in determining the single steps in this constructive process. Psychoanalysis seemed to offer a fundamental approach to psychiatric problems in general. He collected a great amount of data pointing toward such a constructive psychology. He perceived this constructive process particularly clearly in the building up of the experience of one's own body, the body image. This concept was based on Wernicke's idea of the somatopsyche and on Head's ideas on the postural model of the body. Studies on the body image, which he started in 1923, have occupied Schilder up to the present time. Studies on extrapyramidal motility, on the vestibular apparatus and on the postural and righting reflexes have made possible concepts which did not neglect the motor part of experience.

Obviously Schilder's interests did not coincide with those of the psychoanalytic group. He remained un-analyzed. Although his relations to Freud were never particularly close there were no lasting conflicts between the two. Later on, in America, he left the psychoanalytic society, in part because of the different direction of his interests, in part because of some minor local conficts. However, Schilder considers himself a psychoanalyst in the true sense of the word, feeling that he has kept the heritage of Freud better than many of those who were closer to him personally and who followed, at least for a while, his words more or less mechanically.

For Schilder the value of a constructive psychology lies in its approach to the deep problems of science, physics, chemistry, and mathematics. Any problem in physics, for instance, is based on the fundamentals of human experience, which properly belong in the realm of psychoanalytic and constructive psychology.

Schilder's contact with Adolf Meyer, who brought him to this country, gave him a deeper approach to the social problems of psychiatry. He found that psychiatry in America was in closer contact with social realities than psychiatry in Europe. Coming to Bellevue Hospital in 1930 he found himself confronted with many new practical problems. The problems of constructive-psychology in its relation to gestalt psychology took a more definite form. He planned to write a treatise on psychology in several volumes to embrace first the body image; second, perception and thought; third, goals and desires; and fourth, psychotherapy. Of these, the first and fourth volumes have already been published. The other two have not yet been published due to extrinsic circumstances. In addition he has planned further volumes on art and sociology from this general point of view.

Since Schilder believes that theory must lead to action, he has worked out methods of group psychotherapy. In addition, the problem of ideologies has loomed as a problem of great importance without which human life cannot be understood.

A great part of this work has been done in close conjunction with Lauretta Bender, his wife. This is particularly true of his work with children. Whereas Schilder has been previously skeptical of the possibility of understanding children and had felt that there was a danger of projecting insights gained with adults into children, he now feels that the principles of constructive psychology can help in a deeper understanding of the child. The behavior of the child can only be understood as a continuous process of trial and error, which leads to construction and configuration as a basis for action. He feels that behavior difficulties and neuroses are interruptions of this constructive psychological process. Only when an individual strives in his environment and in the world will he have full emotional experiences and a full life as a personality. An individual is truly alive as long as he errs and tries. Human beings drive into the future by trial and error, and thereby find their happiness. Schilder finds the final proof for the irresistible drive into the future in his two sons, Michael, aged three, and Peter, aged two.

Part VI

PERSPECTIVES ON PSYCHOANALYTIC CONCEPTS

Chapter 19

INTROJECTION AND PROJECTIVE IDENTIFICATION[1]

John Frosch, M.D.

INTRODUCTION

The concepts, Identification, Introjection, and Projective Identification require more extensive discussion as to their role in psychic processes. Several authors have pointed to inconsistencies in the use of the term introjection and identification and have attempted to delineate similarities and differences.[82, 127, 69, 183] The confusion is not clarified by the definitions in the Psychoanalytic Glossary.[169]

IDENTIFICATION: — An automatic, unconscious mental process whereby an individual becomes like another person in one or several aspects. It is a natural accompaniment of maturation and mental development and aids in the learning process (including the learning of speech and language), as well as in the acquisition of interests, ideals, mannerisms, etc. An individual's adaptive and defensive reaction patterns are often attributable to indentification with either loved and admired persons, or feared ones. By means of identification with a needed person an individual can often provide for himself the satisfaction of the needs desired from that person. Separation from a loved person becomes more tolerable as a result of identification with him. For identification to oc-

---

[1]Abstracted from *The Psychotic Process*, 1983, Int. U. Press, New York.

cur, sufficient psychic development must have taken place for the individual to distinguish himself from others in his environment. Such differentiation of self and object representations normally occurs in early childhood.[169]

INTROJECTION: — Originally used synonymously with the term identification. Recently it has been differentiated from identification and employed in two different contexts. 1) The assimilation of the object-representation into the self-representation whenever the boundaries between the self and object representations are indistinct. The individual then becomes confused in regard to his separateness and even his identity. 2) The child's taking into himself as a psychic phenomenon the object's (usually parent's) demands as if they were his own, so that he reacts in the same way whether or not the object is present. The child does not copy the object as he would if he identified with it. The regulating, forbidding, and rewarding aspects of the superego are formed by the introjection of parental directions, admonitions and rewards.[169]

INCORPORATION: — A special form of introjection, a taking into the mind of the attributes of another person, which follows the model of the bodily function of oral ingestion and swallowing. It is the primary mechanism in identification (q.v.), the process whereby change in individuality is accomplished through becoming like someone (something) else. Identification accomplished via incorporation implies change by fantasied oral consumption of an object (person), as indicated by cannibalistic wishes in dreams and associations. The mechanism is encountered in psychoses, impulse disorders, severe oral characters, and in less neurotic individuals during states of severe regression in analysis. Although it has some import for psychological understanding (being one way of mentally assimilating interpretations), it is a hazardous basis for mental stability since such incorporative identificatory mechanisms may malfunction or break down easily.[169]

It is clear that such a definition suffers from methodological inaccuracy and considerable overlap. It might be simpler to use the term incorporation in its generic sense, i.e., to include something into the self or the self representation, and then to describe the processes by which this is accomplished, i.e. oral incorporation, etc., rather than to assume that incorporation is always oral. Fenichel (1931) views incorporation as taking place in many modes—anal, epidermal, respiratory, ocular, etc.

CONTRIBUTORY CONCEPTS

Fuchs[82] uses the term introjection in the sense of an instinctive incorporation into the mind and views it as a real "eating up." He restricts the term to this meaning and indicates that this is a process resulting in identification. Schilder (1946) speaks of identification as a form of introjection where the other person becomes incorporated into one's personality. According to Knight[125] introjection is defined as an unconscious inclusion of an object or part of an object into the ego of the subject. It involves previous projections onto the object of the subject's own unconscious tendencies. He defines projection in the more standard dynamic and defense terms whereby the subject attributes his own unacceptable tendencies to an object and then perceives them as tendencies possessed by the object.

Defining it as such he does not take cognizance of the kind of projective process which is coeval with self-non-self dedifferentiation as described for instance by Katan,[112] Tausk[237] and others. Knight differentiates identification from introjection by indicating that identification is a resultant phenomenon, a fact, which may eventuate from many processes. The examples he gives range from the generic use of the term identification to its unconscious role in many situations.

He states his position thus: " ...identification is not a mechanism and is not synonymous introjection. Identification is an accomplished fact, not an act, and may result from several different mechanisms acting separately or together. It may occur by displacement or substitution (with possible projection and introjection also) when we identify one object with another object (misidentification); it may occur mainly by projection as in the case of "altruistic surrender;" it may result mainly from introjection; but in most instances, perhaps, complex interaction of both projection and introjection will have operated to produce the identification.[127] It is clear that Knight views introjection as one of the preliminary steps to identification. Without using the term he describes projective-introjection as playing a role in many processes resulting in identification, e.i., in "altruistic surrender," falling in love, and transference patterns.

Rapaport[172] using the development of object relations as a frame of reference, says

> when reality obliges him to give up these objects, they are not given up intrapsychically: in fact, their intrapsychic existence only then really begins, since their memory-trace instead of their perception is then drive-cathected. This process is conceptualized as introjection. Such introjected objects constitute major sub-organizations within the developing memory-organization . . .These organizations which arise in the ego in the wake of an introjection are conceptualized as identification...On the one hand, these introjected objects become integrated, lose their dependence, and give rise to a homogeneous ego, whose strength is greatly dependent on the completeness of their integration;...Introjection and identification thus enable us to take over, as our own, the feelings and reactions of other people, and later their thoughts also, both those directed specifically towards us and those more general.[172]

Schafer[183] utilizing the general concept of internalization as a frame of reference distinguishes between introjection and identification which are forms of internalization.

> ...introjection should be used to refer to one kind of internalization only, namely, the processes whereby object representations are constituted as introjects or are changed into them... Identification refers to modifying the subjective self or behavior, or both, in order to increase one's resemblance to an object taken as a model; it does not refer, as introjection does, to carrying on certain purely internal relations with an object represented as such (the introject).[183]

There are apparently varying viewpoints regarding the relationship between these two processes as for instance whether introjection has to precede identification. Sandler[182] leans in the direction of viewing introjection as a necessary step on the way to identification. He claims that during regression there may be a decomposition of identification into introjects; however, in psychosis some introjects established early in life have never evolved into identifications. Schaefer's position is expressed as follows:

> Identification and introjection (in the sense of establishing introjects) must be recognized as being two distinct types of internalization. Not all introjects are turned into identifications; identifications may be built out of introjects and so they may regressively decompose into introjects too, but it is not clear that all identifications must be built this way. And the term introjection should be used neither as a synonym for identification or internalization nor as the basic mechanism of identification or internalization.[183]

The confusion in the terms incorporation, introjection, identification, derives to some extent historically and to a larger extent is a result of using different frames of reference, i.e., the processes, from that which eventuates from these processes, i.e., the phenomena or facts.[82, 127, 183] To some extent this developed historically from the attempts to integrate later knowledge by using the language and concepts more in keeping with earlier knowledge. An example is the use of the term and concept incorporation as shown above.

DIFFERENTIATION BETWEEN IDENTIFICATION AND INTROJECTION

I would tend to view all of these processes, incorporation, introjection, identification as part of an overall process, i.e., internalization. This view as was indicated is shared by Schaefer.[183] The term internalization is then applied to the overall process of setting up within ourselves of psychic structures with are derived from an interplay with external sources. Viewed more accurately it is a shift from object representation to inclusion in self representation. Via this process, introjections (or introjects) are created which may be almost anything which derives from the object representation, which in a sense has been abandoned or has become lost and where retention is essential for the organism.

Such introjects may be set up in the psyche in relatively unchanged form in the earlier stages and during such a stage may under certain conditions be ejected or extrajected[243] or projected. Or such situations may persist into later life representing a potential for extrajection, more often as in psychosis. In the course of normal development and maturation, and perhaps with other introjects they become integrated into a homogeneous aspect of the psyche losing so to speak their independent and autonomous operations, and, as such, not ultimately identifiable in their orignial form. It is then that one may speak of identification, which by virtue of its integrated state can under ordinary circumstances no longer be ejected, certainly not in any way resembling its original form. The counterpart to introjection may be projection or extrajection.[243]

We appear to have no equivalent or counterpart in our psychoanalytic language for identification. I have never heard the term to disidentify, to imply this process, and perhaps this is for good reason in light of this discussion. The introject is still to some extent isolated from the rest of the ego and somewhat alien. In the true introject there is still some separation of the introject from the core self. There is, especially in the psychotic, some awareness of distance. In melancholia and in schizophrenia this is not clearly delineated because of some degree of fusion of self and introject. But the latter is still not true identification. Stability of the ego requires for that which is incorporated and introjected to become eventually an integral part of the ego, and for it to be integrated into it in a harmonious fashion. Kernberg[115] speaks of "non metabolized" early pathological internalized object relations. This, in a sense, is equivalent to my own concept in differentiating an introject from a true identification.

I have in some very concrete way analogized the introject to the food bolus which has as yet not been digested or metabolized and can be regurgitated. The regurgitate still has some recognizable feature identifying that which was taken in. So it is with psychic introjects. These can remain in the psyche but are perceived as such or they may be ejected in the form of persecuting delusions, influencing machines, etc., not too unlike their original source.

Once the bolus is digested and absorbed from the intestinal tract, it enters the blood stream and undergoes metabolism. Ultimately it becomes part of the body chemistry and structure. The external sources from which these are derived are no longer recognizable. The substance becomes part of the warp and woof of the body structure, albeit analysis may enable us to reconstruct the sources. So I believe with identification we may reconstruct that with which the organism has identified and from which it has in a sense evolved. But true identification is homogenous with the body psyche. Such an analogy has many defects but in a crude way it serves as a frame of reference to understand these often confused concepts.

INTROJECTED OBJECTS

Rapaport,[173] Isaacs,[104] Bender[21, 25] and others view the persistence of introjected objects in certain forms in childhood as almost pathognomic for schizophrenia. Bender in her discussion of internalization of fantasy objects refer in detail to a child reported by Rapaport (1944) who had many introjected objects. Both these authors laid great stress on the fact that all children had introjected objects in the course of development, a view shared with Susan Isaacs. " ...we have shown that fantasying in the child is part of normal development. Fantasied companions compensate for deficiencies in the child's emotional experiences and is on of the constructive factors in personality formation. Hallucinations, too, often serve a similar function."[25]

A whole spectrum of clinical cases ranging from psychoneurotic to schizophrenics are described, but it was maintained that pathology was determined by the persistence of those introjects into adulthood as well as by their quality. " ...there was a qualititive difference in the type of introjected object as the clinical picture changed. As we turned from the psychoses and approached the neuroses we found instead of the bizarre, primitive, and unrealistic fantasy objects of the former, fantasy objects which were more conditioned by actual experiences and which were more related to the external parents."[25]

I saw a patient who had developed extensive delusions of persecution. Among the many delusions he had was that there existed within him a "power" which had a form and which controlled his behavior both negatively and positively. "I have a power that is an entity within me. He doesn't live on food. Like a mosquito who takes blood, he lives on my body. Maybe he lives on the waste of my body." He had difficulty in locating this "entity" in his body. At first he located it somewhere in his abdomen. He unquestionably gave a shape and form to this object. "Sometimes it's shaped like an orange, sometimes like a Russian potato, like a head, like a tumor, a cancer. One time I began to think maybe it was my heart."

"He is able to talk very loud." (Could I hear him?) "If he talks in a low tone there is a way to use a microphone, to put it on a part of my body and if some one puts an earphone to his ear he could listen to what he says." The discreteness of this introject was further emphasized when I asked the patient, "Does anyone else hear him?" The patient responded, "I'm trying to find that out. Everything sounds crazy but sometimes he acts like a third person. When I'm talking to someone else, he talks in a certain way and if I'm not look-ing at the person he makes me believe that this person talks it." The power in his body was in league with his persecutors. "They are able to persecute me and have a leeway and freedom with me because of the person that I have within me. He lets them do what they want. I'm a very nice character and a lovely human being and maybe they would like to fall in love with me."

This patient had described humiliating childhood experiences of a sexual nature at the hands of an earlier significant figure, essentially an older brother. But as his delusional system unfolded there subsequent-ly entered into the picture older figures such as teachers who also sub-jected him to what he felt were humiliating experiences. This system expanded to include many other figures. But behind all these torturers there lurked the malevolent figure of his seducer brother whom he claims made a murderous attempt on his life at the age of eighteen. This all became internalized as the introject described above who tor-tured him but with mixed reactions.

"It looks on the outside that I should have a lot of relaxation, leisure and easy-going. As a matter of fact he keeps me tense, high-strung, exasperated, and as the saying goes, *Setz und giess kalte wasser*[2] He slays me and then he says I love you. I say to him how can you do this to me, downtrod me to the verge of collapse and then you say you love me. He aggravates me, tortures me, belittles me, makes me a nothing. At the end when he gets me down, he says he loves me."

The patient describes this ambivalence in his previous torturers. Referring to his teachers, he described a good teacher and a bad teacher. The good teacher loved him and praised him, made him feel very proud, the other one criticized and humiliated him in front of others.

"I had two instructors whose relation to me were in direct op-position to one another. Whereas the first teacher always pointed me out to the parents of the other pupils as an exceptional good student, the second teacher, in total contrast, made my life so miserable that I prayed to be dismissed by the school but which tragically for me was never realized." The mixed feelings were felt about his main tor-turer, at present the introjected object, "the power," "the entity."

It is not so difficult to imagine who all the figures represented, who were ultimately crystallized into this "entity." Further explora-

---

[2] This is a Yiddish expression relating to the masseur in a turkisł bath who first smites the client forcefully with a broomlike brush with hot soap and water and then pours cold water over him to soothe him. The process may then be repeated any number of times.

tion led these back to the father about whom he expressed many feelings of ambivalence. There was an ongoing struggle in this man between his love and hostility toward the love object: one which ultimately was incorporated, and internalized in the form of a concrete and discrete introject. Parenthetically I might observe that there were many indications suggesting that he himself was the introject residing in his body. An eleven year-old child described by Rapaport[169] had many introjected objects. One day after ripping apart a small rag doll and removing the stuffing which to him represented various fantasy objects, he attempted to climb into it himself, feet first. Although the author does not explain the implication of introjected objects for womb fantasies this is suggested in some patients I have observed.

PROJECTIVE IDENTIFICATION

It is appropriate at this time to select for more detailed discussion the concept projective-identification which after being suggested by Melanie Klein[126] has been through the years a subject of controversy and, above all, confusion.

I will at this point summarize the views of Klein[126] and her followers on projective identification, a process which she conceives as fundamental to the development of object relations. It should be emphasized that she sees projective-identification as a process present at all stages of early psychic development and it is its vicissitudes that result in the one or the other clinical condition seen subsequently. According to her, "projection, as we know from Freud, originates from the deflection of the Death Instinct outwards and in my view helps the ego in overcoming anxiety by ridding it of danger and badness." As such, self-destruction is avoided. This process is carried out thus:" . . . libidinal and aggressive impulses and phantasies from other sources come to the fore and bring about a confluence of oral, urethral, and anal libidinal and aggressive desires"[126]. She goes on to say, "Much of the hatred against parts of the self is now directed towards the mother. This leads to a particular kind of identification which establishes the prototype of an aggressive object relation. Also, since the projection derives from the infant's impulse to harm or to control the mother, he feels her to be a persecutor. In psychotic disorders this identification of an object with the hated parts of the self contributes to the intensity of the hatred directed against other people."

It is to this process that Klein applies the term projective-identification. A portion of that which is projected therefore still remains, contributing to the infantile superego to which is also added the previously externalized destructive forces via introjection. The back and forth movements of these forces bring in their wake extremes of destructiveness expressed directly externally by the subject as well as retaliative destructive attempts by the object. As Klein says, ". . .the projection of a predominantly hostile inner world which is ruled by persecutory fears leads to the introjection—a taking back—of a hostile external world. Conversely, the introjection of a distorted and hostile external world reinforces the projection of a hostile inner world."[103]. However, not only the bad parts of the self are expelled and projected but equally the good parts of the self which are also introjected.

Rosenfeld[177] summarizes Klein's views as follows: " 'Projective identification' relates first of all to a splitting process of the early ego where either good or bad parts of the self are split off from the ego and are as a further step projected in love or hatred into external objects which leads to fusion and identification of the projected parts of the self with the external objects. There are important paranoid anxieties related to these processes as the objects filled with aggressive parts of the self become persecuting and are experienced by the patient as threatening to retaliate by forcing themselves, and the bad parts of the self which they contain, back again into the ego.' " Melanie Klein gives the name 'projective identification' both to the processes of ego splitting and the 'narcissistic' object relations created by the projection of parts of the self into objects.[126,p.1,2]

Bion[91] describes the mechanism of projective-identification as follows:

> . . . parts of the ego are projected into the object, causing this object to be experienced as controlled by the projected parts and imbued with their qualities. This mechanism, active from the beginning of life, may have various functions: of relieving the ego of bad parts; of preserving good parts by protecting them from a bad internal world; of attacking and destroying the object; etc. One of the consequences of this process is that by projecting the bad parts (including fantasies and bad feelings) into a good breast (an understanding object), the infant will be able—insofar as his development allows—to reintroject the same parts in

a more tolerable form, once they have been modified by the thought (reverie) of the object. . . .he describes a form of pathological projective identification, which takes place in certain psychotic illnesses or which is used by the psychotic personality where there is a predominance of envy and greed. In this case, the splitting of parts of the ego is so severe that it results in a multiplicity of minute fragments which are violently projected into the object. These fragments, which are expelled by pathological projective identification, create a reality populated by bizarre objects and which becomes increasingly painful and persecuting. [91]

Bion adds another component to the projective-identification mechanism: "An evacuation of the bad breast into the real external breast takes place through a realistic projective identification. The mother, with her capacity for reverie, transforms the unplesant sensations linked to the 'bad breast' and provides relief for the infant who then reintrojects the unmitigated and modified emotional experience, i.e., reintrojects an alpha-function, a nonsensual aspect of the mother's love."[35,p.57]. He refers to this as the container-contained model. That which is projected is contained by the object, the container, it is modified, made less dangerous and therefore when reintrojected by the subject because it is less dangerous it is able to be mastered more easily. There have been many subsequent contributions in this area, some highly receptive and others equally critical. To some it is a process applicable to the development of all object relations, to others it is highly restrictive, to psychotic manifestations only. Pacheco[156] for instance assumes that all patients have what he calls a free area, a neurotic area. It is in the latter two that projective identification plays a role but with varying degree. But since all patients have these areas it follows that projective identification plays a role in all such patients. Ogden's[154] use of the concept is quite broad. He views it as a type of defense, a mode of communication, a primitive form of object relations, as well as a pathway for psychological change.

Schilder, although not directly using the term projective-identification nonetheless describes many manifestations which appear to represent aspects of this phenomenon. He says, "For the paranoiac, the dismembered object is basically another multiplicity of persecutors, since very piece turns a persecutor. The object is reduced to many dangerous pieces, which are only appreciated as belonging to the inside of the body, like feces. The persecutors are due to the introjection of partial object.[222,p.58,59]

He describes a patient who had impulses to tear others to pieces. This was also associated with herself falling to pieces. Schilder points out, "It is however remarkable that this sadism directed against others also affects her own body. She does not feel a tendency to hurt herself, but she feels her body falling to pieces. . . . The patient is dismembered under the influence of her own sadistic tendencies against the outside world, and she projects herself into the outside world."[222,p.164] To me this sounds like what Melanie Klein would refer to as projective identification. The impulses are pushed onto others and then felt within the self.

Schilder even broadens the concept in describing the fear of losing parts of the body, pointing out that one never loses the parts. "What has once been part of the body does not lose this quality completely. The bowel movement also separates the feces only physically from the body, psychologically they remain a part of ourselves. We are dealing with a spreading of the body image into the world. . . . Fingernails, everything which comes out of the mouth and nose, hair which has been cut off, always remain in some psychological relation to the body. The organization of the body-image is a very flexible one".(p.188) I wonder whether this is a variant, in a nonpsychotic sense, of self-non-self dedifferentiation. There is no separateness. As such, could this be the soil in which projective-identification develops?

The concept of skybalum as the persecutor[239, 235] has much about it suggestive of projective-identification. This is especially so if one views it within the context of that which is a part of you, or is in your body, never gets lost and still remains part of you, even if expelled from your body. The hardened painful fecal mass, to which the patient reacts by projecting it onto an external persecutor, still remains part of oneself and as such the persecutor is a part of one's self—a bad self. Even if the mass is expelled it is still not lost but returns in the form of the anal persecutor, who will attack, even at times in the very area from which it came. As such, the process may be viewed as a special aspect of projective-identification.

Before proceeding further with the discussion of projective identification as a maneuver in the psychotic process, I should like to make some comments about the terms used. It appears to me that the term projection used here refers to that stage in psychic development in which self-non-self differentiation is quite unclear and what exists internally and externally is not clearly defined. As such it is similar to what Katan[112] refers to as psychotic projection, yet this is not entirely so, as will be discussed presently. I do however wish to comment on the use of the word identification in this process. As I have noted above we are in this process speaking of introjections, and even Klein repeatedly uses this term. In such instances, as I indicated, these introjects are not metabolized into the psychic structures as an integral part, as is true identification, but remain more or less discrete and can be externalized again as is the case in psychotic process. I therefore feel that if we are going to accept Klein's concept at all it is more strictly speaking projective-introjection.

SELF-NON-SELF DEDIFFERENTIATION

I should like to return to the point mentioned above, namely, the state of self-non-self dedifferentiation which exists coeval with projective-introjection, as I prefer to call it. There is some question whether this state of total fusion between self and object is the psychic state which exists for projective-introjection to take place. Jacobson[105] discussing psychotic identification speaks of the diffusion of boundaries between self and object and the resultant fusion between the two. She views this as the state which facilitates primitive introjective or projective identifications evolving out of fantasies of incorporation, devouring, invading, or being devoured by the object. Jacobson sees the projective identification of the adult psychotic as the attempt to split off and project into a suitable external object those parts of the self which unacceptable to the adult ego: The external object would then represent the patient's "bad self."

Rosenfeld[177] feels that "Projective identification which includes ego splitting and projection of good and bad parts of the self into external objects is not identical with symbiosis. For projective identification to take place some temporary differentiation of 'me' and 'not me' is essential. Symbiosis, however, is used by Mahler to describe a state of undifferentiation, of fusion with the mother, in which the 'I' is not yet differentiated from the 'not I.' " It is clear that Rosenfeld feels that for projective introjection to take place some degree of differentiation is necessary. Yet Rosenfeld himself uses the concept of fusion and projective identification interchangeably. But he feels that it is not only excessive projective identification which obliterates differentiation of self and object. On the other hand, in 1964 he says, "Identification is an important factor in narcissistic object relations. It may take place by introjection or by projection. When the object is omnipotently incorporated, the self becomes so identified with the incorporated object that all separate identity or any boundary between self and object is denied. In projective identification parts of the self omnipotently enter an object, for example the mother, to take over certain qualities which would be experienced as desirable, and therefore claim to be the object or part-object. Identification by introjection and projection usually occur simultaneously. In narcissistic object relations defenses against any recognition of separateness between self and object play a predominant part. Awareness of separation would lead to feelings of dependence on an object and therefore to anxiety.''[176,p.170-171].

Freeman[69] in general uses loss of self-non-self differentiation as his frame of reference. As a result he views introjection, projection and identification as used defensively in the nonpsychotic. Introjection and projection as defense, implies the presence of a boundary. Introjection and projection can only occur in the presence of some degree of ego functioning. By contrast, in psychosis the ego which initiates defenses is defective; projection and introjection are really reflective of phenomena during this state of loss of ego boundaries and self-non-self dedifferentiation. Projective identification as a clinical phenomenon to him is really nothing more than lack of self-non-self differentiation.

Schilder[222] although not specifically discussing projective-identification as such, nonetheless implies its role in the paranoiac and in schizophrenics within the context of self-non-self dedifferentiation. It is this state that facilitates the flux back and forth between projection and introjection.

To underline the self-non-self dedifferentiation in the projective-introjective process Kernberg (1975) says

> . . .projective identification is characterized by the lack of differentiation between self and object in that particular area, by continuing to experience the impulse as well as the fear of that impulse while the projection is active, and by the need to control the external object''(p.31).

He continues:

> . . .projective identification may be considered an early form of the mechanism of projection. In terms of structural aspects of the ego, projective identification dif-

fers from projection in that the impulse projected onto an external object does not appear as something alien and distant from the ego because the connection of the self with that projected impulse still continues, and thus the self "empathizes" with the object. The anxiety which provoked the projection of the impulse onto an object in the first place, now becomes fear of that object, accompanied by the need to control the object in order to prevent it from attacking the self when under the influence of that impulse. A consequence of parallel development of the operation of the mechanism of projective identification is the blurring of the limits between the self and the object (a loss of ego boundaries), since part of the projected impulse is still recognized within the ego, and thus self and object fuse in a rather chaotic way.[115,p.56]

Meissner[151] feels that the psychic state of self-non-self dedifferentiation underlies projective-introjection. As such it is a concept applicable only to psychosis. In his discussion of projective-introjection I think Meissner may be troubled by what is problematic to many regarding Klein's concepts. The infantile state during which this phenomenon exists is coeval with self-non-self dedifferentiation. This stage is viewed by Klein as psychosis, or at least alluded to with psychosis language, i.e., the paranoid-schizoid position. This state, if it appears in adulthood, either by regression or fixation, may then appropriately be viewed as psychotic. Even Klein views only excessive projective-introjection as subsequently pathological, leading to psychosis. It is this that leads to a strong confusion between the self and the object, which comes to stand for the self. In this sense she views projective-introjection as leading to self-non-self dedifferentiation, rather than the latter being the psychic state in which projective-introjection develops.

IMPACT UPON THE OBJECT

Floating around in many of the discussions on projective-introjection, is the question of the impact upon the object onto whom the projection takes place. The opinions vary considerably. There are those who view projective-introjection as a fantasy in the subject. The interaction between projective-introjection takes place between the self-representation and the object representation in the internal

psyche of the subject. Meissner[151] emphasizes that what we are dealing with in projective-introjection are fantasies. What derives from
this is an instinctual source of fantasies, which are the substance of
psychosis rather than real object relations interplay. "Consequently
the Kleinian discussion of object relation is cast, not in the language
of real relationship, but rather in the instinctively derived language
of fantasies about objects and their relation to the subject.[151,p.48]

Ogden[157] on the other hand maintains the position that the object projected on, experiences pressure to think, feel, and act congruent with the projection. This then is metabolized in the object,
processed and reinternalized by the projector. In this sense Ogden
views projective-introjection as a mode of communication by making
the other person feel what one is feeling as well as its being a transitional form of object relations. Yet Ogden is not quite consistent
since he defines projective-introjection "as a group of fantasies and
accompanying object relations having to do with the ridding of the
self of unwanted aspects of the self; the depositing of those unwanted
'parts' into another person, and finally, with the recovery of a
modified version of what was extended." It is not quite clear from
this what impact all of this has on the object.

Searles [228] leaves no ambiguity on this subject. He unquestionably belongs to those who feel that the projectee must have a feeling of participation. As the projective-introjection is played out in
therapy the therapist must feel involved in the process. This of course
is not without implications for therapy. The extent to which the
therapist not only accepts and "contains" that which has been projected, and the extent to which he literally feels and experiences this
projection, is not without import. If this is the case this experience
becomes very much a part of the therapeutic process and is even
essential as part of a feeling of participation with the patient in
therapy.

It is not clear what kind of patients Ogden was dealing with.
Searles is obviously dealing with grossly psychotic patients. I
somehow have the impression that Ogden views this as a
phenomenon in all analyses. The view that severe regressive states in
which fragmentation, as well as phenomena akin to projective-
identification, takes place occur in all analysis was expressed by
several participants in a panel on severe regressive states occurring
during analysis.[242, 80, 81]

As I see it, in the psychotic, the whole process is experienced
both internally and externally, so that ultimately real external objects
may become involved, in that the patient reacts to the external object

as literally possessing that which he has projected and his behavior toward that object is thereby influenced accordingly. This behavior may instigate behavior and reactions on the part of the object, which may communicate to the patient the validity of his beliefs that that which he has projected exists in the object. It is this, when it transpires in therapy between the patient and the therapist, that lends itself to the therapist becoming a sort of transitional object, helping the patient deal with the bad part of himself. (I will at some future time deal with the subject of the therapist as transitional object in the treatment of psychotic character disorders.)

CLINICAL DATA

I would like to raise some questions about the overall applicability of the concept of projective-identification. Its view as a process which extends on a spectrum of object relations from that which ranges from the nonpsychotic to the grossly psychotic could perhaps be better examined with clinical material as a guide.

Let us take a not uncommon transference manifestation in the analyses of nonpsychotic patients, also not infrequent among analytic trainees. The patient overidealizes the analyst by projecting upon him his own narcissistic identification (introjection) with an overidealized parental figure or surrogate.[79] He then identifies with (reintrojects) this overidealization and begins to make analytic interpretations wherever he goes. He tends quite excessively to analyze people he comes in contact with, much to their discomfort. In this process there is no loss of self-non-self differentiation. Could this strictly speaking be viewed as projective-identification (introjection)? I doubt whether Kleinians would accept it as such.

I should like to describe a patient's reaction to the information I give here that we were going to terminate and that coeval with this termination, I was giving up my private practice. She became quite panicky and angry. How could I give up treating patients who need me. Why was I so selfish and thinking of my own interest, depriving the world of my services. I would be punished. I would become sick if I did not work at my profession. She then described the nature of my sickness. I would develop all sorts of bowel troubles, constipation, hemorrhoids, bleeding, my whole gastrointestinal system would disintegrate, become cancerous, and I would vomit. I would not be able to sleep and I would consequently be tense and anxious.

When I pointed out to her that all these had been her symptoms, she quite readily acknowledged this. Furthermore, when I pointed out that this was a way of holding on to me she indicated that although she had been free of these symptoms and fears for some time, they would now return but perhaps not with as much renewed power. She would be able to control these fears and dangerous forces in herself.

Why, I asked her, did my having them in me help her? It became clear that through the common experiences she was sharing, she would not lose me. But furthermore, she knew from previous experience that I did not disintegrate when she tried to destroy me (in fantasy) and it was this very indestructability that reassured her and enabled her to deal with her hatreds and hostilities both self- and object-directed. In that sense she would ultimately master and control these forces through introjecting this part of me as well. The hope was that ultimately this healthy component would become part of her self. In a way she was speaking of an ultimate identification. I might say parenthetically that much of this had been experienced with her mother with one major difference. The mother realistically did act in keeping with the patient's fantasies, whereas I did not, and there was a part of me that she could use as a transitional object to work out her separation. This patient, a psychotic character, still retained her capacity to test reality—albeit this was at times quite fragile. All of the above occurred with a basic recognition that these were her fantasies and fears and had little basis in reality. She still kept the boundaries between me and herself clearly defined. There was much in this patient which reminded one of Bion's[35, 91] view of that which has been projected as being contained by the object, the container. That which is projected is, as a result of this containment, modified, attenuated and neutralized and then could safely be reintrojected. To Bion this process reinforces the relationship between child and mother.

A similar process could be seen in a more seriously disturbed patient reported by Nakhla[151,4] who dreamed of one of her aunts murdering another, her sister. She had on previous occasions described her aunt as crazy and as having murderous impulses. Such murderous impulses had been felt by the patient toward her own sister, as was pointed out by the therapist. This was reacted to by the patient with anxiety, fear of going to pieces, and fear that she was seriously ill. In the dream, the therapist who was trying to comfort her, as was the case in reality, was also sick, but he reassured the patient that both he and she were not seriously ill. Nakhla felt that with the murderous feelings which she had projected on the aunt being reintrojected, the patient again felt they were destroying her. In the dream she tried to project her disintegrative fears onto the therapist. There was a projection of the patient's destructive impulses as well as her mutilated self onto the therapist. This was re-experienced in herself with resultant annihilation anxiety. These impulses, however, having been, so to speak, contained, neutralized, and modified in the therapist, could now be introjected and ultimately mastered.

I should like to move on to more obviously psychotic manifestations of this process. Many of the clinical manifestations deriving from this process could be viewed as reflective of self-non-self dedifferentiation. An example is the phenomenon of transitivism, when the patient feels within himself the same phenomena which are going on in another person, such as genital sensations or aggressive feelings. He may, in his delusional system, then ascribe these as being evoked in him by that person. Another example is mutism, which may result because there is no need to speak since the patient and the object are one, undifferentiated. The patient projects her own thoughts on to the object and also feels them within herself. As one patient said to me, "We don't have to speak, because you hear what I hear, you think what I think."

I believe that variations of the influencing machine reflect projective introjective mechanisms. One such patient felt that a highly complicated outside apparatus was capable of experiencing certain sensations, which were also felt by him at the same time. He imagined a mechanical body (which upon description was a duplicate of himself) would lie right next to his bed, and be under the influence of still another machine outside of himself, which was located in a radio station. This machine would broadcast waves influencing and affecting various parts of this phantom body, which would correspond to parts of his own body and he would therefore feel the same sensations.

Another patient described the development of an influencing machine which evolved from feelings of being hypnotized by a given individual. The patient felt parts of her body moving independently so that "I wouldn't know how my hand had got there. I know that I would want to turn on the hot water faucet but I see my hand turning on the cold water faucet." She would find herself falling out of bed, dropping trays, objects, all influenced by this apparatus inside of herself which she had originally externalized. Actually, at this state she had begun to place the influencing object inside of herself. At times she referred to it as an object within herself, or a machine, or a part of herself. She referred to it as the churning evil. It was obvious that at times she objectivated it externally and at other times was willing to accept it as part of herself. It was unquestionably the uterus and the genitals which were the focus and source of the churning, and which apparently influences her. However, the transitional components were already evident since she spoke of forces outside of herself related to this churning. She projected this whole (evil) process and then reintrojected it.

A more obvious manifestation was seen in a patient who had complained of all sorts of peculiar symptoms of the heart, consisting of a peculiar sensation, pain, irregular heart rate, dizziness, etc. He tried to ward these off by somehow influencing his wife's heart. He had, to begin with, felt that his wife's heart disease (whether she had any in reality I do not know) had many peculiar qualities. She had the power to affect other people's hearts through her heart disease, via emanations of rays or other forces, he wasn't quite sure. She had succeeded with her first husband and he had died. He himself felt that this own heart ailment was being aggravated by this process. He tried similarly through emanations to ward off the wife's rays but was not very successful. As the anniversary of her first husband's death approached, he became more and more apprehensive; he felt the power of her heart attacking him vigorously. His counter-moves not quite succeeding, he thereupon killed her.

SUMMARY

The concepts introjection, identification, and incorporation are frequently used interchangeably and in an overlapping fashion. We maintain that they are all manifestations of internalization. Introjects are different from identifications in still retaining a degree of separateness and autonomy in the self-representation, whereas identification is woven into the warp and woof of the self-representation, no longer discrete. Whereas introjection is a process, identification is an established fact which may result from this process.

The concept projective-identification, or introjection as I choose to call it, derives in adulthood from an early infantile stage in psychic development which is viewed by Klein as psychosis—essentially the paranoid position. The problem that one has with Klein's concepts relates to the speculative formulation of the infant's fantasies, made during this stage. There is less of a problem in the application of this concept to adult psychosis.

One is much more comfortable clinically with the concept of

projective-introjection in adult psychoses. But even here I am not quite sure whether to explain all these clinical phenomena one has to fall back on a concept such as projective introjection. So much of it could be understood especially in psychosis as coexisting phenomena, together with others, as deriving from states of dedifferentiation where self-non-self fusion exists.

All the above described psychotic phenomena could be understood within this framework. Therefore, although perhaps for different reasons, I agree with Meissner who said

> . . . the difficulties inherent in the concept of projective identification are particularly methodological in nature, and result from the mixing or confusion of fantasy and process, of metaphor and mechanism, and result in failures in the differentiation of levels and forms of psychic organization and functioning. Consequently, I would urge that the term be abandoned as contributing more confusion than clarification to psychoanalytic thinking and that, in its place, more specific formulations regarding the interactions and relationships of forms of externalization and internalization be employed.[151 p.65]

The phenomenon described by Klein as projective-identification, if used at all, should more accurately be called projective-introjection. However, I feel that it is essentially another manifestation among others, of loss of self-non-self differentiation.

CHRONOLOGY OF
PAUL SCHILDER'S LIFE

Paul Ferdinand Schilder, M.D., Ph.D.

1886 -   February 15. Born to Bertha Fuerth and Ferdinand Schilder, Jews, in Vienna, Austria.

1905 -   Student of Medicine in University of Vienna.

1908 -   Published first paper on neuropathology. (Also attended Freud's lecture.)

1909 -   Published five papers—neuropathology.

1909 -   Graduated University of Vienna, M.D.

1909-1912   Assistant to Anton, Gabriel, in Saale an dem Saale, Germany. Neuropathology.

1912-1914   Assistant to Paul Fleschig, Leipzig, Germany. First studies encephalitis Periaxialis diffusa (Schilder's Disease).

1914-1918   Medical officer in World War I at Front and base hospitals, while studying philosophy at same time.

1917 -   Ph.D. in Philosophy, in absentia, from University of Vienna.

1918 -   Appointed to staff of Neurology and Psychiatry under Wagner von Jauregg.

1919 -   Member of Psychoanalytic Society in Vienna. Read papers, etc.

1921 -   *Privat Dozent* in Neurology and Psychiatry, University of Vienna.

1925 -   Professor *extraordinares* in Neurology and Psychiatry, University of Vienna.

1928 -	Three months as visiting professor to Phipps Clinic, Johns Hopkins University with Adolf Meyers.
1929	Three months at Bloomingdale Hospital (New York Hospital of White Plains). (This may have been same trip to Phipps Clinic.)
1930 -	January through March. Visiting Professor Phipps Clinic, Johns Hopkins University
1930 -	April 1st. To New York via Canada, applying for U.S. citizenship. Clinical Director of the Psychiatric Division of Bellevue, and Research ProfessorNew York University, College of Medicine in Psychiatry.
1936 -	Nov. 27. Married Lauretta Bender.
1937 -	May 21. Son Michael born.
1938 -	Nov. 28. Peter born.
1940 -	Nov. 26. daughter Jane born.
1940 -	Dec. 8. Died following automobile accident.

REFERENCES

1. Adams, R.D., & Richardson, E.P., Jr. The demyelinative diseases of the human nervous system. A classification; a review of salient neuropathologic findings; comments on recent biochemical studies. In J. Folch-Pi, (Ed.), *Chemical pathology of the nervous system.* Oxford: Pergamon, 1961, pp. 162-196.

2. Ades, H.W., & Engstrom, H. Form and innervation of the vestibular epithelia. In NASA SP-77, *The Role of the Vestibular Organs in the Exploration of Space.* 1965, p. 23.

3. Anton, G., Uber die Sebst-Wahernehmung der Herder Krankungen des Gehirns. Archives of Psychiatry, 1900, *32,* 86-103.

4. Arnold, W., Ganzer, U., & Kleinmann, H. Sensorineural hearing loss in mucous otitis. *Archives of Otolaryngology,* 1977, 91, 215.

5. Barber, H. Positional nystagmus, especially after head injury. *Laryngoscope,* 1964, 74, 891.

6. Bartenieff, I. *Effort observation and effort assessment in rehabilitation.* New York: Dance Notation Bureau, 1962.

7. _____, & Davis, M. *Effort-shape analysis of movement.* New York: Dance Notation Bureau, 1971.

8. _____ with Lewis, D. *Body movement: Coping with the environment.* New York: Gordon & Breach, Science Publishers, 1980.

9. _____ *Movement and perception.* Plymouth: McDonald & Evans, 1980.

10. Bast, T.H., & Anson, B.J. *The temporal bone and the ear.* C. C. Thomas, Springfield, Ill., 1949.

11. Bender, L., & Schilder, P. Unconditioned and conditioned reaction to pain in schizophrenia. *American Journal of Psychiatry,* 1930, *10,* 365-384.

12. Bender, L., & Schilder, P. Alcoholic encephalopathy. *Archives of Neurology & Psychiatry,* 29, 990-1053. Reprinted in L. Bender (Ed.) *P. Schilder on Psychoses.* New York: International Universities Press, 1976, pp. 193-258.

13. Bender, L., Psychoses associated with somatic disease that distort the body structure. *Archives of Neurology & Psychiatry,* 32, 1000-1029.

14. Bender, L., & Woltmann, A.G. Puppetry as a psychotherapeutic measure for behavior problems in children. Monthly Bulletin New York State Assoc. Occupational Therapists, 1937, 7, 1-9.

15. _____ A visual motor gestalt test and its clinical use. New York: The American Orthopsychiatric Association, 1938.

16. _____ The Goodenough test (drawing a man) in chronic encephalitis in children. Journal of Nervous & Mental Disorders, 1940, 91, 277-287.

17. Bender, L, & Boas, F. Creative dance in therapy. American Journal of Orthopsychiatry, 1941, 11, 235-245. (Reported in L. Bender, Child Psychiatric Techniques, Springfield, Ill., Charles C. Thomas, 1952, 258-276.

18. _____ Childhood schizophrenia. American Journal of Orthopsychiatry, 1947, 17, 40-56.

19. Bender, L., & Montague, J.A. Psychotherapy through art of a negro child. College Art Journal, 1947, 7, 12-16. Reprinted in L. Bender, Child Psychiatric Techniques, Springfield, Ill. Charles C. Thomas, 1952, pp. 287-302.

20. Bender, L., & Keeler, W.R. The body image of schizophrenic children following electric shock therapy, American Journal of Orthopsychiatry, 1952, 22, 335-355.

21. _____ Child psychiatric techniques. Springfield, Ill.: Charles C. Thomas, 1952.

22. Bender, L., & Freedman, A. A study of the first three years in the maturation of schizophrenic children, Quarterly Journal of Child Behavior, 1952, 4, 245-272.

23. Bender, L., & Woltmann, A.G. The use of plastic material as a psychiatric approach to emotional problems in children. American Journal of Orthopsychiatry, 1952, 7, 283-300. Reprinted in L. Bender, Child Psychiatric Techniques, Springfield, Ill.: Charles C. Thomas, 1952, 221-237.

24. Bender, L. & Helme, W. A quantitative test of theory and diagnostic indicators of childhood schizophrenia, Archives of Neurology and Psychiatry, 1953, 70, 413-427.

25. Bender, L. A dynamic psychopathology of childhood. Springfield, Ill.: Charles C. Thomas, 1954, 85-91.

26. _____ Psychopathology of children with organic brain disorders. Springfield, Ill.: Charles C. Thomas, 1955.

27. Bender, L., & Silver, A. Body image problems of the brain damaged child. Journal of Social Issues, 1948, 4, 84-89. Reprinted in L., Bender, Psychopathology of Children with Organic Brain Disease, Springfield, Ill.: Charles C. Thomas, 1955, 97-104.

28. _____ Problems in conceptualization and communication in children with developmental alexia. In P.H. Hoch & J. Zubin (Eds.), M. Psychopathology of Communication, New York: Grune & Stratton, 1958, 155-176.

29. Bender, L., & Faretra, G. Body image problems of children. In H.I., V.F., &

N.R. Lief (Eds.) *The psychological basis of medical practice.* New York: Haber, Medical Division, Harper & Row, 1963, pp. 431-439.

30. _____ Body image, problems expressed in the art of emotionally disturbed puberty, boys and girls. In R. Volmat & C. Viart, (Eds.) M. Art and *Psychopathology,* Amsterdam Exoyrta, Media Foundation, 1969, 19-27.

31. _____The process of creativity in psychopathological art. *Confinia Psychiatry,* 1976, 19, 77-151.

32. Bender, M.B. Disorders in perception. Springfield, Ill.: Charles C. Thomas, 1952.

33. Bergman, P., & Escalona, S. Unusual sensitivities in very young children. *Psychoanalytic study of the Child,* 1949, *3-4,* 333-353.

34. Bernfield, S. *Psychologic des Sougling,* Brentano 1925. Translated as *The Psychology of the infant.* New York: Brentano 1929.

35. Bion, W.R. Second thoughts. *Selected papers on psychoanalysis.* London: Heinermann, 1967.

36. Borgin, E.G. 1933. Quoted after Schilder, (219) *Mind: perception and thought in their constructive aspects.*

37. Bouman, L. *Diffuse sclerosis (Encephalitis periaxialis diffusa).* Bristol: Wright and Sons, 1934.

38. Bromberg, W., & Schilder, P. On tactile imagination and tactile after-effects. *Journal of Nervous & Mental Diseases,* July 1932, August 1932, *76,* 133.

39. _____ Psychologic considerations in alcoholic hallucinosis, Castration and dismemberment motives. *International Journal of Psychoanalysis,* 1933, *14,* 206.

40. Buelte, A., & Kestenberg, J. Holding the baby (Group studies in progress: Movement patterns: Diagnostic and theraputic considerations). *Presented at the Fall meeting of the American Psychoanalytic Association,* 1971.

41. Caplan, H. Som considerations of the body image concept in child development, *Quarterly Journal of Child Behavior,* 1952, 4, 382-288. Reprinted in Bender, L., *Psychopathology of Children with Organic Brain Disorders,* Springfield, Ill.: Charless C. Thomas, 1955, 104-113.

42. Carlstrom, D., & Engstrom, H. The ultrastructure of statoconia. *Acta Otolaryngologicar* (Stockholm), 1955, *45,* 14.

43. Chaiklin, S. Dance Therapy, In S. Arieti, (Ed.) *American Handbook of Psychiatry,* (2nd ed.), (Vol. 5), Chap. 37, New York: Basic Books, 1975.

44. Clark, G.M., Douglas, R.J., Erway, L.C., & Hubbard, D.G. Vestibular nuclei: neuronal loss in mice with otoconial agenesis and evidence of right-left asymmetry. In T. Gualtierotti (Ed.). *Vestibular function and morphology,* New York: Springer-Verlag, 1980. in press.

45. Curran, F.J., & Frosch, J. The body image in adolescent boys. *Journal of Genetic Psychology,* 1942, *60,* 37-60.

46. Curran, F.J., & Levine, M. A body image study of prostitutes, *Journal of Criminal Psychopathology,* 1942, 4, 93-116.

47. Decker, J.D. The influence of early extirpation of the otocysts on the development of behavior in the chick. *Journal of Experimental Zoology*, 1970, 174, 349.

48. Dell, C. *A primer for movement description using effort-shape and supplementary concepts.* New York: Dance Notation Bureau, 1970.

49. Denison, R.H. The origin of the lateral-line sensory system. *American Zoology*, 1966, 6, 369.

50. DeQuiros, J.B. Diagnosis of vestibular disorders in the learning disabled. *Journal of Learning Disabilities*, 1976, 9, 39.

51. Dix, M. & Hallpike, C. The pathology, symptomatology and diagnosis of certain disorders of the vestibular system. *Annual of Otology Rhinology and Laryngology* (St. Louis), 1952, 61, 987.

52. Douglas, R.J., Clark, G.M., Erway, L.C., Hubbard, D.G., & Wright, C.G. Effects of genetic vestibular defects on behavior related to spatial orientation and emotionality. *Journal of Comp. Physiological Psychology*, 1979, 93, 467.

53. Ellenburger, H.F. A clinical introduction to psychiatric phenomenology and existential analysis. In R. May, E. Angel, & H. Ellenberger, (Eds.) *Existence.* New York: Basic Books, 1958, 92-124.

54. Engstrom, H., Ades, H.W. & Anderson, A. *Structural pattern of the organ of corti.* Stockholm: Almqvist and Wiksell, 1966.

55. Erikson, E.H. *Childhood and society.* New York: Norton, 1950.

56. _____ *Identity and the life cycle. Psychological Issues*, I. New York: International Universities Press, 1959.

57. Erway, L.C., Hurley, L.S., & Fraser, A.S. Neurological defect: manganese in phenocopy and prevention of abnormality of inner ear. *Science*, 1966, 152, 1766.

58. _____ Congenital ataxia and otolith defects due to manganese deficiency in mice. *Journal of Nutrition*, 1970, 100, 643.

59. Erway, L.C., Fraser, A.S. & Hurley, L.S. Prevention of congenital otolith defect in pallid mutant mice by manganese supplementation. *Genetics*, 1971, 67, 97.

60. Erway, L.C., & Mitchell, S.E. Prevention of otolith defect in pastel mink by manganese supplementation. *Heredity*, 1973, 64, 110.

61. Fabian, A.A. Vertical rotation in visual motor performance in relationship to reading reversals, *Psychology*, 1945, 36, 129-135.

62. Farber, M. The foundation of phenomenology. Albany, New York: State University of New York Press, 1967, (Rev. 3rd ed.) p. 19.

63. Fenichel, O. Respiratory introjection, 1931. *In Collected Papers.* New York: Norton, 1933, I: 221-240.

64. Ferenczi, S. Contributions to psycho-analysis. Boston: Richard G. Badger, 1916.

65. Ferraro, A. Primary demyelinating processes of central nervous system, at-

tempt at unification and classification, *Archives of Neurology and Psychiatry,* 1937, *37,* 1100-1160.

66. Fish, B. A study of motor development in infancy and its relationship to psychological functioning, *American Journal of Psychiatry,* 1961, 117, 1113-1118.

67. _____ Neurobiological antecedents of schizophrenia in children, *Archives of General Psychiatry,* 1977, *34,* 1297-1313.

68. _____ Fish, B., & Dixon, W. Vestibular hyporeactivity in infants at risk for schizophrenia, *Archives of General Psychiatry,* 1978, *35,* 963-971.

69. Freeman, T. Aspects of defence in neurosis and psychosis. *International Journal of Psychoanalysis,* 1959, *40,* 199-212.

70. Freud, A. *Normality and pathology in childhood: assessment of development:* New York: International Universities Press, 1965.

71. Freud, S. *The interpretation of dreams,* (Standard Ed.), London: Hogarth Press, 1953, 4 & 5, (Originally published, 1900).

72. _____ *Jokes and their relation to the unconscious* (Standard Ed.), London: Hogarth Press, 1960, *8,* 3-242. (Originally published, 1905).

73. _____ *Introductory lectures on psycho-analysis,* Part III, General theory of the neuroses. (Standard Ed.), London: Hogarth Press, 1963, *16,* 243-463. (Originally published, 1917).

74. _____ *Beyond the pleasure principle,* (Standard Ed.), London: Hogarth Press, 1955, *18,* 3-64. (Originally published, 1920).

75. _____ *The ego and the id.* (Standard Ed.), London: Hogarth Press, 1961, 19, 19-27. (Originally published, 1925).

76. _____ New introductory lectures on psychoanalysis. (Standard Ed.), London: Hogarth Press, 1964, *22,* 1-182. (Originally published, 1935).

77. _____On narcissism: An introduction. (Standard Ed.), London: Hogarth Press, 1957, 14, 69-102. (Originally published 1914).

78. Fromm, E. *Beyond the chains of illusion.* New York: Simon & Schuster, Touchstone, 1962.

79. Frosch, J. Transference derivatives of the family romance. *Journal of the American Psychoanalytic Association,* 1959, *7,* 503-522.

80. _____ Severe Regressive States During Analysis: Introduction. *Journal of the American Psychoanalytic Association* (Vol. 15), 1967a., 491-507.

81. _____ Ibid. *Summary* (Vol. 15), 1967b., 606-623.

82. Fuchs, S.H. On introjection. *International Journal of Psychoanalysis,* 1937, *18,* 269-293.

83. Gelb, A., & Goldstein, K. Zur Psycholgie des Optschen Walornehmunges and Exkunnung— Vorganges. *Zeitschrift ges Neurologie und Psychiatrie,* 1918, *41,* 1-17.

84. Gerstmann, J. & Schilder, P. Studien ueber Bewegungs stoerungen. 1920-1923, I-VII., *Zeitschrift gesampte Neurologie und Psychiatrie.*

85. Gerstmann, J. Fingeragnosia und Isolierte a Graphie, *Zeitschrift gesampte Neurologie und Psychiatrie,* 1927, 108-152.

86. _____ Psychological and phenomenological aspects of disorders of the body image, *Journal of Nervous and Mental Diseases,* 1958, *126,* 499-512.

87. Gesell, A.L. Maturation and infant behavior patterns, *Psychology Review,* 1929, *36,* 307-321.

88. Gesell, A. *Embryology of behavior.* New York: Harper & Bros., 1945.

89. Globus, J.H., & Strauss, I. Progressive degenerative subcortical encephalopathy (Schilder's disease), *Archives of Neurology and Psychiatry,* 1928, *20,* 1190-1228.

90. Gorman, W. *Body image and image of the brain,* St. Louis, Mo.: Warren H. Green, Inc., 1969.

91. Grinberg, L., Sor, D., de Bianchedi, E.T. Introduction to the works of Bion. New York: Jason Aronson, 1977.

92. Gurwitsch, A. In: J. Kocklemans (Ed.). *Phenomenology.* New York: Double-day, 1976, Chap. V.

93. Hanson, N.R. Arts as a language of logic. *Saturday Review,* Dec. 3 1960, p. 22.

94. Hartmann, H. The psychiatric work of Paul Schilder. *Psychoanalytic Review,* 1944, *31,* 287-298.

95. Hartmen H. & Schilder, P. Korperenneres und Koerperschema. *Monatschrift gesampte Neurologie und Psychiatrie,* 1927, *109,* 666-675.

96. Hawkins, J.E., Jr., & Johnsson, L.G. Microdissection and surface prepara-tions of the inner ear. In C.A. Smith & J.A. Vernon (Eds.), *Handbook of auditory and vestibular research methods.* Springfield, Ill.: C. C. Thomas, 1976.

97. Head, S.H. *Studies in neurology* (2 Vols.). London: Frowde, 1920.

98. deHirsch, K., Jansky, J.J., & Langford, W.S. *Predicting reading failure,* New York: Harper & Row, 1966.

99. Hoff, H., & Schilder, P. *Die Lagereflexe des Menschen,* Vienna: Springer, 1927.

100. Hubbard, D.G. *The skyjacker: His flights of fantasy.* New York & London: Col-lier Macmillan, 1971.

101. Humphrey, T. The embryologic differentiation of the vestibular nuclei in man correlated with functional development. *In International symposium on vestibular and oculomotor problems.* Tokyo: Japan Society for Vestibular Research, 1965.

102. Igarashi, M., & Nagaba, M. Vestibular end-organ damage in squirrel monkeys after exposure to intensive linear acceleration. In A. Graybiel (Ed.). *Third symposium on the role of the vestibular organs in space exploration.* NASA, Washington, D.C., 1967.

103. Igarashi, M., & Kanda, T. Fine structure of the otolithic membrane in the squirrel monkey. *Acta Otolaryngologica* (Stockholm), 1969, *68,* 43.

104. Isaacs, S. *Social development in young children.* London: Geo. Routledge & Sons, 1946.

105. Jacobson, E. Contribution to the metapsychology of psychotic identifications. *Journal of the American Psychoanalytic Association,* 1954, *2,* 239-262.

106. _____ Psychotic conflict and reality. New York: International Universities Press, 1967.

107. James, W. *The principles of psychology.* (Vol. II), New York: Henry Holt Co., 1890.

108. Jaspers, K. *Allgemeine Psychopathologic* (2nd ed.). Berlin: Julius Springer, 1920.

109. Johnsson, L.G., & Hawkins, J.E., Jr. Otolithic membranes of the saccule and utricle in man. *Science,* 1967, *157,* 1454.

110. Johnsson, L.G. Degenerative changes in anomalies of the vestibular system in man. *Laryngoscope,* 1971, *81,* 1682.

111. Johnsson, L.G., & Hawkins, J.E., Jr. Sensory and neural degeneration with aging, as seen in microdissection of the human inner ear. *Annual of Otology, Rhinology and Laryngology* (St. Louis), 1972, *81,* 179.

112. Katan, M. Structural aspects of a case of schizophrenia. *Psychoanalytic Study of the Child,* 1950, *5,* 115-211.

113. Kaufman, F. In F. Schlipp, (Ed.), *The philosophy of Ernst Cassirer,* New York: Tudor Publishing Co., 1958, 803.

114. Kaufman, M.R. Schilder's application of psychoanalytic psychiatry. *Archives of General Psychiatry.,* 1962, *7,* 311-320.

115. Kernberg, O. *Borderline conditions and pathological narcissism.* New York: Jason Aronson, 1975.

116. Kestenburg, J. 1965-1967. *The role of movement patterns in development.* I. Rhythms of Movement. II. Flow of Tension and Effort. III. The Control of Shape. New York: Dance Notation Bureau, 1971, (2nd. ed.). 1977. (Reprinted from *Psychoanalytic Quarterly*).

117. _____ From organ-object images to self-and-object-representations. In J. McDevitt & R. Settlage, (Eds.), *Separation-Individuation. Papers in honor of Margaret Mahler.* New York: International Universities Press, 1971, 75-99

118. _____ *Children and parents. Psychoanalytic studies in development.* (2nd ed.). New York: Jason Aronson, 1975.

119. _____ Perspectives psychanalytiques sur la vulnerabilite du tres jeune enfant. Groupe de discussion, Reunion du semestre d'hiver 1973 de l'American Psychoanalytic Association, *Psychiatrie De L' Enfant* (Paris), 1976, XIX 2, 520-522.

120. Kestenberg, J., & Buelte, A. Prevention, infant therapy and the treatment of adults. I. Toward understanding mutuality. II. Mutual holding and holding oneself up. *International Journal of Psychoanalytic Psychotherapy,* 1977, *6,* 339-396, 369-396.

121. Kestenberg, J., & Weinstein, J. Transitional objects and body-image formation. In Grolnick & Barken, (Eds.), *Between reality and fantasy-transitional objects and phenomena.* New York: Jason Aronson, 1978, 75-95.

122. Kestenberg, J., c Marcus, H. Hypothetical monosex and bisexuality—A psychoanalytic interpretation of sex differences as they reveal themselves in movement patterns of men and women. In M. C. Nelson & J. Ikenberry, (Eds.). *Psychosexual imperatives,* The Self-in-process series. New York: Human Sciences Press, 1979.

123. Kestenberg, J. & Sossin, M. *The role of movement patterns in development II. Epilogue and glossary.* New York: Dance Notation Bureau, 1979.

124. _____ Ego-organization in obsessive-compulsive development. A study of the rat-man, based on the interpretation of movement patterns. In *Volume commemorating the 25th anniversary of the psychoanalytic division of Down State University.* New York: Jason Aronson, 1980.

125. _____ The inner-genital phase. In D. Mendel, (Ed.). *Early feminine development, Contemporary psychoanalytic views.* New York: Spectrum Publications, 1980a.

126. Klein, M. Notes on some schizoid mechanism. *International Journal of Psychoanalysis,* 1946, *27,* 99-110.

127. Knight, R.P. Introjection, projection and identification. *Psychoanalytic Quarterly,* 1940, *9,* 334-341.

128. Kohut, H. *The analysis of the self.* New York: International Universities Press, 1971.

129. Kolb, L.C. Disturbances of the body image, In S. Arieti. (Ed.). *American handbook of psychiatry.* (1st ed.). New York: Basic Books, 1959, Chap. 38, 749-779.

130. Kovach, J.K. Spatial orientation of the chick embryo during the last five days of incubation. *Journal of Comp. Physiological Psychology,* 1968, *66,* 283.

131. Laban, R. & Lawrence, F.C. *Effort.* London: MacDonald & Evans, 1947.

132. Laban, R. *The mastery of movement.* (2nd ed.). L. Ullman, (Ed.). London: MacDonald & Evans, 1960.

133. _____ *Choreutics.* L. Ullman, (Ed.). London: MacDonald & Evans, 1966.

134. Lamb, W. 1961. *Correspondence course in movement assessment.* Unpublished.

135. _____ *Posture and gesture.* London: Gerald Duckworth, 1965.

136. Lamb, W., & Turner, D. *Management behavior.* New York: International Universities Press, 1969.

137. Larsell, O. The cerebellum of myxinoids and petromyzonts including developmental stages in the lampreys. *Journal Comp. Neurology,* 1947, *86,* 395.

138. Lim, D.J. Formation and fate of the otoconia. *Annual of Otology, Rhinology and Laryngology* (St. Louis), 1973, *82,* 23.

139. _____ The statoconia of the non-mammalian species. *Brain Behavior and Evolution* (BASAL) 1974, *10,* 37.

140. Lim, D.J. & Erway, L.C. Influence of manganese on genetically defective otolith. *Annual of Otology, Rhinology and Laryngology* (St. Louis), 1974, *83,* 565.

141. Lindeman, H. Studies on the morphology of the sensory regions of the vestibular apparatus. *Ergeb. Anat. Entwicklungsgesch,* 1969, *42,* 1.

142. Lipps, T. Das Wissen von fremden ichen. *Psycho. Untersuch,* 1907, *1,* 694-722.

143. Lyon, M.F. Hereditary absence of otoliths in the house mouse. *Journal of Physiology,* 1951, *114,* 410.

144. _____ Absence of otoliths in the mouse: an effect of the pallid mutant. *Journal of Genetics,* 1953, 51, 638.

145. _____ The developmental origin of hereditary absence of otoliths in mice. *Journal of Embryol. Exp. Morphology,* 1955a, *3,* 230.

146. _____ The development of the otoliths of the mouse. *Journal of Embryol. Exp. Morphology,* 1955b, *3,* 213.

147. Machover, K. *Personality projection in the drawing of the human figure.* Springfield, Ill.: Charles C. Thomas, 1949.

148. Magnus, R., & deKleijn, A. Die Abhangigkeit des Extremitationmuskein von der Tonus der Kopfstellung, *Arch. ges Physiol.,* 1912, *145,* 455-548.

149. Magnus, R. Some results of studies in the physiology of posture, *Lancet,* 1926, *2,* 531, 585.

150. May, R., Angel, E., & Ellenberger, H. (Eds.). *Existence,* New York: Basic Books, 1958.

151. Meissner, W.W. A note on projective identification. *Journal of the American Psychoanalytic Association,* 1980, *28,* 43-67.

152. Miller, I. *Imitation and identification.* Paper presented before the American Psychoanalytic Association, 1962.

153. Montague, A. In H. Anderson & G.L. Angerson (Eds.). *The art of the schizophrenic child.* Projective Techniques, New York: Prentice Hall, 1951, 370-385.

154. Nakhla, Fayek. *Personal Communication,* 1980.

155. Niederland, W.G. Schreber and Flechsig. *Journal of the American Psychoanalytic Association,* 1968, *16,* 740-748.

156. Obersteimer, H. On allochisia, a peculiar sensory disorder. *Brain,* 1882, *14,* 153-164.

157. Ogden, T.J. On projective identification. *International Journal of Psychoanalysis,* 1979, *60,* 357-373.

158. Ornitz, E. Neurophysiological studies, 117-139, In M. Rutter & E. Schopler, (Eds). *Autism,* New York: Plenum Press, 1978.

159. Pachedo, M.A.P. Neurotic and psychotic transference and Projective identification. *International Review of Psychoanalysis,* 1980, *7,* 157-164.

160. Paparella, M.M., Oda, M., Hiraide, F., & Brady, D. Pathology of sensorineural hearing loss in otitis media. *Annals of Otology Rhinology and Laryngology,* 1972, *81,* 632.

161. Pare, A. *The Works of That Famous Chinuvgion, Ambrose Parey* (Trans. from the Latin and compared with the French by T. Johnson), London: Cotes, 1969.

162. Parker, S. Character of Modern Psychiatry. A synthetic Presentation of the Work of Paul Schilder, *Journal of Nervous & Mental Diseases,* 1926, *63,* 313-342.

163. Parker, S., & Schilder, P. Das Koerperschema in Lift. *Zeitschrift fur de gesampte Neutologie und Psychiatrie,* 1930, *129,* 250-279.

164. Peto, A. To cast away. *Psychoanalytic Study of the Child,* 1970, *25,* 401.

165. Piaget, J. *Judgment and Reasoning of the Child.* New York: Harcourt, Brace & Co., 1928.

166. Preston, R.E., Johnsson, L.G., Hill, J.H., & Schact, J. Incorporation of radioactive calcium into otolithic membranes and middle ear ossicles of the gerbil. *Acta Otolaryngologica* (Stockholm) 1975. *80,* 269.

167. Preuss, K.T. *Der Ursprung der Religion und Kunst.* Globus, 1902-5, 86-7.

168. Preyer, T.W. *Die Seele des Kinder.* Lepzig, 1882. Trans. *The Mind of the Child.* 2 vols. New York, Appleton, 1888, 1889.

169. Psychoanalytic Glossary. A Glossary of Psychoanalytic Terms and Concepts. B.F. Moore & B.D. Fine, (Eds.). New York: Psychoanalytic Association, 1968.

170. Ramsden, P. *Top Team Planning: The Power of the Individual Motivation in Management,* London: Associated Business Programmes, 1973.

171. Rapaport, D. *Organization and Pathology of Thought.* New York: Columbia University Press, 1951.

172. Rapaport, D. Paul Schilder's contribution to the theory of thought processes. *International Journal of Psychoanalysis,* 1951, *32,* 1-11. Reprinted in P. Schilder, *Medical Psychology,* trans. by D. Rapaport. New York, International Universities Press, 1953, Appendix 340-356.

173. Rapoport, J. Fantasy objects in children. *Psychoanalytic Review,* 1944, *31,* 1-6.

174. Riopelle, A.J., & Hubbard, D.G. Prenatal manganese deprivation and early behavior of primates. *Journal of Orthomolecular Psychiatry,* 1978, *6,* 327.

175. Robbins, E. & Soodak, M. Personal communication, 1972.

176. Rosenfeld, Herbert, On the Psychopathology of Narcissism in Psychotic States, 1964. In *Psychotic states.* A psychoanalytical approach, New York: International Universities Press, 1965.

177. _____ On Projective Identification. *Scientific Bulletin of the British Psychoanalytical Society and the Institute of Psycho-Analysis.* London, 1970.

178. Rosenhall, U., & Rubin, W. Degenerative changes in the human vestibular sensory epithelia. *Acta Otolaryngolica.* 1975, *79,* 67.

179. Ross, M.D., Johnsson, L.G., Peacor, D. & Allard, L.F. Observations on normal and degenerating human otoconia. *Annals of Otology, Rhinology and Laryngoly* (St. Louis), 1976, *85,* 310.

180. Ross, M.D., & Peacor, D. The nature and crystal growth of otoconia in the rat. *Annals of Otology, Rhinology and Laryngoly* (St. Louis). 1975, *84,* 22.

181. Sandler, J. On the Concept of Superego. *The Psychoanalytic Study of the Child.* New York: International Universities Press, 1960, *15*, 128-162.

182. Sartre, J.-P. *Being and Nothingness.* H. Barnes (trans.) New York: Citadel Press, 1964.

183. Schafer, R. *Aspects of Internalization.* New York: International Universities Press, 1968.

184. Schilder, P. Zur Kenntnis der sogenannten diffusen Sklerose (Uber Enzephalitis periaxialis diffusa), *Zeitschrift fur de gesampte Neurologie und Psychiatrie.* 1912, *10*, 1-60.

185. _____ Uber das Selbstbewsstsein und seine Storungen, *Zeitschrift fur de gesampte Neurologie und Psychiatrie.* 1913, *20*, 511-519.

186. _____ *Selbstbewusstsein und persönlichkeitsbewusstsein,* Berlin: Springer, 1914.

187. Schilder, P. & Weidner, H. Zur Kenntnis symbolahnlicher Bildungen im Rahman der Schizophrenic, *Zeitschrift fur die gesampte Neurologie und Psychiatrie,* 1914, 26, 201-244.

188. Schilder, P. *Wahn and Erkenntnis.* Berlin: Springer, 1918.

189. Schilder, P. Ueber Gedankenentwicklung. *Zeitschrift fur die gesampte Neurologie und Psychiatrie,* (Vol. 59), 1920, 250-263 and *Studies concerning the psychology and symptomatology of general paresis,* Berlin: Karger, 1930. D. Rapaport, trans. On the development of thought, In David Rapaport *Organization and pathology of thought* New York: Columbia University Press, 1951, pp. 497-580.

190. _____ The nature of hypnosis (Orignally published as *Ueber das Wesen der hypnose,* Berlin: Springer, and *Lehrbuch der Hypnose,* with Otto Kauders, Berling & Vienna: Springer, 1922). G. Covin, trans. New York: International Universities Press, 1956.

191. Schilder, P. *Das Koerperschema.* Berlin: Springer, 1923.

192. _____ *Seel und Leben.* Berlin: Springer, 1923.

193. Schilder: *Medical psychology* D. Rapaport, trans. New York: International Universities Press, 1953. (Originally published as *Medizinishe Psychologie* fur Aerzte und Psychologen, Berlin: Springer, 1924).

194. Schilder, P. *Introduction to Psychoanalytic Psychiatry.* Trans. B. Glueck, New York: International Universities Press, 1951. (Originally published in German Internat. Psycho-analytic Vienna: Verlag, 1925).

195. _____ *Gedanken zur Naturphilosophie.* Vienna: Springer, 1928. Schilder, P. *Psychotherapy.* New York: Norton, 1938.

196. Schilder, P. *A case of loss of unity of the body image,* 1930. *In The Image and Appearance of the Human Body.* New York: International Universities Press, 1978, pp. 158-168.

197. Schilder, P. & Parker, S. Das Koerperschema in Lift, *Zeitschrift fur de gesampte Neurologie und Psychiatrie,* 1930, *128,* 777-783.

198. Schilder, P. Neurasthenic hypochondriac character, *Medical Review of Reviews,*

1930, 35, 164-176. Reprinted in Schilder, P., *On Neuroses*, L. Bender, (Ed.), New York: International Universities Press, 1979.

199. Schilder, P. Unity of body, sadism and dizziness, *Psychoanalytic Review*, 1930, *17*, 114-122.

200. _____ "Vestibulo - Optik und Koerperschema in der Alkohalhalluzinose," *Zeitschrift fur de gesampte Neurologie und Psychiatrie*, 1930, 128, 784-791.

201. Schilder, P. 1931. *Brain and personality*. New York Nervous and Mental Disease Publishing Co.; Monograph Series, No. 53 (2nd ed.) New York: International Universities Press, 1951, paperback 1969.

202. _____Localization of the body image (Postural model of the body), *Proceedings of Association for Research, Nervous and Mental Diseases*, 1932, *13*, 466-484.

203. Schilder, P. & Eslter, B. Death and dying: Comparative study of attitudes and mental reactions to death and dying. *Psychoanalytic Review*, 1933, *20*, 133-185.

204. _____ The vestibular apparatus in neurosis and psychosis, *Journal of Nervous and Mental Disease*, 1933, *78*, 1-23; 137-164. Reprinted in Schilder, P., *Mind, Perception and Thought in Their Constructive Aspects*, New York: Columbia University Press, 1942, 83, 134.

205. Schilder, P., & Wechsler, D. The attitudes of children toward death. *Journal of Genetic Psychology*, 1934, *45*, 406-451.

206. _____ The somato-psyche in psychiatry and social psychology, *Journal of Abnormal & Social Psychiatry*, 1934, *39*, 314-327. Reprinted in Schilder, P., *Psychoanalysis, Man and Society*, L. Bender (Ed.), New York: Norton, 1951, 36-51.

207. _____ Children's concepts of the inside of their body, *International Journal of Psychoanalysis*, 1935, *16*, 355-360.

208. _____ *The image and appearance of the human body, studies in the constructive energies of the psyche*, 1935. London: Kegan Paul, French, Trubner & Co. Reprinted New York: International Universities Press, 1970, (paperback, 1978).

209. _____Psychoanalysis of space, Psychoanalalytic Review, 1935, *22*, Reprinted in *Mind: Perception and thought in their constructive aspects;* New York: Columbia University Press, 1942, 189-212.

210. Schilder, P. Analysis of ideologies in psychotheraputic method, especially in group treatment, *American Journal of Psychiatry*, 1936, *93*, 601-617.

211. Schilder, P: The psychology and development of language and the symbol, In L. Bender, *A dynamic psychopathology of childhood*, 3-15, Springfield, Ill.: Charles C. Thomas, 1954. Reprinted from The child and the symbol, *Scientia* July, 1938, 21-26, and Language and the constructive energies of the psyche, Scientia, March 1936, 149-158.

212. _____Psychoanalytic remarks on Alice in Wonderland and Lewis Carroll, *Journal of Nervous and Mental Diseases*, 1938, *87*, 159-168, Reprinted in Bender, L., *A dynamic psychopathology of childhood*. Springfield, Ill.: Charles C. Thomas, 1954.

213. _____ *Psychotherapy*, New York: Norton, 1938, 191-192.

214. _____ Preface to L. Bender, *A visual motor gestalt test and its clinical use*, New York: American Orthopsychiatric Association. 1938.

215. _____The psychology of schizophrenia. *Psychoanalytic Review*, 1939, 26: 380-398. Reprinted in Schilder, P., *On psychosis* L. Bender (Ed.). New York: International Universities Press, 1976, 30.

216. _____Vita and bibliography of Paul Schilder, *Journal of Criminal Psychopathology*, 1940, *2*, 221-234.

217. _____ The body image in dreams, *Psychoanalytic Review*, 1942. *29*, 113-126. Partially reprinted from Schilder, P., *Psycho Therapy*, New York: Norton, 1938, revised ed. L. Bender, 1951.

218. _____ *Goals and desires of man, a psychological survey of life*. New York: Columbia University Press, 1942.

219. Schilder, P. Mind: *Perception and thought in their constructive aspects*. New York: Columbia University, 1942a.

220. _____ *Psychoanalysis, man and society*. New York: Norton, 1951, 12.

221. Schilder, P. Contributions to developmental neuropsychiatry, New York: International Universities Press, 1964.

222. _____ *On psychoses*, L. Bender (Ed.). New York: International Universities Press, 1976.

223. _____ *On neuroses*, L. Bender (Ed.). New York: International Universities Press. 1979.

224. Schorske, C. E. *Fin-de-siecle Vienna*, New York: Vintage Books, 1981 Chap. VI, VII.

225. Schrader, R.K., Erway, L.,C., & Hurley, L.S. Mucopolysaccharide synthesis in the developing inner ear of manganese-deficient and pallid mutant mice. *Teratol*, 1973, *8*, 257.

226. Schuknecht, H., Igarashi, M., & Gacek, R. The pathological types of cochleo-saccular degeneration. *Acta Otolaryngologica* (Stockholm), 1965, *59*, 154.

227. Schuknecht, H. *Pathology of the ear*. Cambridge: Harvard University Press, 1974.

228. Searles, H. Transference psychosis in the psychotherapy of chronic schizophrenia. *International Journal of Psychoanalysis*, 1964, 44, 249-281.

229. Silberpfennig, J. (Kestenberg, J.) Eye Movements in Insulin Coma. *Confinia Neurologia*, 1938, 1̀3, 188-200.

230. _____ Recovery from bilateral gaze paralysis. *Confinia Neurologia*. 1939, II1, 2, 15-31.

231. _____ Disturbances of ocular movements with pseudo-hemianopsia in frontal lobe tumors. *Confinia Neurologia.* 1941. IVì, 2, 1-13.

232. Silver, A. Postural and righting responses in children, *Journal of Pediatrics,* 1952, *41,* 493-498.

233. Silver, A., & Gabrel, P. The association of schizophrenia in childhood with primitive postural responses and decreased muscle tone. *Developmental Medicine and Child Neurology,* 1964, *6,* 495-497.

234. Soodak, M. Movement training for parents. Group studies in progress: Movement patterns: Diagnostic and therapeutic considerations. Presented at the fall meetings of the *American Psychoanalytic Association,* 1971. Unpublished.

235. Staercke, The reversal of the libido sign in delusions of persecution. *International Journal of Psychoanalysis.* August 1920, *1,* 231-234.

236. Sullivan, H.S. *The Interpersonal Theory of Psychiatry.* New York: Norton, 1953.

237. Tausk, V. On the Origin of the Influencing Machine in Schizophrenia, In R. Fliess (Ed.) *The Psychoanalytic Reader,* New York: International Universities Press, 1948.

238. Teitelbaum, H. Psychogenic body image disturbances associated with psychogenic aphasia and agnosia, *Journal of Nervous and Mental Diseases,* 1941, *93,* 581-597.

239. Van Ophuijsen, J.H.W. On the origin of feelings of persecution. *International Journal of Psychiatry,* 1920, *1,* 235-239.

240. Veenhof, V.B. The development of satoconia in mice. *Akademie van Wetenschappen,* Amsterdam, 1969.

241. Watanuki, K., & Schuknecht, H.F. A morphological study of human vestibular sensory epithelia. *Archives of Otolaryngology,* 1976, *102,* 583.

242. Weinshel, E. Panel report: Severe regressive states during analysis. *Journal of the American Psychoanalytic Association,* 1966, *14,* 538-368.

243. Weiss, E. Projection, extrajection and objectivation. *Psychoanalytic Quarterly,* 1947, *16,* 357-377.

244. Wentinck, C. *Modern and primitive art,* Oxford: Phaidon Press, 1979, 13.

245. Wernicke, C. *Grundriss der Psychiatrie,* Leipzig: F. Barth, 1906.

246. Winkler, J.K., & Bromberg, W. *Mind explorers.* New York: Reynal & Hitchcock, 1939.

247. Wislocki, G.B. & Ladman, A.J. Selective and histochemical staining of the otolithic membranes, cupulae and tectorial membrane of the inner ear. *Journal of Anatomy,* 1955, *89,* 3.

248. Wittles, F. In Memoriam: Paul Schilder, 1886-1940, *Psychoanalytic Quarterly,* 1941, *10,* 131.

249. Wright, C.G. & Hubbard, D.G. Observations of otoconial membranes from human infants. *Acta Otolaryngologica* (Stockholm), 1978, *86,* 185.

250. Wright, C.G., Hubbard, D.G., & Clark, G.M. Observations of human fetal

otoconial membranes. *Annals of Otology, Rhinology, and Laryngology,* 1979. *88,* 267.

251. Wright, C.G., Hubbard, D.G., & Graham, J.W. Absence of otoconia in a human infant. *Annals of Otology, Rhinology and Laryngology* (St. Louis), 1979, *88:* 779.

252. Yakovlev, P.I., & Lecours, A.R. The myelogenetic cycles of regional maturation of the brain. In A. Minkowski (Ed.), *Regional Development of the Brain in Early Life.* Philadelphia: F.A. Davis, 1967.

NAME INDEX

SUBJECT INDEX